Living Next Door to the Death House

Living Next Door to the Death House

Virginia Stem Owens *and* David Clinton Owens

WILLIAM B. EERDMANS PUBLISHING COMPANY

GRAND RAPIDS, MICHIGAN / CAMBRIDGE, U.K.

Published 2003 by
Wm. B. Eerdmans Publishing Co.
2140 Oak Industrial Drive N.E., Grand Rapids, Michigan 49505 /
P.O. Box 163, Cambridge CB3 9PU U.K.

Printed in the United States of America

07 06 05 04 03   7 6 5 4 3 2 1

Library of Congress Cataloging-in-Publication Data

Owens, Virginia Stem.
Living next door to the death house /
Virginia Stem Owens and David Clinton Owens.
p.   cm.
ISBN 978-0-8028-3998-5
1. Capital punishment — Texas — Huntsville.
2. Capital punishment — Social aspects — Texas — Huntsville.
3. Huntsville (Tex.) — Social life and customs.
I. Owens, David Clinton. II. Title

HV8699.U5O94 2003
364.66′09764′169 — dc21

2002192283I

www.eerdmans.com

Contents

Introduction

THOUGH THIS book is authored by the two of us, Virginia and David, the voice you hear narrating is hers; mine is muted in the background in editing and additions, and, occasionally, in interview dialogue. And that is as it should be, for hers is the voice of greater experience with the town of Huntsville, its people, its history, and its prisons. As she says in the first chapter, both her mother and her grandfather worked for a time in the system. So have others of her mother's extended clan. Members of that family have lived in Walker County, of which Huntsville is the county seat, for four generations.

Virginia herself was actually born in Houston. It was not until she was seven that her father moved the family to Walker County. Her father's career in the U.S. Air Force, however, took the family to several different locations, including El Paso, Texas, where we met and married. It would be another twenty-three years, spent in other parts of Texas and in four other states, before she was able to come back to Huntsville.

Nevertheless, the town has always seemed like home for Virginia. We often visited her grandparents and other close relatives in the area. Her parents had retired here while our own children were quite young. We spent many holidays and summer vacations here. Because we moved so often ourselves, they too identified this place as the real family homestead. For Virginia, if there was any place on earth that had the feel of home, Huntsville was it.

I, on the other hand, had some adjusting to do. Raised in a desert city, and later having become enamored of rugged terrain and crisp, dry air after thirteen years in the Rocky Mountains, I was unimpressed with the heavy, humid heat, the billions of sometimes gargantuan bugs, the rank undergrowth of vine and weed everywhere that characterized summers in Huntsville. Our visits to Virginia's family over the years were generally either in the summer or at Christmas. I felt uncomfortable during the stifling summers and missed snow at Christmas.

But I felt most uncomfortable all those years every time with the high mesh fences topped with razor wire and the harsh floodlighting that defined the prison unit.

Since those early years, however, my feelings about Huntsville's climate and terrain have changed. Experiencing some of the gorgeous springs and autumns and the mild winters of the area has done that. Summer heat turns to a comfortable mid-70s average from October through early June, interrupted by only a few weeks of winter cold. I have learned that Huntsville is a registered wild bird sanctuary and thus have come to realize that the many bugs feed the many birds. I also now appreciate the fact that the same soil and climate that produces the summer tangle of weed and vine also makes for wonderful gardening, both vegetable and floral.

But I still have difficulty accepting the fact that, in or near what is now my adopted hometown, thousands of men live imprisoned. Until Virginia and I married, I knew little or nothing about Huntsville or the Texas prison system. As I grew up in El Paso, almost eight hundred miles to the west, crime and punishment was something I read about in the newspapers; what actually happened to people who were convicted of crimes, other than those who were jailed locally, I had very little idea. In this I am sure I am typical among fellow citizens all over the country. Out of sight, out of mind

This is not to say that my El Paso did not know crime. On the border of Mexico, it did then and does now have a high crime rate. In the neighborhood I grew up in, we mainly worried about theft and burglary. Syndicates of auto thieves were particular nuisances, but home burglars ran a close second. I remember how horrified I was to learn that while friends of my parents were at church one Sunday morning, thieves had backed a big truck into their driveway, loaded up the contents of their house — furniture, appliances, clothing — and driven off.

In any event, whatever El Paso's crime statistics, I grew up not thinking much about prisons or death row or executions. The only prison I knew anything about was across the border near Juarez, Mexico. And all I knew about that place was that you definitely did not want to go there. Up river from El Paso, on the Texas-New Mexico border, was La Tuna Federal Prison, a minimum-security facility of very attractive, white-walled, turreted Spanish-mission architecture. I suppose I wondered at times what it would be like to be locked up in La Tuna, but the exterior looked so pleasant that I did not think living there would be so especially terrible, except for one's loss of freedom.

My marital connection to Huntsville, however, has over time diffused some of my ignorance about prisons. In the 1970s, when my mother-in-law worked in what was then the women's prison unit, Goree, just two miles from our present home, I attended a Christmas pageant produced by prisoners. Though not allowed to roam freely, I nevertheless saw enough to understand for the first time that prison was not, as many Texans were complaining in those days, a tax-supported Hilton Hotel. Later, in the 1980s, I taught some English courses in two nearby units, Wynne and Ellis. I had been hired by one of the colleges that contracted to provide post-secondary education to inmates. This time, I had to go through cellblocks and common rooms to get to the classroom areas. Despite the noise and heat, I must say, I do not believe I ever taught a more attentive, participatory, and appreciative set of students in my life.

Recently, I attended a Kairos prison ministry event at the Hobby unit for women near Marlin, Texas. During that visit, I was particularly struck by how solicitous the women were of their visitors' comfort. They apologized for the lack of air conditioning in the big gym where we gathered. Several kept getting up to move big fans around, hoping somehow to spare us the broiler effect of a typical mid-summer day in Central Texas, even though we would soon be riding in air-conditioned cars back to our air-conditioned homes while they were stuck with the heat for the rest of that day and many more to come.

Though these experiences are few, I now know firsthand things about Texas prisons that had been only vaguely a part my consciousness before. I know that incarceration means austere confinement without many amenities. Everyone wears prison whites. No other clothing allowed. Cells contain bare essentials for two, sometimes four. In the cellblocks there is heat for the winters but no air-conditioning for the blistering summers. Cells, hallways, latrines, classrooms are all stark, bare concrete and steel, sometimes freshly painted, sometimes not, generally clean but not always, and, until lights out at night, extremely noisy. Living conditions are not brutal but are definitely spartan.

I learned, in short, that Texas prisons are not designed to encourage a comfortable lifestyle beyond three square meals daily, a regular shower, and a clean change of clothes from time to time. Offenders can have other things within limits, but they have to earn them and they have to earn the right to keep them. Nothing extra comes easily, especially privileges like college courses.

I do not know anything firsthand about the violent brutality that the media reports some prisoners — and occasionally some correction officers — inflict upon one another in prison units around Huntsville. But, assuming some of those reports are true, they only add to my sense of paradox about this place. Yet what has disturbed me more year by year are the legal executions that take place in downtown Huntsville — more executions than in any other place in the United States since 1982, and, indeed, more than in most countries of the world.

Virginia and I decided to collaborate on this book about living next door to the death house because, despite our different histories with the town, we have both become sensitized to the paradoxes that surround us here. She has the roots and involvement with the town that make her a native. I now have the greater familiarity with the inside of nearby prison units, and I provide the perspective of a relative newcomer to Huntsville, still something of an outsider looking in. We have discovered that the differences in our perspectives have been just enough to leaven what could easily have turned this book into either a polemic on the death penalty or, conversely, into a PR treatise on the reasons (quite valid) that led *Money* magazine once to declare Huntsville one of the thirty-five ideal communities in which to live — an honor I am sure got a good laugh among offenders in the Walls unit downtown.

Between us, the book came into focus fairly quickly. It did not let either of us completely direct its aim. As a consequence, as it grew, *Living Next Door to the Death House* became not primarily a book about Huntsville or about prisons or even about the death penalty, but more about how the death chamber behind the Walls in the center of town has affected the lives of our fellow townspeople and visitors who, for a variety of reasons, have had to confront its presence. We chose an interview format as the means for getting this story told so that the real voices of the people this book presents get heard.

You will not hear the voices of the people on death row here, however. Their lawyers have recently advised many residents of death row against granting interviews, especially while appeals are still pending. Also, the rules now governing visitors to death row, which include full body searches of the offenders following the visit, make many reluctant to accept interviews. Besides, our focus was not on death row but on the ripples that radiate outward from Huntsville's prisons, especially from the execution chamber inside the Walls, and that eventually affect us all.

The voices you hear narrating this book are many more than just Virginia's and mine. We are deeply grateful for those who have been willing to participate in this project, and we thank them for their candor and graciousness. From their homes and workplaces in or near this small town in East Texas, these men and women have spoken with frank honesty words that all citizens — of Huntsville, of Texas, and of many other places in the world — need to hear.

1

The Town

From battle and murder, and from sudden death, Good Lord, deliver us.

The Book of Common Prayer

THOUGH IT'S BEEN fifteen years since the events occurred that permanently marked a couple of otherwise unremarkable locations in my hometown, I still shudder whenever I pass them — a strip mall along an interstate access road and a carwash near the sheriff's office on the north end of town. The strip mall has other tenants now, and newcomers to Huntsville use the carwash with none of the misgivings the natives feel. But back in 1987, the abduction of a young woman from an optical shop and the murder of a woman in front of her three-year-old child made us all profoundly uneasy. Especially since both murders went unsolved for two years.

Ours is a quiet town. Murder is rare here, and when it does occur, there's usually no mystery about who did it or why. But the fate of these two women appeared to be entirely arbitrary, senseless, and consequently terrifying to the people — especially the women — of Huntsville. A lot of cars went unwashed that winter.

IT WAS a hot July afternoon in 1987, and business was slow at the Robinson Creek Center, a row of small shops and offices near the town's hospital. Surrounded by a stand of tall yellow pines, the long concrete building housed, among other businesses, an optical shop. Its storefront windows looked east toward the uninviting view of the interstate access road.

The Vision Center had only recently opened its doors to the public — in fact, earlier that day carpenters had still been trimming out the woodwork in the office. They had left for the day, though, and now twenty-seven-year-old Debra Ewing was alone in the shop, the wall behind her filled with ranks of blank glasses frames. In another half hour Debra would be able to lock up for the day and go home too.

Glancing out at the parking lot where sun was turning the asphalt mushy, she saw an old Chevy Impala pull in and a clean-cut fellow, probably in his thirties, get out. He stood by the car for a moment, the driver's door still open, scanning the row of shops. The man seemed disoriented, as if he weren't quite sure what he was looking for. After a moment, he reached in to retrieve something from the car, then slammed the door and started across the parking lot. That's when Debra saw the gun.

Her first thought was that he intended to rob one of the shops. But instead of grabbing the keys and locking the doors, Debra grabbed her purse and dashed out of the Vision Center and down the sidewalk toward the Prudential Insurance office, where she expected other people would still be at work.

Inside the Prudential office, however, the twenty-year-old secretary was also alone that afternoon, rinsing out coffee cups in a kitchenette at the rear of the building. When she heard someone burst yelling through the front doors, she turned off the water and stepped out into the hall to see what the ruckus was about.

"There's a man outside with a gun!" Debra screamed.

Panicking, the Prudential secretary fled down the hall toward the back of the building, then dived into one of the empty offices and locked the door. Crouching under the desk, she dragged the phone down by its cord and called 911.

When the Huntsville police arrived, they found the secretary still

2

huddled under the desk. But the only sign of Debra Ewing was her purse and shoes lying out on the sidewalk. Had she kicked off her shoes in an attempt to outrun the man?

"Once I was inside the office," the Prudential secretary told the investigating officer, "I couldn't hear a thing." And no one else in Robinson Creek Center had seen or heard anything either.

Using tracking dogs, the police searched the wooded area, thick with underbrush, behind the strip center. No luck. Using the optical shop's log, they called every customer who had been in that day. The last appointment had been scheduled for 3:30, at least an hour before Debra disappeared.

People in Huntsville read their morning paper the next day aghast at the abduction. If abduction it was, some said. Surely, if Debra Ewing had been forced into the car, someone must have seen or heard her. For the next several days people speculated that she must have gone off voluntarily with her alleged kidnapper. After all, the sheriff and police had still found no trace of her.

On Wednesday, Ewing's disappearance was still a front-page story. As the days passed, it became obvious that pressure was being brought to bear on the local police department.

An FBI spokesman who arrived on the scene told a local reporter that the agency "would not be averse" to running a check on their national database of serial killers. The town's police chief had declined, however, saying that as yet they had no hard evidence of anything like a serial killing.

Soon after that, both the FBI and the Texas Rangers officially opened their investigations on the case. The hunt for Debra Ewing was extended to include neighboring counties.

The Huntsville Chamber of Commerce had organized and promoted a celebration of the town's 152nd anniversary for Sunday, but among the crowds attending the activities the conversations circled inevitably toward the latest rumors about Debra Ewing's disappearance. The whole thing had been staged to cover up her elopement with another man. It was an insurance hoax. A jealous lover had kidnapped her and fled with her to Mexico.

But while the crowds milled around the ice cream freezers and listened to local musicians in the park's gazebo, a real estate agent was showing some development property called Paradise Point, about twenty miles south of Huntsville, to prospective clients. The potential buyers, an off-duty Houston police officer and his wife, were particularly interested in lakefront property, so the agent pulled off the interstate and took a dirt road back through the woods about three miles.

He parked in a clearing, and the trio set off on foot through the dense pine forest toward the lake. They had not gone more than a hundred yards when they came upon a woman's body, nude from the waist down. Her chest had two gaping wounds, probably made by a knife. Because of the intense Texas heat, the body was already badly decomposed. So badly, in fact, that the medical examiner in Houston could not determine the approximate time of death, though he did confirm that it was what remained of Debra Ewing.

All week, updates of Debra Ewing's disappearance had carried in the local paper. Now her story returned to the front page. However, after three more days, it drifted from the front to the third page. None of the law enforcement agencies involved had been able to come up with any clues to the murderer's identity. Debra Ewing's friends, acquaintances, and family members were all questioned, but none of them could think of any enemies or jilted lovers who might have done such a deed.

It was the sheer irrationality of the murder that made the citizenry of Huntsville so uneasy and fearful. And which accounted for the variant speculations about Debra Ewing's connection to her abductor. We demanded reasons, and when none were forthcoming, some invented them. Debra Ewing must, some insisted, have somehow been complicit in the crime. After all, who would murder a person they didn't even know? The fear that haunted us all was this: If such a senseless horror could overtake this woman, it might befall any of us, might strike anywhere.

And indeed, events would bear out the truth of this conclusion.

Weeks, then months went by. About the middle of October, the heat began to moderate, and by Halloween the days had become quite pleasant, no longer stifling but not yet chilly. Perhaps because the weather was still so mild, Mary Risinger decided to stop by a self-service carwash before taking her three-year-old daughter trick-or-treating that Halloween. The little girl was beside her, already dressed for the evening in her frilly ballerina costume.

As Mary Risinger drove her white car into one of the bays, she perhaps noticed a brown pickup parked behind the carwash. If she did, she would have had no reason to suspect danger. The sheriff's department had newly relocated their offices right down the road from the carwash.

Taking some quarters from her purse to feed into the machine, she probably had to reassure her little girl, eager for trick-or-treats, that washing the car wouldn't take long. Then they would be on their way to the fun part of the evening.

Mary Risinger's attacker must have struck just as she was getting out of the car, grabbing her from behind and plunging a knife into her throat. Mary Risinger, however, put up a surprisingly tough fight, examiners would later surmise from the angles and numbers of her wounds. After all, she was protecting not just her own life but her child's.

Passersby later reported that they had indeed seen a couple having what they took to be a tussle at the carwash, but they had not stopped to check it out since they thought it was only a lovers' quarrel.

However desperate Mary Risinger's resistance proved, it was no match for a man with a knife who struck blow after blow. Finally, she fell in a heap by the cement drain beside the car. The man ran to the brown pickup, jumped in, and roared away just as another vehicle drove up. The people just turning into the carwash noticed a white car in one of the bays, seemingly unattended. Then they saw the bloody body lying beside the car. Terrified, they reversed out of the carwash drive and sped down the road to the new sheriff's office to report what they had seen.

A deputy told the dispatcher to put in a call for an ambulance, then rushed off to the carwash. But as he knelt beside the savaged body of Mary Risinger, he could tell she was already dead, stabbed multiple times in the throat. He was just getting slowly to his feet when he spotted a movement inside the white car. He took a step closer and saw a small, frightened face. Peering into the window, he saw a little girl wearing a ballerina costume. It was soaked with blood.

It took some doing for the deputy to convince the child to unlock the car doors and let him in.

As I said, ours is a quiet town, a pretty town. Nestled in a national forest, it has a state park and lake on its southern border. When a trader named Pleasant Gray founded the town in 1835, he described the area as a "natural prairie in the middle of a vast forest with a mighty pretty stream running near by." In fact, he found it so much like the place he had left in Alabama that he gave it the same name as his former hometown.

Huntsville's attractions have not faded with the years. The Rating Guide to Life in America's Small Cities ranked Huntsville forty-first in the nation and first in Texas in 1990. In 2000, Demographics Daily, an online publication of Bizjournal.com, put Huntsville among the top "dreamtowns" in the nation with the highest quality of life. The state university here leavens the intellectual and cultural lump, which might otherwise prove a bit leaden. In an ordinary year, only two or three people are killed here. That is, if you don't count the several dozen people executed in Huntsville by the state of Texas each year.

This pleasant town has another, less appealing side, one represented by a single room — the death chamber — at the Walls, the prison compound that sits just a few blocks east of the county courthouse square. Unfortunately, that room provides the only picture most people have of Huntsville. But the effect of what goes on in that small room reaches out like tentacles to touch the lives of everyone who lives here.

According to the last census, Huntsville has a population of slightly over 35,000. That number includes more than 8000 prisoners housed in the five prison units located within the city limits. In the outlying rural areas, another 5300 prisoners live in two additional units. About 8500 people are employed in various capacities by the prison system, the Texas Department of Criminal Justice (TDCJ). Huntsville is a company town.

How did the incarceration industry come to dominate the economy and culture of this town? The reason is rooted in the state's history. When Texas became a state in 1846, Huntsville made an early, and unsuccessful, bid for the capital. It lost out to the more centrally located

Austin, then a frontier town on the edge of Comanche territory. As a kind of consolation prize, Huntsville was awarded the state penitentiary. And the prison system remains to this day the only state agency headquartered outside of Austin.

In some ways, these two cities — Huntsville and Austin — epitomize a certain tension that still characterizes the state. Located in the eastern pine forests, Huntsville held longer to customs and attitudes associated with Southern states, while Austin, sprawling across the limestone hills of Central Texas, is wedded to the ways of the West. Lynchings, for example, especially of African-Americans, occurred with some frequency in East Texas well into the 1930s. West Texas, by contrast, served as headquarters to the Buffalo soldiers, African-American recruits in the U.S. Army. Another telling statistic: over the years, West Texas has sent only a handful of men to Huntsville for execution.

Huntsville did not become the sole site of the state's executions until 1923, however. Until then, each county had carried out its own executions. Following the frontier tradition of using available technology, these were most often public hangings. To get an idea of how frequently these hangings were, consider these numbers: between 1608 and 1991 — a span of 383 years — 14,634 people were executed in the entire territory that is now the United States. That's about thirty-eight a year. But between 1919 and mid-1923, less than four years, 394 people were hanged in Texas — a rate of more than a hundred a year.

As the state gradually became more urbanized, however, its citizens grew increasingly uncomfortable with the local hangings, associated as they were with vigilante justice and racist lynchings. Thus in 1923 the state legislature mandated that all future executions be carried out under the supervision of state officials at the Walls unit in Huntsville.

A few months later, Texas began to execute by electrocution, a method considered more civilized and humane than public hanging.* Three hundred sixty-one men eventually met their maker sitting in the original Old Sparky, the electric chair that is now the crown jewel of the Texas Prison Museum's exhibits.

---

* In 1890 New York privately executed its first criminal, after Thomas Edison performed public demonstrations of the method.

The grade school I attended in Huntsville was about four blocks from the Walls. The playground gossip was always full of tales about the lights dimming at midnight whenever a prisoner was electrocuted. "Old Sparky sucks up all the juice," a deputy's son told us, his voice husky with an insider's authority.

Of the 361 men who died in Old Sparky, 229 were black, 108 were white, and 23 were Hispanic. None were women. Until 1998, when Karla Faye Tucker died by lethal injection, no woman had ever been executed at the Walls in Huntsville.

MY OWN family has a long history with the prison system. During World War II my grandfather worked for a while as a guard. "Herding convicts," he called it. Three decades later, my mother was assistant to the warden at the women's prison, still located then in Huntsville. But the family connection goes back even farther, and down a darker path.

Long before I was born, even before my grandfather was born, my great-great-uncle rented convicts from the state to pick cotton on his farm. One day a rented prisoner tried to run away. He only made it as far as the river before he was caught. The uncle warned him that he would be whipped if he tried to escape again.

Undeterred, the convict somehow got his hands on a shotgun several days later and fled the cotton field a second time. The uncle, figuring the man would not try the river route again, began the search by checking his outbuildings. As he opened the door to a little board-and-batt tool shed, the prisoner stepped out of the shadows and shot him in the chest. Then the man flung down the gun and fled.

When he heard of the shooting, the sheriff rode out to the farm, fearful that the victim's brothers might find the runaway before he could and take their own revenge. So he swore all four brothers as deputies, trusting their oaths as agents of the law to keep them within its bounds. The convict was soon found, tried, and given a life sentence.

Many years later, when the prisoner was old and sick, prison officials contacted the surviving brothers and asked if they would cause trouble if the convict were released so he could spend his last days with his family. By then the brothers' passions had cooled, and they agreed to let their brother's murderer go home to die.

The moral ambiguities in the story are, of course, daunting. As you probably suspected, the convict was black and probably born in slavery. What his original crime was, I have no idea. Nor do I know why, in this part of the country, he was only given a life sentence instead of the death penalty for shooting a white landowner.

But what surprises me most about this story is its ending — the brothers' clemency in agreeing to let the dying man return home.

It's a story that could never happen today. First of all, the practice of renting convict labor ended long ago. Second, should an inmate kill someone during an attempted escape today, he would automatically get a death sentence. Certainly he would not be released to return to his family just because he was near death, no matter how compassionate the victim's family. Today, victims' families have no say in such matters.

A LOT of other things have changed since then as well, not least the media coverage — or lack of it — that surrounds executions. The old-time hangings may have been public events, but today only the family of the murder victim and the prisoner's family or spiritual advisor are allowed to view executions. Three media representatives — two print and one broadcast — are also in the viewing room, their job being to disseminate information about the execution to the state's citizenry in whose name the sentence is carried out.

The presence of the media has rarely posed a problem for Huntsville. The story of a crime committed years ago was old news. Even the murderer's execution rarely held the attention of most news consumers. Then came the execution of Karla Faye Tucker in 1998.

Tucker's crime had been sufficiently brutal — she had hacked at least one person to death in Houston with a pickax — for the press to cover every graphic detail of the crime and Tucker's life as a prostitute. But it was neither the crime nor her former life that brought squads of TV vans to Huntsville, satellite dishes rotating on their roofs. It was her religious conversion and drastically altered life that raised the national consciousness about the death penalty in a way that decades of earnest abolitionist rhetoric had not been able to do. For a week before Tucker's execution there was not a vacant motel room or restaurant table to be found in Huntsville. Swarms of celebrities, reporters, and film crews, both foreign and domestic, descended on the town. TV vans clogged the streets. Shoppers were accosted for man-on-the-street interviews.

But while the media's presence boosted the city's income considerably, it made most Huntsville residents profoundly uncomfortable. We may be proud of the lovely grounds of our state university, we may be glad when the historical museum has its annual festival celebrating our connection to Sam Houston, the George Washington of Texas, but we did not enjoy the questionable fame that Karla Faye Tucker's execution brought us. Not even the most ardent supporter of capital punishment boasts about our international reputation as the execution capital of the Western world.

Another sort of high-profile execution two years later reinforced Huntsville's notoriety. And this time it wasn't even good for business. Gary Graham, thirty-nine years old, had spent nearly nineteen of those years on death row for a 1981 robbery-murder. He had also been charged with ten other robberies, two shootings, ten car thefts, and eight more robberies — most committed on the same day as the fatal incident that resulted in his death sentence. Because he maintained to the end that he had not committed the particular crime for which he was condemned — though his other deadly exploits hardly qualified him as a poster child for the abolitionist cause — Graham became a *cause celebre* among the New Black Panthers.

June 22, 2000, the day of Graham's execution, a number of the brothers, some of them armed, along with other, more pacific abolitionist groups, streamed into town. Businesses on the courthouse square, mostly antique shops, shut down for the duration. Some boarded up their windows. Sharpshooters were stationed on the roofs of downtown buildings in case a riot broke out. People in Huntsville still shake their heads at the memory. Thank heavens nothing happened, they say.

BUT, OF COURSE, something did happen. Prison officials waited for two hours while three courts ruled on Graham's last-minute appeals. When they were all denied, Gary Graham made his desperately lengthy last statement, claiming to the last that he was innocent of the crime for which he was being executed. It was a quarter to nine that evening before he was finally pronounced dead.

Such high-profile executions are few and far between. No protesters, for example, showed up yesterday to protest the execution of John Wheat, a former church janitor, though his crime was surely as barbarous and tragic as any.

In 1996 John Wheat had been living in an apartment complex a few doors down from a single mother and her three small children. He sometimes babysat the children — Lacey, nineteen months old, Eddie, her eight-year-old brother, and Ashley, her sister, who was six. But Ashley reported to their mother that the man had, as the newspaper account circumspectly put it, "touched her inappropriately."

On hearing this, the mother immediately confronted John Wheat, threatening to call the police. The two exchanged angry words. Then she left and returned to her apartment. A few minutes later, John Wheat came to her door carrying two guns, a .22 caliber pistol and a semi-automatic handgun.

Terrified, the woman ran out of the apartment and down the walkway, then ducked into another apartment whose door was open. John Wheat followed her inside and shot her twice in the head. Then he returned to the family's apartment and shot all three children. Afterwards, he stood outside, shooting randomly at the bystanders who had collected. A policewoman answering the call for help was also shot.

Despite her head wounds, the mother somehow survived, as did four of the others John Wheat had wounded. The children, however, were all dead when the police arrived. Wheat was charged only with the murder of the toddler. Texas law requires the death penalty for killing a child under the age of six. The mother suffered severe brain damage; her sister came to John Wheat's execution as the family's witness.

Last night, from the gurney in the execution chamber, John Wheat smiled and waved to members of his own family on the other side of the viewing window. "I deeply regret what happened," he said in his final statement. "I did not intentionally or knowingly harm anyone. I did not do anything deliberately. That's it."

If there was ever a man who deserved to die it was John Wheat.

Even Jesus said that it were better for anyone who offends against the little ones to be thrown into the depths of the sea wearing a millstone around his neck. Yet this momentous occasion, supposedly intended to vindicate three innocent lives, proved of no particular interest to society at large.

As for Huntsville, most people here were grateful for the public's lack of interest.

A woman who works as a victim's advocate in the county told me recently how being identified with Huntsville affects her high school children. One of them plays on a ball team, another plays in the band. They both go on road trips to other towns around the state.

"It's hard on them sometimes," the woman said. "They get called names. People yell, 'Go back to Prison Town.'" She paused to smile wryly. "Most people are in favor of executing murderers. Not where they live, of course, but someplace else. Huntsville is that place."

BECAUSE HUNTSVILLE is that place, a small group gathers at St. Stephen's Church on Wednesday afternoons when executions are scheduled. Some weeks, though, have more than one on the calendar, so we come on Tuesday or Thursday as well. Among us are three professors, a secretary, a college chaplain, a woman with a small videography business, the rector, and me. Most are members of this Episcopal congregation; some are not.

We arrive at five-thirty, scatter among the pews, and pray the Liturgy for an Execution, a service devised by several members of the congregation. We all know that, while we pray, a man on the other side of town is being strapped onto a gurney and needles are being inserted into the vein at the crook of his elbow. That picture takes shape in our mind's eye as we say the words we've all but memorized by now. Sometimes, however, the man's sentence is stayed at the last moment, and we leave, wondering what the man, the threat of death temporarily deferred, is feeling at that moment.

The litany we use covers just about everyone involved in the process. We pray for the murderer's "sincere contrition and confidence in Jesus Christ." We pray for his victim's eternal peace. We pray for both the murderer's and the victim's families. We pray for the attorneys, the

judge, and the jury who decided his fate. We pray for the prison personnel, including the guards, the warden, and the chaplains, all waiting up
there at the Walls. We pray for the governor and the state's Board of
Pardons and Paroles. Finally, we are exhorted to pray "for the people of
the State of Texas, who carry out this sentence."

That's when I can feel the words begin to stick in my throat. I like
the litany so long as we're praying from the moral high ground. My
heart stretches magnanimously, imagining the prisoner's dread, the
families' anguish, the burden on those inside the death chamber, the
strain on officials making life-and-death decisions. But as a Texan, and
thus at least a part, however small, of the body in whose name the execution is carried out, this unnerves me. The next petition is even closer
to home: "for the people of Huntsville, that we remain distressed and
avoid complacency."

One afternoon last spring, however, the group gathered, not for an
execution, but to wait for a film crew to arrive. As we stood around the
narthex, we spoke in nervous undertones.

Weeks ago, a producer from WDR German public television had
called me about a documentary he was making on how Christians deal
with the death penalty. He said he wanted to place that particular issue
within the larger context of Christians' attitudes toward the value of
life, including abortion, euthanasia, stem cell research, and so on. He
had read some articles I had written about the death penalty. Would I
agree to be interviewed?

"I'm not really the best person to talk to," I told him. I suggested
some better prospects, including the rector of St. Stephen's.

"If you want to film the people who come to the service here, it'll
have to be just a conversation," the rector warned. "Several other crews
have been here already. But we don't allow filming during services."

Jim looks a little too normal to be your stereotypical Episcopal
priest. He's not tall, and his nose isn't sharp and thin nor his hair sil-
vered. I suspect he wears his clergy collar around town so he won't be
taken for a high school math teacher or the owner of an office supply
store. He's been at St. Stephen's only seven years, so he's still considered
a newcomer.

Two of the professors in the group have taught at the state university in Huntsville for thirty years, and they're still not insiders either. In fact, of all the people at the church this afternoon, I probably have the longest history with the town.

People usually raise an eyebrow or grin when I identify my hometown as Huntsville. "When did you get out?" they joke. At least they used to. Lately, they just raise an eyebrow. In other parts of the country, and especially in Europe, claiming this town as your home is almost like saying you grew up in Three Mile Island or Chernobyl.

Most people in Huntsville, like most people in the nation — around seventy-eight percent — support the death penalty. That is, unless, they are presented with other options, such as a sentence of life without parole. But generally, people here are reluctant to talk about the subject. They feel somehow personally stigmatized, as if their physical proximity to the Walls has stamped their foreheads with the mark of Cain. If asked about the executions, most simply frown and shake their heads. It's easy to read into that gesture a protest against the unfairness of being singled out. After all, it's not Huntsville's fault.

I've had the same feelings myself. When the German film crew finally showed up that spring afternoon, they set up the shoot on the front lawn of the church. Both the cameraman and audio engineer were Bosnians, slightly built, with dark hair and multiple earrings. I don't think they spoke much English.

The reporter, on the other hand, was large, fair, and German. His English was simultaneously quaint and passionate. Placing me in the shade of a blossoming pear tree in order to get a shot of the church in the background, he begins asking his questions. "We simply do not understand this, we Europeans," he says. "I mean, as a Christian, how you can justify executions?"

"I don't," I say. "But I can understand why some people do."

"Okay, so tell me about that." He gestures to the soundman to move in closer with the boom.

"They probably rely on Bible verses from the Old Testament. An eye for an eye." Then I add, "But I think you should find some of them and let them speak for themselves."

He frowns. "But are these executions not state-sponsored killing — right in your own neighborhood? As a Christian, how can you stand to let that sort of thing happen here?" His voice registers a barely contained moral outrage.

"You're from Germany," I snap, "and you ask how that can happen?"

ANOTHER REPORTER, another interview, this time from the now-defunct *George* magazine. This time we've met for lunch at a local restaurant. "Finally," he says, loading his plate at the salad bar, "some vegetables besides french fries and iceberg lettuce." We sit in a back room in the restaurant, overlooking the tops of redbud trees, where we can talk more easily.

"I can't believe people's attitude here," he confides from across the table. "They call the Walls unit 'the death house.' Those are the very words they use. And they're not even being ironic."

I raise what I hope is a suitably ironic eyebrow at the observation. The young reporter is handsome and well-spoken. He might have just stepped out of the glossy pages of his own magazine. I can tell he has led a life sheltered from iceberg lettuce. Also, there's not a store in Huntsville that sells the brand of shirt he's wearing.

"How can they stand to call it that?" he goes on, inserting the tines of his fork into a cherry tomato.

My eyebrow sinks and my irony deserts me. I stare at him blankly. "Because," I say, "that's what it is."

DAVID AND I are both so familiar with the prison culture that pervades Huntsville, we wonder what it looks like to new arrivals in town. How do the executions affect them? While we were having dinner with a couple of newcomers one evening, David asked them how they felt about living in a town that has the reputation of being the nation's execution capital.

Caroline, a native Minnesotan with Scandinavian blond hair and melting blue eyes, came to Texas by the circuitous route of England and Arizona to teach in the university's music department. Her husband John, a British transplant, took early retirement from a medical career to pursue several avocational interests, including seventeenth-century history.

"I remember when I was interviewing for the job," Caroline says, "I asked one of my colleagues about the executions, and he said to me, 'you don't even notice it.'"

She shifts her glass a fraction of an inch on the table. "And during my first year of teaching, that was true. I didn't notice. Yet, somehow, I always managed to turn left before I reached the Walls. I didn't even realize I was doing that for a while. But now, whenever I go past there in the car, I do think about it."

"And, of course," her husband puts in, "one does see those people in their white outfits pulling weeds from the flowerbeds on the courthouse lawn. That scene does take one aback at times."

"I guess living in England for twenty years has changed my perspective, too," Caroline continues. "They, of course, think it's appalling. But I'm sure that, if I'd spent my entire life in America, I would simply assume it was normal. The death penalty wouldn't seem all that strange to me. From the European perspective, however, it's barbaric."

"It's not merely a question of the death penalty, is it?" John adds. "These people are incarcerated for a long time before they are ever executed. They have no hope, have they? They've got nothing to lose by bad behavior."

"I think most of them file appeals," I say. "That's where their hope must lie."

"I had to examine prisoners in Wansworth, one of the rougher prisons in London," John recalls. "In treating them, in treating any of my patients, I try to make contact with them, meaning I physically touch them. Patients always respond better if there is some form of physical contact. But, when I touched the prisoners at Wansworth, they reacted as if they had received an electric shock."

"When we first got here," Caroline adds, "people would ask John, 'Why don't you work for the prison system?' They didn't understand that John doesn't have the proper kind of personality for that."

"How so?" I ask.

"I've spent the whole of my life running around after people," John says. "I worked in the kind of medical system where you don't get paid very much, so it was kind of obligatory. Of course, I was trying to help people, put them back together again. But, in the prison system, you only survive if you're a skilled manipulator. So I was the wrong candidate."

Caroline nods. "John has the kind of personality that would be very manipulable."

"I was educated to perform a service," John goes on. "People in prison are much more skilled manipulators than I would ever be. They would run away with me."

David turns to Caroline. "How does it make you feel when, on any given day, maybe when you're preparing for a concert at the university, just a few blocks away someone else may be preparing for their execution?" He puts up a hand. "Of course, I know that when you're at work, you're not necessarily thinking about these questions. But does that affect you? Or your students?"

Caroline shakes her head. "I don't think it affects the music department or our students much. They're all too busy creating their own little worlds. Whether something like that was happening two blocks or two thousand miles away, it wouldn't matter. Musicians, you know, they live in their own world."

———

MAYBE EVERYONE else in America lives in a different kind of world than we do in Huntsville. Maybe you never have to remember that, on any given Wednesday, just when you're sitting down to supper, a syringe is being inserted into a man's vein, its contents deliberately and methodically calibrated to cause death. Maybe you even live in one of the twelve states that have abolished the death penalty and thus feel untouched by the dilemma. Nevertheless, you have thought about capital punishment, studied the arguments for and against it, taken a moral position on one side or the other. Even so, capital punishment probably remains a distant abstraction, rather than a part of your neighborhood's landscape. And you'd like to keep it like that — distant and theoretical.

But consider this: On June 11, 2001, two days before the state of Texas executed John Wheat, the United States executed Timothy McVeigh in Terre Haute, Indiana. John Wheat killed three children. Timothy McVeigh killed nineteen — along with 149 adults — when he set off the bomb at the Murrah Federal Building in Oklahoma City.

He was put to death not during the dinner hour, but early in the morning, when most people in the Central time zone were eating breakfast. At that moment on the east coast, people were already on their way to work. Farther west, folks were just waking up.

Despite the early hour, whether they had eaten breakfast yet or not, almost everyone in the country knew it was national execution day. The news media had covered first the trial, then the delay in the execution, in close detail. It would have been difficult to find anyone who had not heard of or did not have an opinion about the crime or the culprit. Timothy McVeigh was not just a local villain; he had sinned against us all. This was America's execution. And for that one day at least, everyone lived in Huntsville, Texas.

Curiously, however, June 11, 2001, came and went with scarcely a ripple on the surface of our national consciousness, just as executions in Huntsville go largely ignored. A man whose life had been exhaustively chronicled, whose every word appeared in print, sank below the threshold of our collective consciousness with scarcely any notice. The execution seemed strangely anticlimactic. No one except representatives of the victims' families watched Timothy McVeigh die on closed circuit television. With no new pictures to show, only that all-too-familiar clip of McVeigh in his orange prison jumpsuit being led down a prison ramp, the major networks that evening carried only a brief announcement that the court's execution order had indeed been carried out.

In a statement to the press, Jannie Coverdale, the grandmother of two of the nineteen children Timothy McVeigh killed, said she had been looking forward to watching his execution, assuring herself that then he would be gone from her life forever. On the other hand, Robert Welch, whose daughter was also among the victims, said he believed the execution would bring neither him nor other Oklahomans the relief and release they had been hoping for.

And what about the rest of us — the commuters, the coffee-drinkers, the people just picking up the newspaper off the steps or shutting off alarm clocks? We scarcely realized that the sentence was being carried out in our name. We just went on about our business.

IN HUNTSVILLE, on execution Wednesdays, the local paper usually runs a story describing the crime the condemned committed, the appeals made for his case, and their outcome. On Thursday, the paper tells us what he ordered for his last meal, and records his final statement. Some readers study those last words to see if he died insisting on his innocence or apologizing for his crime. If he claimed innocence, we may suffer a twinge of discomfort brought on by a fleeting uncertainty. If he showed signs of remorse, we feel a longer-lasting relief. Then we too go about our business.

However, should our business take us past the death house on the east end of Eleventh Street, we glance uneasily at the plain red brick building, knowing that what goes on inside is no abstraction, but a reality so palpable it suddenly makes the air around the Walls heavy and harder to breathe.

An execution touches not only the wives, parents, siblings, and children of both the victim and the murderer, but also the attorneys who prosecuted and defended the prisoner, as well as the people who, ten or more years ago, served on the jury that convicted him. It affects the law enforcement officers who investigated the crime; the people who cleaned up after it; the guards who have lived alongside the prisoner for years; the wardens who oversee the execution; the chaplains and spiritual advisors who have learned the prisoner's most intimate secrets; the technicians who prepare the syringe and prick the vein.

These are the ones who daily bear the burden of execution's reality for the rest of us, so we can go on about our business, unperturbed and unfettered. Nevertheless, we should not forget that they bear that burden in our name.

2

Crime and Punishment

Had I a hundred tongues, a hundred mouths, a voice of iron
and a chest of brass, I could not tell all the forms of crime, could
not name all the punishments.

VIRGIL, *Aeneid*

WHEN IN *The Mikado* Gilbert and Sullivan's Lord High Executioner sang that his intention was "to let the punishment fit the crime," he was echoing a much older aphorism of Cicero that crime and punishment should be equal. All systems of justice, modern and ancient, have made at least rudimentary attempts to weigh the punishment against the crime.

Though it has not always been the case, nowadays we only execute people for murder. None of the fifty states puts anyone to death for a crime of lesser magnitude, though federal law allows for the execution of traitors and the military code of justice for mutineers. On the face of it, matching crime to punishment looks simple. But as with any human project, balancing the scales of justice is seldom easy. Not all murders are equal under the law. And each of the fifty states applies its laws differently.

Currently in Texas, a district attorney can ask for the death penalty when a murder has been committed during the course of a robbery or other felony such as rape, when the victim is a law enforcement officer or a fireman, when there are multiple victims, or when the victim is a child under six. This last category — murders of children — is one to which we react with special and universal horror.

About the time David and I began writing this book, a young suburban mother, Andrea Pia Yates, drowned her five children in the bathtub of their home in Clear Lake, less than a hundred miles from Huntsville. The first one she drowned was six-month-old Mary, her only daughter. Then she forced Mary's brothers Luke, Paul, and John, aged two, three, and five respectively, into the bathtub and under the water. Afterwards, she carried the four bodies to the back bedroom and laid them out on the bed, covering them with a sheet. Finally, she chased her oldest child, Noah, seven, through the house, wrestled him into the tub, and held him under the water till he stopped thrashing. She left his body in the tub while she called the police to report what she had done. Then she phoned her husband, Rusty, at his NASA office in the Johnson Space Center where he worked as a computer engineer. She told him to come home, saying that something was wrong with the children.

We have been following the development of her case, trying to understand how it is possible — for society, for her husband, for her — to absorb the enormity of such a crime. How should we respond? Is there any way to repair the many lives shattered on that June day in 2001?

Some people believe that her husband, Russell Yates, shares the blame for their children's death. After all, following the birth of her fourth child, she had taken an overdose of Trazodone and was subsequently hospitalized in a psychiatric ward with a severe depressive disorder. Discharged the next week, she had to be hospitalized again a month later after Russell Yates had found her holding a knife to her throat and had wrestled it from her. Back in the hospital, she was treated with the powerful anti-psychotic drug, Haldol, to which she seemed to respond so well that she was released in less than three weeks, though she continued her daily outpatient care for another ten days.

The psychiatrist who treated Andrea during this episode counseled the couple not to have any more children, as further pregnancies would threaten Andrea's already precarious mental condition. But within months of that warning, Andrea conceived another child.

Andrea's best friend, a fellow nurse who had worked with Andrea at a large cancer hospital in Houston, worried about her friend's state of mind. When Andrea began displaying symptoms of severe depression after the birth of her fifth child, the friend became alarmed. She called Russell Yates several times, begging him to take Andrea to see her psychiatrist. He dismissed her concerns, however, saying that his wife was merely sad about her father, who was on the point of death. During the three weeks after Andrea's father died, the friend visited her numerous times. She found Andrea unbathed and thin, wandering mutely through the house, paying no attention to anyone, not even her children.

A few weeks before Andrea killed her children, she was hospitalized twice in a psychiatric treatment center where a new psychiatrist, a man this time, treated her. After she was dismissed for the second time, this doctor called Russell Yates and advised him to begin decreasing Andrea's doses of Haldol. Russell did as he was told. Two weeks later, Russell took Andrea for her scheduled appointment with the doctor. It had been eleven days since her last dose of Haldol, and Russell told the doctor that his wife was not doing well. Nevertheless, the doctor did not prescribe any more Haldol.

Two days later, Andrea Yates drowned her five children.

In her confession, Andrea told police she killed the children because they were not "righteous" and therefore "doomed to perish in the fires of hell."

A crime like Andrea Yates's smashes into the imagination with the force of a tidal wave, then leaves us emotionally marooned somewhere between shock and outrage. To kill one's own children strikes us as so counterintuitive, so unnatural, that we instantly recoil from the thought. Mothers provide the archetype for trust and security in practically all cultures. They harbor us in their bodies, then nurture us through our most defenseless years. Therefore, hearing of a mother who methodically drowns five of her own children — most of whom, the coroner reported, had obviously struggled for their lives — sets up cosmic shock waves in our psyches.

What is to be done in the aftermath of such an enormity? As Andrea Yates's fellow citizens, how are we to respond to her crime?

How does the justice system repair the hole she has ripped in the social fabric?

Actually, maternal filicide — a mother murdering her own child — is not as rare as we would like to think. According to a special report by the Bureau of Justice Statistics, when women kill, they most often kill family members. And the family members they most often kill are their children. Over half — 55 percent — of children killed by some member of the family are murdered by their mothers.

Currently, fifty-five women are on death row in this country. Nine of those fifty-five were convicted of killing their children. None of those nine pled insanity as a mitigating factor except Christina Riggs, an Arkansas mother with a history of depression who injected her two little boys with potassium chloride, the same chemical used to execute prisoners. Riggs then tried to kill herself immediately afterward. Her lawyers failed to convince the jury that she was mentally incompetent. She was executed last year.

In addition to Andrea Yates, two other mothers in Houston have killed their children during the past decade. Claudette Kibble, who as a child of thirteen had been abducted and repeatedly raped, bore five children, including a set of twins, within four years. In 1986, when her first child was still a toddler, she drowned him, then reported to the authorities that he had died at home of a seizure. She would eventually kill two more of her babies and attempt to kill a fourth. All the victims were boys. Her only daughter, one of the twins, was not harmed. When she was twenty-three, Kibble, at the urging of her mother, finally confessed to the murders. Waiving her right to a jury trial, she received a life sentence in exchange for a guilty plea.

Also in 1986, a Mexican immigrant named Juana Leija threw six of her seven children into Buffalo Bayou, a sluggish stream that meanders through downtown Houston. Passersby managed to save four of the children, but two drowned. Leija had twice before tried to kill herself in order to escape her abusive husband. Her lawyer argued that she had chosen to take her children with her so as not to leave them to the mercy of a sadistic father. When she pled no contest to the murder charges, she was given ten years of deferred-adjudication probation. Her oldest child, Eloisa, seeing her mother pitching her siblings into the bayou, had run for help. Eloisa is now in her twenties with children of her own. Leija sometimes baby-sits those grandchildren. She has never committed another act of violence.

At least two other cases of maternal murder in the past decade show that immigrant mothers living with abusive men are particularly at risk. Maria Amaya, a Salvadoran living in New York, cut the throats of her four children, then tried to kill herself by drinking lye. Like Leija, she believed she was sending her children to a better place where they would escape the torture she had undergone. Maria Amaya was judged legally insane, and the murder charges were dropped.

Khouma Her did not get off so easy. A Hmong refugee living in Minnesota, she strangled her six children three years ago when her estranged husband threatened to take them away from her. After killing the children, she tried to hang herself, believing they would all be reunited in an afterlife. Though she had lived with domestic abuse for years, because Khouma Her had no medical diagnosis of depression, her lawyers decided not to mount an insanity defense. She received a sentence of fifty years in prison.

Many maternal murderers are women who have borne a number of children over a short period of time. These women often end up killing themselves later, even if they receive relatively lenient treatment by the justice system. In a case very similar to that of Andrea Yates, a mother in Honolulu whose husband was frequently away on missions during the Vietnam War also drowned her five children in the bathtub. She was judged not guilty by reason of insanity and remitted to a psychiatric hospital. Six months later she hanged herself.

Some mothers kill their infants serially over an extended period of time. Marie Noe finally confessed in 1999 to killing eight children over a nineteen-year period. But, as she had been treated for mental illness for a long time, she was charged only with second-degree murder and received a sentence of twenty years' probation. No doubt her age, 77, was also taken into account in sentencing.

Given these precedents, one could hardly predict what the jury would decide about Andrea Yates. She was neither a poor immigrant nor the victim of domestic abuse but a white, middle-class, well-educated, suburban mother. On the other hand, her history of severe depression, including recent hospitalization, was well documented. Nevertheless, Houston's new district attorney asked for the death penalty. Though Harris County is known as the "capital of capital punishment," up until the Yates case, the prosecution had never sought a death sentence for maternal murderers. Kibble got a life sentence in exchange for a guilty plea, and Leija has already finished her ten years of deferred-adjudication probation.

A month after the murder of his children, Russell Yates discovered via the Internet James Young, the husband of a woman in Honolulu who had killed their children. On November 22, 1965, Maggie Young drowned their five children in the bathtub and laid them out in the bed, much as Andrea had done with hers. Like Andrea, Maggie had been hospitalized for postpartum depression and psychosis following suicide attempts. Like Russell Yates, Young was anxious for his wife to return home, and never saw disaster coming. And like Andrea, Maggie killed her children because, according to her husband, "she thought she was saving them from an awful world and a mother who couldn't take care of them."

Maggie Young was charged with first-degree murder and placed in the Honolulu State Penitentiary. Psychiatrists for the court found her unfit for trial, however, and she was sent to a state mental hospital, where she responded well to treatment. But the return of reason had its consequences. Maggie Young hung herself in a shed on the hospital grounds a few months later.

What remains unclear about both the Young and Yates cases is the mothers' motives. However irrational such acts seem to us, they make sense to their perpetrators. Most motives for murder seem plain enough — greed, jealousy, fear. Medea supposedly killed her children in revenge for her husband's unfaithfulness. Did suppressed rage against her husband seethe beneath Andrea Yates's visions of bloody knives and the voices urging her to kill her children? Did physical and emotional fatigue from bearing in close succession, then caring for, even home schooling, five lively children without adequate help from husband and family overwhelm her? Did her brain fall prey to psychosis caused by unbalanced chemicals? Or is Andrea Yates an aberrant human being, a conscienceless member of our species of a kind frightening to contemplate, a female counterpart of men like Theodore Bundy and Jeffrey Dahmer?

We have an inherent and abiding need to make sense of murder, to connect cause to effect. But how will we explain to ourselves the horror of those four small bodies laid out on the bed and the one floating face down in the bathtub?

And what about juries' reasons for meting out widely varying sentences to mothers who murder? Do juries feel sorrier for some women than others? What makes jurors vote to send one person to a mental hospital and another to the death chamber? Is postpartum depression a less convincing mitigating factor than domestic abuse and poverty? Certainly, Texas juries are notoriously reluctant to accept an insanity defense. We hesitate to diminish anyone's responsibility for his or her actions. Yet they believed in Leija's impaired mental state. Was it because of her lack of education? If so, Andrea Yates's case was in trouble, since she is a college graduate and a registered nurse.

Indeed, not many people on death row fit Andrea Yates's profile. Most murderers are men, their crimes so conventional that they make poor copy for the newsroom. Statistically, most murders are committed with a handgun during the course of a robbery. Consequently, in most cases the murderer does not know the person he is killing.

Between these two extremes — drowning one's children, an act so aberrant we find it difficult to imagine, and, say, a convenience store killing, now so commonplace we don't bother to read the particulars in the newspaper — lies the entire bleak spectrum of violence, variously shaded by avarice, revenge, and testosterone. Disgruntled employees who take out their rage indiscriminately on their bosses and coworkers. Dissatisfied clients of drug dealers or gamblers with big debts. Abused wives. Jealous husbands. Rapists drunk with rage and power.

Our laws try to take into account such differences in motive. Murder committed in a fit of passion usually brings a lighter sentence than one that has been carefully planned — what is variously called murder aforethought or with premeditation. But making such distinctions has only come about after thousands of years of juridical evolution.

Before civilization developed a complex justice system with legal codes and appellate courts, clans or tribes avenged injuries, insults, or murder of their members. Indeed, in some societies today, it remains a matter of honor to punish an offense against one's family by inflicting even greater damage on the malefactor and his kin. This retaliation then raises the stakes and calls for another cycle of even more ingenious methods of punishment, usually involving mutilation or protracted death.

Such a state of affairs, however, does not make for particularly stable societies. Business cannot be transacted with foreign markets or travel accommodated if safety cannot be insured outside a clan's turf or village. For civilization to flourish, a central authority must be able to control the countryside and roads.

Thus, the rule of law eventually supplanted *lex talionis,* and the right to punish was taken from family or clan groups and vested in the state. In our own society today, we tend to think of revenge as a personal passion. Modern secular states are generally more interested in maintaining security and order. But we have recently seen how cadres of the disaffected, fueled by moral outrage, can disrupt the stability of even the most powerful of secular states. Ancient ways are still active in the world.

Hammurabi, the Babylonian king who united Mesopotamia almost four thousand years ago, first began the practice of writing down laws to insure legal continuity. Discovered in modern Iraq at the beginning of the twentieth century, a seven-foot pillar of black basalt inscribed with 3600 lines of cuneiform writing contains what we know today as Hammurabi's Code. The text is illustrated with a bas-relief of Hammurabi receiving a ring and staff from the Babylonian sun god, Shamash, as tokens of his authority to render justice.

The inscription does not make up a complete legal code but appears to be an addendum to the common, or unwritten, law of the land. It deals with a variety of issues — property rights, borrowing and lending, and marital and domestic law. It establishes penalties for such personal injury claims as a botched surgery and provides redress for unsafe working conditions. And for twenty-five different crimes, including building a shoddy house that collapses and kills the occupant, raping a betrothed girl, and allowing conspirators to meet in one's tavern, the code stipulates a punishment of death.

Many laws in Hammurabi's Code are similar to laws in the Hebrew Bible, especially to the Mosaic law in Exodus and Leviticus. Unlike the Bible, however, Hammurabi's Code prescribes no religious rituals. These two ancient legal documents, the Babylonian and the Hebrew, establish the principle of equal retribution, exacting injury for injury, life for life. But they also distinguish between classes when setting penalties. The murderer's life must be forfeited when a citizen is killed, but if the victim is only a freedman or a slave, the murderer gets off with a fine.

Today we would find both the laws in Exodus and Leviticus as well as Hammurabi's Code harsh, especially as they impose the death penalty for any number of offenses less than murder. Nevertheless, for their time they proved a milestone in humane jurisprudence. The very fact that they limit retribution to only an eye for an eye shows a good deal of progress compared to ancient tribal practices of wiping out an entire clan in retaliation for an injury done to a member of one's own clan. Hammurabi's Code ends by proclaiming its purpose to be "that the strong may not oppress the weak, that justice may be dealt the orphan and the widow," a sentiment expressed also in the biblical texts.

The wheel of justice does not always turn in the same direction, however. A thousand years after Hammurabi and Moses, the Draconian Code declared that every crime committed in Athens, even the most trivial, must be punished with death. And in Rome, the Law of the Twelve Tablets prescribed notoriously cruel executions — drowning, beating to death, burning alive, impalement, and crucifixion being but a few.

On the other hand, in 1066, William the Conqueror brought a surprising leniency to Britain when he invaded and subdued the island. He outlawed capital punishment altogether, except in times of war. To accomplish this, he first broke up the old feudal system and forced the powerful warlords to submit to the authority of the official courts.

In many other parts of medieval Europe, however, powerful families still governed as independent fiefdoms, and were content to leave reprisals in the hands of individuals or their kin. Nor did the ban on capital punishment in England long survive William the Conqueror. During the reign of Henry VIII (1509-1547), an estimated 72,000 people (among them two of the king's wives) were executed for crimes ranging from marrying a Jew to treason.

The list of execution methods expanded beyond England's traditional hanging to include boiling, burning at the stake, beheading, pulling apart with horses, and cutting the condemned into quarters while still alive. One could be put to death for crimes such as cutting down a tree without permission, robbing a rabbit warren, or any of 220 other crimes. The scientist and mathematician Isaac Newton, appointed Master of the Mint in 1699, sent a number of people to the gallows for the crime of counterfeiting coins.

Meanwhile, across the Atlantic in the ill-fated Jamestown Colony, Captain George Kendall, convicted of spying for Spain, became the first European to be executed in the New World. The Virginia colony's first legal code allowed the death penalty for such crimes as stealing grapes, killing chickens, or engaging in trade with the Indians.

Soon after the Revolutionary War, state legislatures began reducing the number and types of crimes for which a malefactor could receive a death sentence. The concept of "degrees of culpability" found its way into American jurisprudence, and as early as 1794, Pennsylvania began limiting the death penalty to first-degree murder. Michigan abolished the death penalty altogether (except for treason) in the mid-nineteenth century, the first state to do so.

Still, in several states people have been sentenced to death for lesser crimes than murder until quite recently. As late as 1971, the year before the U.S. Supreme Court ruled capital punishment unconstitutional, Texas was still executing for rape. Robbery was also punishable by death.

Today, thirty-eight of the fifty states retain the death penalty, though modes of execution in these states vary. Lethal injection is the most common, but Delaware, New Hampshire, and Washington also may hang their condemned prisoners, while Idaho, Oklahoma, and Utah can still use firing squads. Alabama, Florida, Georgia, Nebraska, South Carolina, Tennessee, Virginia, and Ohio allow electrocutions, although some of these use the electric chair only when the capital crime was committed before their laws permitted lethal injection. Some states avoid having their methods of execution declared unconstitutional by providing alternative methods. Oklahoma, for instance, allows for lethal injection, electrocution, or firing squad.

The twelve states that have done away with the death penalty altogether are Alaska, Hawaii, Iowa, Maine, Massachusetts, Michigan, Minnesota, North Dakota, Rhode Island, Vermont, West Virginia, and Wisconsin.

———⟋⟋⟍⟍———

I HAVE never been the victim of a violent crime, though I did have a cousin who was shot, supposedly during a drug deal, and I have a friend who was raped. That's as close as I've come to the murky world of murder and mayhem. Nor as a sixty-year-old white woman do I belong to a sociological category at high risk of being murdered.

According to the FBI, men are three times more likely to become murder victims than are women. Also, people in my age category are less likely to meet a violent end than are younger people. In the high-crime years of 1992-1994, one out of every fifty Americans was the victim of a violent crime. Yet the numbers more than doubled — one in twenty-three — for those between the ages of twelve and twenty-four.

I am also less likely to be murdered because I am not black. African Americans make up about 12 percent of the U.S. population, yet they account for 51 percent of all murder victims, making them eight times more likely to die a violent death than their white counterparts. If I were an African American man under twenty, my chances of being murdered would be bone chilling. The odds of finding myself in the dock, charged with murder, would be likewise disquieting.

A close look at the current landscape of crime and punishment can be unnerving. During the month of January 2000, seven convicted murderers, all men, were executed in Huntsville, a record-breaking number for one month in Texas. The first man, a truck driver named Earl Heiselbetz, stole eight dollars from a neighbor, then killed her and her two-year-old daughter. Spencer Goodman carjacked a red Cadillac, killed its owner, and stole her credit cards. David Hicks raped and beat to death his eighty-seven-year-old grandmother. Larry Robison decapitated his male lover and four other people in a lake cottage. Billy

Hughes shot a state trooper who had stopped him to question him about stolen credit cards. Glenn McGinnis shot a clerk at the dry cleaners for $140. When he was twenty-two, James Moreland stabbed two men in the back multiple times. He lived on death row for sixteen years before he was executed.

I look at the official prison photographs of these men and try to imagine them in ordinary clothes on an ordinary street. I ask myself if, had I passed any of these men on the street, would I have spotted them as criminals? Is there some special configuration of their features that marks them as malicious or dangerous?

Not that I can tell. Given a ball cap and a smile, any of them might be the man who reads my electric meter. Or dress one in a button-down shirt and tie, and he could be an insurance salesman. For the most part, murderers look so ordinary that the ancient practice of branding criminals, the way God set a mark on Cain, makes a certain amount of sense.

If we can't single out murderers with the naked eye, is there some other means that might tell us who is likely to become one? Can we predict who is likely to kill, and thus prevent the crime?

Sociologists debate this question. Some warn that an American underclass, cut off from the national institutions of family, education, work, and neighborhood, will produce "super predators." They argue that the drop in the crime rate has not come about from "socializing the underclass" but from locking them up — 1.8 million of them, to be exact. Behavioral scientists claim they can predict which preschool boys will become violent adult criminals by testing their testosterone levels. Such notions make racial profiling appear almost benign.

Yet even if we are leery of sociologists' ability to predict criminality, the numbers they compile tell a sad story. According to the FBI, after declining markedly since 1992, the number of violent crimes in the United States has leveled off with the advent of a new millennium. Across the nation, it seems we have now hit a plateau. In 2000, homicides were actually up again in Boston, San Diego, and Los Angeles. As James Alan Fox, who analyzes crime data for the government, put it, "We have squeezed all the air out of the balloon." Improved law enforcement practices have diminished crime about as far as can be expected.

Curiously, however, during the decade of the nineties when crime rates were falling, the incarceration numbers were going in the opposite direction. We were putting more people, including murderers, in prison every year despite the declining crime rate. In 1985, the nation's combined prison and jail population was less than 800,000. By 1999, those same institutions held 1,860,520 inmates, an increase of 133 percent. This means that one in every 147 Americans lives behind bars. Only Russia has a higher level of incarceration — one in 146. By 2000, three percent of our fellow citizens were living under some type of supervision by law enforcement.

In Texas, the incarceration figures are even higher. According to the U.S. Justice Department, Texas's prison population has increased 173 percent since 1990, almost 12 percent every year during the 1990s — twice the rate of other states. Texas closed the millennium with 163,090 of its citizens in state or federal prisons, surpassing California's incarceration numbers for the first time.

But while the national rate of murders, along with other violent crimes, was dropping, the population on death row rose exponentially. Fewer murders were being committed, and more murderers were getting a death sentence. In 1975, fewer than 500 people were housed on the federal and state death rows. By 2000, that number had exploded to 35,000.

Some analysts believe these two trends — murders going down and incarceration going up — is a sign that our get-tough-on-crime attitude during the 1980s — more convictions and stiffer sentences — is working. They may be right. In Houston, murders went from an all-time high of 608 in 1991 to less than half that number — 254 — in 1997. Meanwhile, the death row populations in state and federal prisons burgeoned to 3,452 by the beginning of 2000. And more of those were sent to death row from Houston than from any other city in the nation.

Vince Schiraldi, who directs the Justice Policy Institute in Washington, D.C., observed that "Texas chooses to solve its crime problem with executions and by locking up more people." To which Larry Todd, the Texas Department of Criminal Justice's official spokesman, responded, "That's what we need, people in Washington telling us how to do things in Texas."

IN SOME ways, Napoleon Beazley, scheduled for execution later this week, fits all the statistically derived crime categories. He was young, only seventeen, when he killed a man for his car eight years ago. Beazley is an African-American. But he was also an honor student at his small-town East Texas high school, well liked by his fellow students and teachers, and president of his senior class. Who would have predicted that Napoleon Beazley would shoot sixty-three-year-old John Luttig in a neighboring town?

According to the two brothers who went joy riding with Beazley, he had boasted that he would steal a Mercedes that night. What he hadn't counted on was that his victim would turn out to be the father of Judge J. Michael Luttig of the Fourth U.S. Circuit Court of Appeals.

The two brothers with Napoleon Beazley that night testified against their companion, testimony they have recently recanted. While not denying that Beazley did the shooting, they now claim that the prosecuting attorney threatened to give them death sentences too if they did not make Beazley "look as bad as possible in front of the jury." Their recent affidavit says that Beazley did not shoot John Luttig out of anger as the prosecutor urged them to say. Instead, they say that afterwards, Beazley "couldn't really explain it, even to himself." According to them, Beazley's only explanation was, "I guess I was just tripping and wanted to see what it was like to shoot somebody."

The U.S. Supreme Court has already refused to issue a stay of execution while Beazley's case is further appealed. Three justices abstained from voting because of prior involvement with the victim's son, the federal judge. Three others voted to issue the stay, and the remaining three denied it, even though the American Bar Association has taken a position against imposing the death penalty for crimes committed when the defendant was under eighteen — an age Beazley was shy of by three months when he shot Luttig.

Thirty-one men currently on Texas's death row were seventeen when they committed murder. Nine others have already been executed since the state reopened its execution chamber in 1982.

Members of the Luttig family have declined to come to Texas to view the execution. "I don't want any more pain," the son told a reporter, adding that the execution would be "a horrible tragedy for both families."

This is a sentiment we rarely hear publicly expressed in Texas, especially by the murder victim's family. The number of our citizens supporting capital punishment runs about the national average. Indeed, 57 percent of the U.S. population find the punishment meted out by our courts "too soft," and 53 percent feel the death penalty is not imposed often enough.

Certainly politicians running for office vie for the honor of being tougher than their opponents when it comes to the death penalty. And for good reason. A national poll taken in 2000 by Rasmussen Research found that 40 percent of the population said they would not even consider voting for a candidate who opposed capital punishment. Though 60 percent believed that the wrong person is sometimes executed, 70 percent agreed that we should retain this form of punishment even if the wrong person was "occasionally" executed.

Punishment, not deterrence, appears to be the primary goal of the death sentence in most people's minds. Only 44 percent believe that the death penalty actually reduces the number of violent crimes committed.

Examining poll results carefully, however, one can sometimes sense a certain shift in public attitudes. For instance, despite Texans' still high approval rate for capital punishment, it has dropped from an even higher 81 percent in 1995. And if a sentence of life without parole were available to juries, the approval rate drops to 60 percent.

Also, the national poll showed that 77 percent of respondents felt that DNA tests should be available to defendants charged with capital murder. Fifty-three percent support a moratorium on executions until issues of uneven distribution of the sentence among minorities and the poor are resolved. We have also become a bit more squeamish about the means of execution employed. By far the instrument of choice now is lethal injection — 57 percent — with hanging, firing squad, gassing, and electrocution all coming in at under 10 percent.

Of course, none of these figures mean much to Napoleon Beazley. No DNA test was needed to convict him. He confessed to his crime. He has not claimed that his race affected his sentence. His youth at the

34

time he shot John Luttig is the only mitigating circumstance in his favor — one that seldom impresses Texas juries.

Meanwhile, "prayer warriors" from Napoleon Beazley's small East Texas town, about a hundred miles east of here, have been gathering at Mount Zion Baptist Church four times a day for the past several weeks to pray for him. Angie Dickson, the pastor, told reporters last week, "If we go around seeking revenge, if we have an eye for an eye, tooth for a tooth, then eventually we'll all be blind and we'll all be toothless." Dickson maintains that her "prayer warriors are not only praying for Napoleon, but we are also praying for the victim and his family. Whatever happens next week, I can't imagine watching another man die will make them feel better."

3

The Pawn and the Perpetrator

May the bad not kill the good
Nor the good kill the bad
I am a poet, without any bias,
I say without doubt or hesitation
There are no good assassins.

PABLO NERUDA

BY RIGHTS, the first voices that deserve to be heard in this story belong to murder victims. Did not the blood of that first murder victim, Abel, cry out to God from the ground? Isn't the whole justice system designed to vindicate the victim?

Unfortunately, however, murder victims never really get their day in court. Victims of other crimes survive, take part in the prosecution, and testify in court about their experiences. But the voices of the murdered have been silenced forever. By the time their violent deaths are written up in the newspaper or broadcast on TV, their corpses have already been hauled offstage. Now little more than stage props, evidence for the prosecution, they are unable to take an active role in their own drama. For them, the denouement has already happened before the curtain even goes up.

"Victim" is one of those terms about which we feel ambiguous these days. For one thing, we have applied the term so widely and indiscriminately that it has lost the weight it once carried. One can be a victim of an earthquake, schoolyard bullies, leukemia, or credit card fraud.

Victimhood is characterized by passive inertia, not a quality much admired in our culture. On that score, however, the term is regrettably apt for murder victims who become little more than pawns in the game of justice. Even the people they leave behind — mothers, fathers, wives, children, brothers, sisters — are pushed to the edges of the game board. Survivors have no say in the investigation of the crime or in the prosecution of the killer.

In Texas, as in most states now, the law allows people who have been robbed, swindled, assaulted, or raped to deliver Victim Impact Statements. After their assailants have been found guilty — and, in Texas, after sentencing — victims can, at the discretion of the judge, confront the person who has wronged them and articulate their outrage and loss. Murder victims never get that chance. Families of the murdered may give vent to their own trauma and suffering, but they are only able to imagine the surprise, terror, pain, or consternation the victims themselves experienced. No reporter records murder victims' last words.

To add insult to injury, the very person responsible for silencing the victim's voice now takes center stage. Because our justice focuses on punishment, the criminal gets the lead role. During the investigation, the arrest, and the trial, the spotlight is on the murderer. It is his life story reporters recount, him the cameras focus on, his the motives we ponder, his future that hangs so dramatically in the balance. The person he killed is all but forgotten in the unfolding narrative. The victim is merely evidence.

The families of murder victims, angered by a justice system that ignores them, have formed numerous victims' rights groups, the most famous probably being MADD — Mothers Against Drunk Drivers. Susan Herman, executive director of the National Center for Victims of Crime, has twenty-five years' experience in the field of victims' rights. She began by working primarily with women, teaching self-defense in a crisis center for rape victims and organizing shelters for battered women and their children. In 2000 she addressed the National Press Club on the need to ensure that the voices of victims are heard, that we pay more attention to their wounds, both physical and psychic. The culture of our current jurisprudence generally ignores victims, she pointed out, except during the prosecution process, and then only when they are valuable as witnesses.

Herman presents an appalling picture of what victims of violent crime have to face after already enduring the trauma of the crime itself — everything from broken windows and blood-soaked carpets to hospital bills, lost wages, and, worst of all, the loss of loved ones.

"The clear focus of the criminal justice system is the offender," she told the National Press Club, "and not the victim. We don't usually think about victims in our conception of justice. Justice is what happens to an offender."

Herman believes we should develop a system of what she calls "parallel justice" that would focus on relieving the suffering and loss of victims, helping them rebuild their lives, much as the Red Cross moves in to help flood or storm victims. "In my view," she said, "we need to separate the pursuit of justice for victims from the administration of justice for offenders. We need to create two distinct visions of justice. One for victims and one for offenders."

The National Press Club was a fitting audience for her remarks. In large cities the press often ignores ordinary murders — barroom brawls, convenience-store killings, drug deals gone awry — unless it's a slow news day. Only if the victim is distinguished or notorious does the story appear on the front page. Or if the victim was killed by some particularly gruesome means that can be described in macabre detail. Hostages murdered by their captors receive at least local coverage on the evening news, especially if the victims are children. But of the more than three hundred annual murder victims in Houston, few get more than a column inch of coverage, some none at all.

In small towns like Huntsville, though, the case is somewhat different. People are murdered in Houston almost every day of the year, but in Huntsville murders are rare — two or three a year. When they do occur, they always show up on the front page of the local paper. Though we live in a town containing hundreds of convicted murderers, we are as shocked by our own homegrown homicide as any other small town would be.

Mary Risinger's murder at the carwash, coming so soon after that of Debra Ewing, put the entire county on edge. Because a small child had witnessed her mother's slaying, this killing affected the community even more deeply than the first. Yet, as in Debra Ewing's case, the search for Mary Risinger's murderer led nowhere. The police questioned several suspects, but had too little hard evidence to arrest any of them.

Another year went by. It was October again, and students on the Texas A&M campus, fifty miles west of Huntsville, were already well into the fall semester. A twenty-one-year-old coed, having finished her morning classes, was just unlocking her car when a man grabbed her and forced her inside it. Then he tied her hands to the seat belt and held a knife to her throat. All he wanted, he told her, was her car.

The young woman was terrified as he drove her out of town to a secluded park. There he dragged her from the car, raped her, tied her to a tree, and slashed her throat from ear to ear. Then he sat in the car watching her for a while, before he drove away.

When he was gone, the coed managed to untie herself and, covered with blood, stagger to a nearby road used by gravel trucks.

"I collapsed and prayed that someone would come get me or that I'd be found, so my body just wouldn't lay there for weeks," she later reported. Fortunately, it wasn't long until a county employee came along and found her.

This time, however, the attacker did not escape. Her car was found abandoned and fingerprints lifted from it matched those of a convicted rapist out on parole, Daniel Lee Corwin.

Eight days after the attack on the coed, he was arrested in his Huntsville home where he had worked as a carpenter. Identified by the young woman he had tried to kill, he was charged with attempted murder, not a capital offense in Texas. Corwin pled guilty.

Despite his guilty plea, however, despite his previous conviction for rape, many people who knew Daniel Lee Corwin refused to believe he was guilty, including the carpentry crew he worked with in Huntsville. Likewise, a group of Huntsville students with whom he had commuted to Texas A&M also vouched for Corwin. And his current girlfriend swore that Daniel would never try to kill anyone. She complained to the press that authorities were picking on him because of his past prison record. Even a College Station policeman who had been in on his arrest described Daniel Lee Corwin as soft-spoken, with the demeanor of "the boy next door."

Nevertheless, the jury was so shocked by the brutality of the crime and convinced by the coed's identification of him that they handed down a 99-year sentence.

Meanwhile, Huntsville authorities were no closer to discovering who had killed Debra Ewing and Mary Risinger. Those questions still remained unanswered. And their murderer might have never been found if an alert prison sociologist named Lew Davis hadn't dug a little deeper during Daniel Lee Corwin's intake interview at the TDCJ's diagnostic unit.

The sociologist, like most people in Huntsville, had followed the newspaper reports of the investigations into the Ewing and Risinger murders. He remembered that Corwin had been questioned by police in both instances. So during his evaluation of Corwin, he asked what he knew about The Vision Center murder. The prisoner claimed to know nothing about it. He gave the same response when Davis asked him about the carwash murder. Yet to Davis, Corwin's denial sounded tentative, and the man couldn't look the sociologist in the eye.

Convinced there was more to be learned from Corwin, Davis arranged for a Huntsville police detective, a fellow church member, to meet with Corwin. "I think this guy's good for The Vision Center and the carwash cases," Davis told the detective. "I think he's ready to talk."

Over time, the detective and Corwin developed a strange rapport. Corwin eventually told the detective that he wanted to confess to the murders of Ewing and Risinger to "get it off my chest." Finally, he was ready to give a full confession on videotape to the Texas Rangers.

In the process, he also told about raping a thirteen-year-old babysitter at knifepoint in 1974, when he was a boy of only fourteen. Suspicion had fallen on another boy with an arrest record, but the girl failed to identify him in a lineup. When she pointed out Danny Corwin to friends at school as the one who looked most like her attacker, they all told her she must be mistaken. Danny was a good kid. Still, police followed up her identification by giving the boy a lie-detector test. The results were inconclusive. He was never charged.

As for Danny's parents, Nancy and Philip Corwin, they never quizzed their fourteen-year-old son about the incident. "It was so out of character for Danny that we just couldn't believe it," the father would say later.

Thus Corwin's initial crime had gone undiscovered and unchecked. At sixteen, he committed an even more violent crime. Not only did he abduct and rape a fellow student at Temple High School, he also stabbed her twice in the chest and twice slashed her throat. Then he left her for dead in a gravel pit outside of town. The girl managed to drag herself onto a road where she was picked up by a passing motorist. Fighting for her life, she managed to tell police, with no hesitation, that Danny Corwin was her attacker, adding that he had intentionally aimed the knife at her heart and twisted it, all the while staring her straight in the eye.

Nevertheless, many people still found it impossible to believe that such a nice kid as Danny Corwin could be capable of such a vicious act. Indeed, some of them hinted that the girl must have been to blame somehow, must have "asked for it."

It is easy to see why folks in his hometown were incredulous about any evidence that pointed to Daniel Lee Corwin as a sadistic criminal. He came from the kind of family any community would be proud of. His parents were decent, hard-working people who were regular churchgoers. Growing up, the second of four children, Danny was obedient, loving, and eager to please. He had always been active in church activities and Boy Scouts. He even volunteered to clean up around the First Presbyterian Church in Temple because, he told the pastor, he could not afford to tithe.

The boy had had to repeat third grade because of reading problems, but since then had been a good student. And he was, after all, only sixteen. Looking at a possible life sentence for aggravated rape and attempted murder, Corwin plea-bargained — a confession in exchange for a forty-year sentence, which in the '70s would probably have meant no more than ten years.

In prison, he proved to be a model inmate, just as he had been a perfect son. His father advised him to "make the best of a bad situation" and take it a day at a time. He encouraged his son to finish high school and take some college courses in prison. And Corwin did indeed receive his GED as well as earning a junior college diploma while he was behind bars. He also took part in prison church activities and even taught himself to play the organ. And he learned the carpentry trade.

He was such a model prisoner, in fact, that he served less than ten of his forty-year term. In fact, he had not been out on parole for long before he abducted Debra Ewing from the Vision Center. And he was still out three months later when he stabbed Mary Risinger to death in front of her three-year-old daughter.

But even before murdering Ewing and Risinger, he had raped and stabbed to death seventy-two-year-old Alice Martin as she walked her dog along a country road one February morning. The elderly woman's body had been found in a field. Though Corwin admitted to the rape during his questioning by the detective, in his confession he said he did not recall the murder. His attacks on women were random, he explained, and were preceded by several days of intense anxiety during which "pressure built up" in his head and sexual urges became intense. He described himself as having "tunnel vision" during these episodes.

In 1990, it took the jury only twenty-five minutes to decide that Daniel Lee Corwin should be executed, the first person given a death sentence under the state's new serial-killer law.

"I think they invented the death penalty for people like him," the district attorney said. "He's a bona fide serial killer. And I think the events surrounding him point out how lousy the parole system here was in the 1980s. He's just bad, bad, bad."

But at fourteen, Danny hadn't looked like a potential murderer or even a bad boy. And at thirty-one he still seemed, from all outward appearances, a mild-mannered carpenter. Could anyone have predicted that the good boy, Danny Corwin, would turn out to be a serial killer?

Indeed, he seemed unable to believe it himself. He told the detective who originally heard his confession that he didn't want to be labeled a serial killer because people would lump him in the same category as the infamous Henry Lee Lucas.

Lucas, a one-eyed drifter, had confessed to over six hundred murders, though he later recanted and said he had only killed one person, his mother. Ironically, in 1998, four days before Lucas's scheduled execution, his death sentence was commuted to life imprisonment by then Governor Bush, the only time Bush ever used his power to pardon a criminal or commuted a sentence during his six years in office. Henry Lee Lucas lived another three years before suffering a fatal heart attack in prison at the age of sixty-four. He had served seventeen years of several life sentences. He took with him to the grave the actual number of his victims.

Later that same year Lucas died, the potassium chloride injected into Daniel Lee Corwin's arm collapsed his lungs as he lay on the gurney in the death chamber at the Walls. Daniel Lee Corwin was forty years old when he died and had been on death row for seven years. His last meal consisted of steak, potatoes, peas, cake, and root beer. We have no idea, of course, what Debra Ewing or Mary Risinger ate for their last meal.

———*~~*———

SINCE 1984, all county and district attorney offices in Texas have been required to have on their staff a Victim Assistance Coordinator. In Huntsville, ours is Denise Vogler, a middle-aged woman with three grown children who looks more like a teacher or businesswoman than someone who deals daily with the seamier side of life in Walker County. As she invites me into her office, she tells me she knows my parents from church. I tell her that my father thinks her husband, a state trooper, should run for sheriff in the next election.

The Victim Assistance Coordinator in Walker County for over ten years, she is required by state law to send, within ten days of a felony indictment, a packet of information about their rights to any victims harmed by the crime. These rights include the right to receive updates on the progress of their case, continuing protection by law enforcement from stalking or threats of violence, the right to be present and secure at all public proceedings concerning the offense, the right to referrals to social service agencies for counseling and medical attention, and the right to financial compensation for certain expenses.

The Victims Compensation Fund, established in 1979, receives a portion of every court-assessed fine in the state, even traffic tickets, as well as other sorts of fees like court costs. The fund pays victims for medical expenses not covered by insurance, funeral costs, psychological counseling, relocation (usually in domestic violence cases), travel to trials, and child care and lost wages during the trial.

To some people, the right to make a Victim Impact Statement is even more important than monetary compensation. Vogler points out the blue sheet in the information packet she hands me on which victims are to write out such statements. Though some of Vogler's other services start up as soon as the defendant is indicted by the grand jury, the Victim Impact Statement can only be delivered after the conviction and sentencing. (District attorneys across the state are working to make the VIS available to the jury after conviction but before sentencing.) The judge who presides over the trial determines what use may be made of this statement. Sometimes it is read aloud in open court, though the judge determines who will read it. Sometimes the judge has the victim read it to the offender privately in his chambers.

"I was asked to be a part of a private reading once," Vogler says. "The secondary victim, the mother of a murdered girl, asked to confront the murderer in a room with just the four of us — her, the defendant, the bailiff, and me. I was a little nervous about that, I admit," she goes on. "But the woman handled it very graciously. She looked him right in the eye and said, 'I despise what you did, but I love you. I don't ever want anyone, even you, to experience the pain I feel now. But I never want you to have the same freedom to move around that I have either.'"

When defendants hear Victim Impact Statements in open court, she says, they usually don't show much response. "They just sit there with no expression, staring straight ahead. But that day, in private, everyone in the room was in tears."

I ask if making a Victim Impact Statement seems to help these family members who have had a loved one murdered.

"I think so," she says slowly, after studying the question a while. "But just sitting through the trial, watching the process work, is beneficial, too. One victim told me that going through the investigation and trial was like climbing a mountain. But then you get to the judgment phase, and there's a sudden sense of relief. As if everything that could be done, has been done. There's simply nothing more to do."

"If you could change one thing about the justice system, what would it be?"

She doesn't have to think about this one. "More judges," she says instantly. Walker County shares two judges with two other counties. "The grand jury indicts on average fifty crimes a month," she says. "That means a backlog, so that trials are delayed way past the patience of the victims. And I can understand that."

"Justice delayed is justice denied?"

"Yes. And that means a lot of anger I have to deal with as the VAC. I always tell the victims the first time I meet with them that at some point they are going to get extremely angry with me. Some of them refuse to believe it at first because I'm giving them help then. But when the case is delayed getting on the docket, or if the defendant pleads to a lesser charge, or if they can't get the information they want, it's me they vent their frustrations on. I had to learn to deal with that when I started this job."

Vogler estimates that she mails between four and twenty-eight information packets a month. Most of the recipients are victims of assault or domestic violence. In 1993, however, Denise sent out seven packets to families of murder victims. "Seven murders," she exclaims. "That's the most Huntsville has ever had in any one year. Usually there's just two or three."

Nevertheless, direct murder victims are beyond the help of any assistance program — which makes murder a category apart. There can be, quite simply, no restitution adequate to restore a life, no compensation fund to bring back the voice of Mary Risinger or Debra Ewing.

And what about the little girl in the blood-spattered ballerina costume who witnessed her mother's murder that Halloween night? Maybe she eventually got counseling that helped her accept her loss. But this year she will be a senior in high school, and Mary Risinger won't be there to see her daughter graduate. What can make up for that?

"People talk about 'closure' and 'getting on with their lives,'" Vogler says, "but I don't think 'closure' is the right word. It's not like you can close the door on something as traumatic as the murder of a loved one and forget about it, because it never goes away. You can't ever forget what happened. The word I use, the best that I can come up with, is 'acceptance.' Some people do get to where they can accept the fact that something this terrible has happened to them, after which they can begin to focus on other parts of their lives again."

Some, but not all. Two weeks after Daniel Lee Corwin was finally sentenced to die, Debra Ewing's father, Tommy Black, who for three years had been carrying his anger and bitterness over his daughter's savage slaying, died of a heart attack at fifty-three.

So what do we, the citizens of Huntsville, do, we who witness near at hand both crime and punishment? Here, in the center of our city, the ultimate penalty is exacted. And no matter how we try to ignore that fact, ripples start from that center and spread outward in ever widening rings that sooner or later reach each of us.

I never knew Debra Ewing or Mary Risinger, much less Daniel Lee Corwin. Probably only a handful of people in Huntsville ever did. Nevertheless, justice is left to us, their survivors. What do we owe Debra Ewing, Mary Risinger, and Alice Martin? What do we owe Mary's daughter, or any of their family members? And what about Mr. and Mrs. Corwin, the murderer's parents?

These questions keep circling in my mind, and I wonder what answers the victims themselves would give us if they could.

4

Capital Offense and Ultimate Penalty

There's not any horses that need stealing, but there's some people that need killing.

PERCY FOREMAN

WHEN I VISITED Denise Vogler, the Victim Assistance Coordinator, I had been surprised to discover that her office was in the buff brick building across from the northeast corner of the courthouse square — the same building that had been the city post office when I was in grade school just down the hill. In Huntsville we have the odd habit of locating places by what they used to be. We give directions by saying, "the old Minimax" (now a Dollar Store), or "the old Raven Café" (now Carousel Fabrics), or "the old hospital" (now a nursing home).

As I push open the door today, I find that what had been the spacious lobby of the old post office, replete with art deco flourishes, is now a small anteroom stocked with pamphlets about drug abuse and victim's rights. A young woman at a teller's window has to buzz open the locked door for me — a precaution against disgruntled defendants, she tells me. Then she leads me through a maze of cubicles and hallways, a second line of defense meant to confuse hostile intruders. When we reach the DA's office at the back of the building, David Weeks is standing outside his office door waiting for me. I had learned a good bit about victims from Denise Vogler on my earlier visit. Now I want to find out just how someone accused of murder begins the long march to the death house.

David Weeks, a stocky man in his mid-forties with thick, dark hair waving symmetrically back from his forehead, is possessed of sufficient self-confidence to also sport a heavy dark beard in this conservative town. Under the beard his face remains purposely impassive as he ushers me in and gestures toward the two empty chairs facing his desk. A friend of mine, an assistant DA, has set up this interview, but I restate my purpose to David Weeks and ask if he minds if I use a tape recorder. He shrugs and shakes his head laconically, as if the answer were obvious.

Weeks has been a prosecuting attorney since June of 1982, and district attorney in Walker County since January 1991. He has an unusual background for a DA. His Mennonite parents raised him to be a pacifist.

"I didn't start off with prosecution in mind," he says. "I was planning on becoming Perry Mason. I wanted to protect poor downtrodden innocents. But as I gained more experience in the system, I learned what the real truth was, which is that most defendants are guilty."

Weeks interned as assistant DA for the Twelfth Judicial District, which encompasses three rural counties, and then as special prosecutor for the Texas prison system. He now serves as both county and district attorney for Walker County.

County attorneys, he explains, deal with misdemeanors, civil cases, juvenile matters, and Child Protective Services, as well as advising the county on contracts and other legal matters. District attorneys, on the other hand, do nothing but prosecute felonies. Their bailiwick is the criminal courts. Weeks's office combines both jobs.

"What kind of crime," I ask, "qualifies for the charge of capital murder? What distinguishes it from, say, first-degree murder?"

"For one thing, the maximum sentence for anything less than capital murder is life," he begins. "In Texas at present, any prisoner, regardless of his crime or the length of his sentence, is eligible for parole after serving fifteen years, sometimes less. This includes a life sentence for murder. Thus, the only choice available to a jury, if they want to ensure that a murderer is never set loose again, is capital punishment."

"But what kind of crime qualifies for a capital charge?" I ask again.

"In deciding what charge to go for, I have to consider the nature of the crime," Weeks says, leaning back in his chair now. "State law mandates that the death penalty can only be imposed for murders committed under certain conditions. These include the murder of a child under six, a police officer, a fireman, a correctional officer, or a murder committed in the course of an aggravated robbery, kidnapping, sexual assault, or arson." He ticks these off on his fingers, then adds, "Oh yes. And multiple murders and homicides committed in order to gain or maintain membership in a prison gang."

"But the DA isn't obliged to ask for the death penalty, even for those murders," I say, making it a question.

"No. Not necessarily." He hesitates a moment before he goes on. "I was opposed to the death penalty until I came to the conclusion that we need it," Weeks says, "though I still believe it should be reserved for only the worst crimes. But you've got to have that ultimate punishment to make the rest of the system work. You talk about the war on crime. Well, you don't win a war by saying we're not going to hurt anyone."

I ask him to tell me about the process of charging someone.

"It works this way," Weeks says. "First, the grand jury indicts the person accused of the crime."

I interrupt to ask how the grand jury is chosen.

"In Walker County," he says, "the county judge appoints a commission of five people. Those five people each submit a list of names, supposedly representing the entire spectrum of registered voters. That list is winnowed to forty from whom fourteen are chosen. There's twelve on a grand jury, and we have two serving as alternates."

"Doesn't that build a certain elitist layer into the judicial process?" I ask.

"I'm a strong believer in the grand jury system," Weeks says. "It's the conscience of the community."

This isn't really an answer to my question, but I decide not to mention that, of the fourteen current members of Walker County's grand jury, only three are women, one of whom is also the sole African-American, though twenty-four percent of the county's population is black.

"Those fourteen people serve a term of six months," Weeks continues. "They decide which cases go to trial and which are dismissed."

Of course, even before the grand jury considers the case, the district attorney has already been at work, preparing evidence to present to them. The defense counsel plays no part in the grand jury process, of course, since there has as yet been no charge.

Weeks swings his chair around and leans over his desk now. "In drug cases, the first thing I try to do is get the person treatment, help with their problems. But as far as I'm concerned, when a person walks into a store with a gun, they've made the decision to kill somebody, or somebody's going to get killed — them or somebody else. I can understand some kind of murders a lot easier than I can understand someone going in to rob a convenience store or raping a child."

Besides deciding which cases to present to the grand jury, the district attorney must also, when the crime is homicide, decide whether or not to ask for the death penalty. Weeks says he considers three aspects of the crime when making this decision. First, the offense itself: was the murder committed in cold blood, that is, with planning and preparation? Was it committed by a particularly heinous method? What was the relationship between the murderer and the victim? Were there any special circumstances or mitigating factors?

Next, Weeks looks at the defendant. What is his background? (I refer consistently to defendants in murder cases as "he" since men make up over 99 percent of the inmates on death row.) Will he be a future danger to society? Does he have a previous record of violence?

And finally, Weeks considers the jury. "Capital cases are the hardest to try," he notes, "because, let's face it, nobody wants to be responsible for somebody else's death." If the case is weak or circumstantial, he doesn't seek the death penalty. "The jury's going to hold you to a higher standard. You better be able to prove it to them, really beyond all doubt. I feel it's my responsibility to give the community the opportunity to speak through the jury."

During his years as a special prosecutor for the Texas prison system, Weeks tried eight capital cases. Five were murders committed inside prisons and three were committed by parolees.

David Weeks was still in the TDCJ special prosecutor's office when he hired the Huntsville police detective who got Daniel Lee Corwin to confess to the murders of Debra Ewing and Mary Risinger.

"Those kind of people, serial killers," Weeks adds, shaking his head, "are just a different breed."

David Weeks has asked for the death penalty only twice in his ten years as district attorney. Five months into his first term, he retried a capital case that had been reversed by the appellate court and sent back to district court. "The second time around the jury hung on punishment," he says. "One dissenting vote is all it takes, you know."

Weeks's other capital case as district attorney was that of Raymond Cobb.

Seventeen-year-old Raymond Cobb, a senior at Huntsville High School, lived north of town with his mother. Their nearest neighbors, Lindsey and Margaret Owings and their sixteen-month-old daughter, Kori Rae, lived just across the highway. Raymond seemed a good kid, never in trouble at school, and active in the youth group at University Heights Baptist Church, where he sang in the choir. My parents and several of my cousins have been members of University Heights Church since its founding. Some of them remember Raymond as a quiet boy, a little on the outskirts of the teenage clique.

Two days after Christmas in 1993, Raymond was alone at home, still out of school for the holidays. In another week, he would be starting his last semester in high school. He would later claim that he drank several beers that afternoon, smoked some marijuana, and topped it off with tequila. Then he went across the road and entered the Owings home. He was in the midst of dismantling a stereo and a VCR in the living room when, by his account, Margaret Owings, a twenty-three-year-old decorated Navy veteran, rushed out of her sewing room, saw what he was doing, and leapt on his back. Raymond had come prepared, however, with a double-edged stiletto, a black widow engraved on its handle. He stabbed her in the abdomen and then again, according to the coroner, in the heart.

After he was sure the woman was dead, he dragged her body a half-mile into the woods. Then he went back to his house across the highway and retrieved a shovel. On his way back to the woods where he had left the body, he reentered the Owings home, picked up the sleeping toddler, and carried her with him.

While he was digging the grave for Margaret Owings, Kori Rae woke up and, according to his later statement, stumbled into the hole. Raymond then rolled the mother's body into the grave on top of her baby. After he had buried them both, Raymond remembered sobbing and stabbing the grave with another knife he had brought along. Then he went home.

That evening after his shift as a maintenance carpenter for the Texas Department of Corrections, Lindsey Owings pulled into his driveway, puzzled as to why no lights shone in the windows. When he entered the house, he saw Kori's toys scattered about the living room and Margaret's sewing project still out on the table. Thinking they might be outdoors, he went outside again and called their names. When he went back inside, he noticed for the first time that the VCR and stereo were missing. That's when he called the sheriff.

The sheriff and his team were unable to find any further trace of Margaret and Kori Rae. They did, however, find the missing stereo and VCR in Raymond Cobb's home across the road and arrested the boy for burglary. At the advice of his court-appointed attorney, Raymond confessed to stealing the stereo and VCR but denied knowing anything about the missing mother and child. Nor was there any physical evidence linking him to their disappearance.

In fact, as the days went by and no other leads turned up, suspicion fell for a while on Lindsey Owings himself. Spouses are, after all, usually the first suspects in such disappearances. But when his shift ended every day, Owings would drive the country roads around his home, keeping alive an irrational hope of finding his wife and child. "I would get out and call her name, trying to find her," he later testified.

Meanwhile, Raymond Cobb, free on bond, went back to school after the holidays, and, despite the cloud hanging over him, his grades improved considerably that second semester. He graduated from high school on schedule in the spring of 1994. Then, still awaiting trial on the burglary charge, he went west to live with his father, Charles Cobb, and to look for work in Odessa, Texas.

It was not a move, on the face of it, likely to improve Raymond Cobb's future. The elder Cobb had already served two sentences in prison himself. Who knows what dynamics were at work there in Odessa between father and son? Did Raymond seek out his father, hoping to reestablish some long lost relationship? Or did he see Charles Cobb as a mentor, perhaps a future partner, in crime?

Did he feel a compulsion to tell someone about what had happened two days after Christmas in 1993? Did he choose his father as confessor, believing his own prison record would make him a more indulgent judge? Or did the two begin swapping stories of their criminal capers one night, each trying to top the other, until Raymond's pride in what even DA Weeks admits was an almost perfect crime got the better of him?

Whatever the son's motives for seeking out his father, as the second anniversary of the murders drew near, Raymond Cobb, now twenty years old, told his father that he had killed Margaret Owings and buried her, along with her living child, in a shallow grave in the woods.

The tenor of Charles Cobb's testimony at his son's trial indicates that Raymond did not get a sympathetic hearing from his father. "I told him I was tired of lies," the elder Cobb testified. "I told him the only way I could help was if he told me the truth." Yet after hearing the truth, Charles Cobb nevertheless waited several hours before notifying the authorities. Five hundred dollars had been offered for information about the crime, but the elder Cobb insisted on the witness stand that the reward had not influenced him to turn in his son. However, he did accept the reward, explaining that he turned over the money to his own father in reparation for Raymond's having stolen his late grandmother's gold wedding rings from the old man.

Whatever the nature of the relationship between father and son, it was an Odessa police officer, Harold Thomas, who elicited the official confession from Raymond Cobb. After Cobb had undergone intense questioning, all to no avail, Thomas came into the room and quietly offered him a cup of coffee. Then, speaking softly, the police lieutenant, who obviously knew his man, asked, "Son, if you were to die tonight, where would you go?"

At first, Cobb again denied knowing anything about the Owings murders. But Thomas kept up his gentle prodding. "God disapproves of Christians killing, you know. It's a terrible burden to carry in your heart."

At that, Cobb began to cry and tremble. Finally, reaching for a cigarette, he said, "Light my cigarette and I'll go ahead and tell." Not only did Cobb confess to the murders; he also led the police to another gold wedding ring hidden in his Odessa apartment, one he had taken from Margaret Owings's finger before dumping her in the shallow grave.

Brought back to Huntsville to stand trial, Cobb took officers on a tramp across pastures and into heavy pine woods around the Owings home. At first he could not identify the location of his victims' graves. In the intervening two years, new growth had changed the look of the site. The police brought in dogs trained to scent cadavers, but, after an hour and a half, they had still come up with nothing.

Finally, late in the day, Cobb saw a pine tree that he remembered using as a landmark when he had brought the sleeping baby from the house. From that point, a phalanx of lawmen crawled forward on their hands and knees through the woods, clearing it of debris and undergrowth. Then, shoulder to shoulder, they advanced, searching the cleared ground for signs of a recent grave. Floodlights were brought in when the winter light began to fail.

The first thing they found was a pink bedroom slipper. Then a toddler's blue quilted coat. Next a woman's red jogging suit, then a baby shoe. Also scattered through the underbrush were Margaret Owings's bones. Within another hundred feet, the searchers came upon the grave.

The officers spent the rest of the night excavating the grave a quarter inch at a time, using plastic spoons. But all it yielded was the matted blonde hair of Kori Rae. Dogs had evidently dug up the bodies long ago.

In court, Lindsey Owings was asked to identify the wedding ring found in Cobb's apartment as well as the items of clothing found in the woods near the shallow grave. Last of all, the DA held out a pair of tiny shoes. "Those are Kori's moccasins," Lindsey said, his voice breaking. "The ones I had made for her."

As HE RECOUNTS the trial of Raymond Cobb, the only person he has sent to death row, David Weeks makes no pretense of sympathy for the defendant, who, ironically, had become a father himself just two days after his arrest in Odessa. By the time of his trial, Cobb's son, Nicholas

Wayne, was about the same age Lindsey Owings's daughter had been when he killed her.

The jury took only forty-five minutes to find Raymond Cobb guilty of murder. The punishment phase took a bit longer. Weeks presented as an expert witness a psychology professor who said there was no proper category for baby killers like Raymond Cobb who put no value at all on human life.

Appearing for the defense was Agnes Williams, Cobb's mother who had worked in the nursery at University Heights Baptist Church. In tears, she pled with the jury not to take her only son. He had always seemed perfectly normal and loved animals and children, she told them. The psychologist hired by the defense testified that Cobb would present no further danger to society, that what he needed was the structured environment of prison. Several of Raymond's high school teachers also spoke up for him, as did members of University Heights Baptist Church and their pastor, who called him a model youth. The pastor's wife, turning to address the jury directly, said that Cobb needed to be punished but that there was no reason for yet a third person to die.

Weeks, however, still believes, as he told the jury that day, that certain details about the crime mark Raymond Cobb as an incipient serial killer. "Taking trophies from victims, for one thing — in this case, Margaret Owings's wedding ring," he says. "And he kept a collection of newspaper clippings about the murders. That fits the serial killer profile. I think if we hadn't gotten him when we did, he would surely have killed again."

—⁓⁓—

DENISE VOGLER, the Victim Assistance Coordinator, whose office is just down the hall from Weeks's, has a different take on Raymond Cobb, however. She and her husband, a state trooper, were Raymond Cobb's Sunday School teachers for four years — another of those quirks of co-incidence in small-town life. Though Cobb attended church regularly, he was, she remembers, always something of an outsider. "The day of the murders, Raymond had been drinking, you know," she tells me. "And smoking marijuana. I don't believe he would have done such a thing otherwise."

She pauses a moment, as if considering. "I just know he was a Christian. He made a profession of faith and got baptized." She shakes her head. "But then none of us ever knows for certain about another person, do we? But I think Raymond was sincere."

"Obviously no one expected this," I say. "Even his mother."

"No. Well, you see," she brightens momentarily, "Raymond went out to West Texas after he graduated to live with his dad. I think he just got hardened out there."

That move, of course, came after the murder, but I do not point this out. Instead, I ask, "He's still on death row, waiting for a date?"

"Oh, yes. Now don't misunderstand me. I am definitely for the death penalty," she says, her right hand chopping the syllables emphatically into her flattened left palm. "But after his execution," she adds, letting both hands drop, "I fully expect Raymond to be up there in heaven waiting for me. Along with all the other thieves and murderers."

—◦◦◦—

DAVID WEEKS hired Kay Douglas, an African-American woman from Chicago, as his first assistant DA not long after he won his first election as district attorney. It is a testament to his open-mindedness that he chose her, because she has never kept secret her opposition to the death penalty.

Douglas came to Huntsville twenty years ago to work on her master's degree in criminal justice. Douglas's career took a detour, however, when she married, had a child, then divorced. Faced with reentering the job market, she shifted her focus and got a law degree from the University of Houston. Nevertheless, she remained interested in her earlier research in criminal justice — the interviews she had done with two hundred men on death row.

"This was at a time when most death row inmates had no further legal representation after their first automatic appeal," she tells me. She sits, not behind her desk, but in the other visitor's chair in her office. Her hands lie perfectly still in her lap, an outward sign of her inner serenity and self-possession. "There was a lot of concern then about adequate representation in general," she adds.

In her interviews she asked the inmates what sort of capital case they had, where their appeal was in the system at that point, and if they had any current representation. "The feeling I always left with," she says, "was, there but for the grace of God go I. Everybody in there was somebody's son, somebody's father, somebody's husband."

Most of the men had been on drugs when they committed the crime that brought them there, but after years of having no access to drugs, as well as time to reflect, these men did not seem particularly frightening to Douglas. "As a matter of fact," she says, "the one guy who actually frightened me, who made me want to get up and run at first, ended up crying during the interview. He said that his mother had died and he knew she was looking down from heaven, disappointed in him."

In all her years in the DA's office, Douglas has worked on only one capital case. It involved a woman who hired a hit man to kill her husband. Weeks, however, eventually decided to waive the death penalty.

For the most part, Douglas specializes in child abuse and domestic violence cases. She deals with Child Protective Services, commits substance abusers and the mentally incompetent to state and private facilities, and obtains protective orders for battered women — the bulk of work in most DA's offices, but the kind that rarely ends up on TV dramas.

I ask Douglas if domestic violence often or ever escalates to murder in this judicial district.

"Sometimes," she says, "but we haven't prosecuted many, because they're most often murder-suicides." She tells me that just such a murder case is coming up the following month involving a man who killed his wife, the only eyewitness being a four-year-old child. But such cases are unusual, she says, and they are difficult to prosecute, since in a capital case the DA must prove that the killer poses a future danger to society.

"They may have killed the person they're mad at, but after that, they may not be likely to kill anyone else. After all, as the old lawyer joke goes, how many spouses can you kill?" She smiles wryly. "Now Betty Lou Beets was convicted of killing two of her husbands. She buried one in the front yard and one in the back. But she did it for the insurance money."

Douglas pauses a moment while the smile turns into a frown. "The funny thing was, when they executed Betty Lou Beets, women's rights groups came up here at the last minute, claiming she was a battered woman. Well, if she'd only killed one husband and hadn't done it for the insurance money, you might make a case for that. But I think frivolous protests like that detract from those who are seriously concerned about the death penalty."

I've noticed that a recent string of executions were for murders of women. So I ask Douglas if some kind of prevention measures might keep some of these from happening.

She is silent while she considers the question. "Probably not," she finally says. "I work with victims of violence a lot. The cycle of violence is so hard to break. First, there's the actual abuse, followed by a period when they make up and he says he's going to change. He'll start going to church, buy her a car, whatever. Then something happens — the trigger — and he does it all over again. It's hard to convince women that people actually get killed in such situations. They all think, oh, he wouldn't do that. He loves me. I love him. That would never happen. I don't care how often they see it in the paper."

Douglas does mention that women's shelters are now trying to get women to devise a safety plan, something as simple as putting a lock on the laundry room door and keeping it stocked with food, water, and bedding so they can stay there till it's safe to come out again.

"You'd be surprised how much violence there is among older people in their sixties and seventies, too," she adds. "It's been going on for decades and the wife thinks, I have absolutely no resources. Where am I to go?" Douglas compresses her lips into a grim line and shakes her head. "People have this false sense of security. I know I do. I've lived here so long, I think nothing is ever going to happen to me, that it couldn't happen here. I don't know how you make people see this could happen without making them paranoid."

"So education's not the answer?" I ask.

"We're already educated," she replies. "Think about it. Women are trained to be quiet, not to make a public scene. And when something happens, how do you suddenly start yelling, calling out, calling attention to yourself? It goes against all we're raised to be."

This elegant woman surprises me now by suddenly sitting back and laughing. "We were in JP [Justice of the Peace] court the other day when I suddenly realized all the troopers had their duty weapons on them." Douglas points two fingers downward from her waist, miming revolvers. "They even had holsters in their boots. One guy had one knife in each boot too. They advised us women that we ought to start wearing guns in our bras." She interrupts her story to explain that almost everyone in the DA's office owns a gun except her.

"But I told those guys, you know what? I just don't think I'm going to do that. I'd probably fall and shoot myself. That whole idea that somehow I can prepare enough. . . ." She shakes her head. "I have to weigh that against my belief that God really runs the world, that nothing happens to you unless he allows it. Not that I'm an idiot, but how much precaution can you take?"

"Speaking of women," I say, "how do you predict the Andrea Yates trial will turn out?"

Douglas sighs and clasps her hands atop one knee. "If there had been only one child, or if the autopsies hadn't shown what a serious struggle those kids put up, it might not go too hard for her. But with that many kids, and considering that she called the police right afterward, it kind of gives you a hint that maybe she thought there was something wrong with what she did. So I'm not sure that she's the right person to choose as the poster child for postpartum depression."

When I raise my eyebrows in surprise at her answer, she adds in an even firmer voice, "And I don't think that Andrea Yates is being well served by the National Organization for Women raising money for her defense fund and holding candlelight vigils. That could lose her public sympathy."

I have been struck by how much "public sympathy" affects our pursuit of justice. Obviously Judge Belinda Hill, in whose court the Yates case will be tried, is also worried about the public's attitude, sympathetic or otherwise. She has issued a gag order for all parties, concerned their comments could influence prospective jurors.

I tell Douglas that I'm still not certain about the underlying assumptions of our justice system. "I'm not sure whether our purpose is vengeance or retribution or rehabilitation. The single point I feel fairly clear about is public safety. I know we have to isolate people who disrupt society or endanger the rest of us. But then that leads to the practical problem of our ever-expanding prison population in this country. The numbers are staggering."

"We've got to wake up to the fact that we can't build our way out of this," Douglas responds immediately. "The one thing voters are willing to raise taxes for is prisons. If you ask the community for a new elementary school — wait, no, taxes will go up. Can't do that. But that's where the money needs to be going."

Douglas leans back and looks thoughtful. "Most people on death row grew up in an atmosphere of domestic violence. Of course, if you grow up with violence, me telling you in school that violence doesn't work isn't necessarily going to help you. Beyond school, we've got to get into the homes. We've got kids coming in from kindergarten who are so angry they're just time bombs waiting to explode. That's scary."

Douglas tells me about a scholar in Dallas who has studied the children of the Branch Davidians in Waco. He found that the brains of such children who grow up in violent or chaotic surroundings develop differently.

"They're constantly in a flight-or-fight mode," she explains. "They never relax. They never attend to verbal cues. Instead, they're constantly watching for visual clues. At home they've learned not to trust what they're told, but to watch movements or manners. That's how they know when they're about to get hit."

Thus, a teacher will be frustrated at such a child's failure to follow directions and not realize that making direct eye contact can terrify the child. Also, these children live only in the moment. The future is too unpredictable to posit.

"They have no concept of the future promise," Douglas continues. "'If the class is good for a week, we'll have a party.' They have no concept of a week. They may not be in the same town in a week, or even alive then. That's not something you can deal with in counseling. Teachers are prepared to do crisis counseling if your father dies or your house burns down. But this is ongoing, it's all they know. It's embedded in the structure of their brain."

She gives an involuntary shudder. "It's not as though you can move all those kids out of your community and put them in a leper colony."

Douglas regards safety measures such as metal detectors as a poor excuse for controlling school violence. "It's far more important," she says, "to have somebody there who cares about you, someone who checks in with each child every day and says, 'How are you doing?' Someone who can pick up on when something's gone wrong." Some schools, she reports, are assigning an adult to each child — the janitor, a school bus driver, the teacher — who can make the child feel connected.

"Of course," she adds, "if their parents had someone to talk to as well, some outlet, that might defuse a lot of frustration and anger, too. For a lot of people, church does that. But with kids, too often it's gangs. People are going to find whoever will accept them."

Douglas recognizes that changes in family structures have affected children as well. "Few kids today don't have a stepmother or stepfather. Which could be a good thing, if only the parents would do the work it takes to continue the relationship. Kids could have two moms and two dads who love them instead of making it a battlefield. A lot of people, when they get a divorce, think, fine, I'll never have to see him again. As long as you have children together, you'll have to see him."

Douglas, however, did not get much support from her church when, on their annual Family Day, she said she still considered her ex-husband family. In most quarters, she feels, it's not socially acceptable to get along with an ex-spouse. "Regardless of what consequences it has with God," she says, "you don't get to hate somebody just because you used to be married to them. If the faith community can't accept that, what do we expect from people who don't have that foundation?"

Years ago, before she was assistant DA in Walker County, Douglas asked to be allowed to witness an execution by lethal injection. "If something happens that's part of the real world," she says, "I want to see it. Even the worst."

She left the Walls that evening, however, thinking she had seen worse sights on television. "It was like watching somebody go to sleep," she says. "The next day I felt bad because I hadn't felt bad."

I mention that some people argue we should actually televise executions as a deterrent.

"I can tell you what would happen," Douglas responds. "No one would watch. They'd just say, what was that? I've seen worse than that in cartoons."

Nor does Douglas feel that the victim's family gets much satisfaction from watching the execution. "What the family members most often say after an execution is, 'But he didn't suffer. My loved ones suffered. He just went to sleep.'"

I asked Douglas how the criminal justice system could be changed so that justice is served without our having to execute criminals.

"I don't know that we do have to execute people." The words come quickly and crackle with conviction.

"Okay," I say. "Then what change would convince voters that executions aren't necessary?"

Douglas frowns when she considers the question, the answer to which seems to include everyone. When she finally speaks, her response is oblique. "When there's an execution, our office gets phone calls from people yelling and screaming about the death penalty. They don't realize that we have nothing to do with it. The crime wasn't committed in our district, and we didn't try the case. I think that shows just how little most people understand about how the criminal justice system works. I wouldn't myself, if I didn't work here. Most people don't know that some inmates get off of death row, most of them on retrials. Sometimes they have several retrials."

"If a length of time has elapsed since their last trial," she goes on, "things can happen to change the outcome. Witnesses die. They move away and can't be found again. The court rules that a piece of evidence was used improperly. And then there's money. Capital cases cost a lot to prosecute. Does a county want to spend its resources for retrial? Sometimes inmates may get credit for time served and get out. Or get commuted to a life sentence. And then sometimes, they didn't do it. With DNA testing there are going to be a lot more retrials, though it won't change verdicts nearly so often as people think." She pauses a moment, then adds, "But then most people don't know that not everyone convicted of murder gets the death penalty. In fact, most don't."

"So is educating voters the answer?" I ask.

Doubt deepens her frown. "Not necessarily. Because I think we have this basic need to say that people on death row are different from us, that we could never do what they have done. And that the ones on death row are worse than other murderers. That they don't deserve to live in society again. That may be true, but. . . ." She lets the sentence trail off.

"Once in a while an inmate on death row says that himself," I interject.

"Yes." Douglas nods. "Some of them will tell you that everyone there is a scumbag and deserves to die. Like that fellow who asked for a lot of dirt for his last meal." She takes a deep breath. "But there's a way to separate people from society without killing them."

"Life without parole," I say.

"Yes. And I know all the reasons my boss gives for why that's not a good idea. He thinks it will make them more violent, and that they'll end up killing somebody in prison. Almost all prosecutors fight against life without parole. But if you really want to punish someone, the idea of living the rest of your life knowing you'll never get out of prison is the worst punishment."

"So that's the change you'd like to see?" I say.

"There's something else that needs to change too," she adds. "It's hard to hear, because we're not so rehabilitation-oriented anymore. It's all punishment now. That's why we've got the numbers we have in prison and why our recidivism rate is so high. We need to change the way we view the offender. If we do that, then we'll be better able to make a decision about the death penalty."

———

RAYMOND COBB's first trial, was, of course, not his last. As Kay Douglas pointed out, the first trial never wraps up a capital case. All capital convictions must go to the Texas Court of Criminal Appeals. It took till the spring of 2000, five years after his original conviction, before Raymond Cobb's case was reviewed there. Cobb's attorney on the burglary charge claimed that he should have been present when the Odessa police questioned his client. The lawyer contended that, while Cobb had been read his Miranda rights, he was nevertheless deprived of the right to counsel at that time. Presumably, a lawyer would have advised him not to confess to the murders of Margaret and Kori Rae Owings. Thus Cobb's confession was obtained illegally, the lawyer argued, and so could not be used against him. The Court of Criminal Appeals agreed with him, reversing the original decision.

The state then appealed the appellate court's ruling to the U.S. Supreme Court, which split along its usual five-to-four line and reinstated the original verdict.

Raymond Cobb was seventeen when he committed murder, the same age Napoleon Beazley was when he shot John Luttig for his Mercedes. Raymond Cobb was an outsider; Napoleon Beazley was president of his senior class. They are both twenty-five now. Only Beazley is not likely to get any older.

Like Cobb's, Beazley's case went to the Supreme Court, which only yesterday declined to issue a stay of execution, despite an affidavit submitted by his lawyer, Robin Norris, that states he failed to give his client adequate representation, that he did not prepare essential briefs, and that he failed to file necessary appeals in time to do his client any good.

The Texas Board of Pardons and Paroles, not surprisingly, refused to give Beazley a sixty-day reprieve so that the lawyer's claims could be investigated. And the governor, Rick Perry, has so far chosen not to use his discretionary power to grant a thirty-day stay. Noting that his own seventeen-year-old son knows right from wrong, the governor said, "The citizens of the State of Texas have sent a clear message that when you reach seventeen years of age, you're going to be held responsible for your actions, just like you're an adult." A spokeswoman for the governor also reported that of the 332 letters the office received opposing Beazley's execution, only 23 came from Texans. Almost two-thirds of the total came from foreign countries.

As I come out of the old post office after my interview with David Weeks, I glance up the street in the direction of the Walls. TV crews are already snaking cables from their vans in the parking lot as the hour for Napoleon Beazley's execution approaches, staking out the best spots for their reporters. In a couple more hours, protesters and supporters of the death penalty will be gathering in their designated spaces across the street from the prison.

So, in six more hours Napoleon Beazley will take his last few steps to the gurney waiting for him in the death chamber. At his request, his family will not witness his execution. "I don't want to put them through that," the local newspaper quoted him as saying this morning. Beazley compared waiting for an execution to dying of cancer. "It eats away at you piece by piece, and then you get to a point where you don't care if you live or die."

Beazley has never denied his culpability. He admits that he alone is responsible for his predicament. "The only reason I'm here is because of me."

Even Jeffrey Doughtie, the man scheduled to die tomorrow, told our local reporter that it bothers him to see someone so young die. "If anybody should be executed," Doughtie said, "it should be me, because I had one million chances and I blew every one. The death penalty was made for people like me." Beazley, on the other hand, could stand a second chance, he believes.

I'M ON my way home from the grocery store, hurrying in order to make the five-thirty execution service at our church, when I hear the news on the radio. The Texas Court of Criminal Appeals has unexpectedly issued a reprieve for Beazley. The brief two-page statement does not specify the reasons for the decision. The newscaster reports, however, that the district judge who presided over Beazley's original trial has appealed to the governor to commute the death sentence, based on Beazley's age at the time of the murder. This, the voice on the radio speculates, may have tipped the scales.

Whatever the reason for the reprieve, Beazley was stunned by his good fortune. He had been writing a last letter in his cell next to the death chamber when the prison chaplain brought him the news of the stay. Beazley stared blankly, then asked for a few minutes alone to take in this sudden shift in his fate.

The next morning, the newspaper has a front-page photo of the chaplain, his face beaming as he leaves the Walls.

THE NEXT DAY, Jeffrey Doughtie is not so lucky. No word arrives at the last moment to stay the executioner's hand. Stretched on the gurney, he gives his final statement, saying, "It started with the needle and it's ending with the needle." With a $400-a-day drug habit to support, Doughtie had beat to death an elderly couple in their antique shop in 1993 when they refused to give him money.

"For about nine years I've thought about the death penalty, if it's right or wrong," he continued. "I don't have the answer. But I don't think this world is a safer place without me in it." He added, "Killing me now ain't hurting me. It gave me time to say goodbye to my family."

Then he looked at his friends on the other side of the window who came to witness his execution and thanked them. "If you leave crying, you don't do me justice," he told them. "If you don't see peace in my eyes, you don't see me."

So WHAT are the differences between these three men, one dead now, one with an appeal still in process, one in uncertain judicial limbo? All three are undeniably guilty. All three murders were brutal. Doughtie was drug-befuddled and driven by addiction. Beazley murdered, ostensibly, for a car. Cobb for no reason I am able to understand. It is absurd to call Doughtie's motive reasonable, but at least it is comprehensible. He actually seems to have profited from his time on death row, his final statement showing a clarity he might never have attained otherwise.

As for Napoleon Beazley, perhaps he killed a man not so much for his car as to gain the admiration of his friends. He doesn't say. But he admits that he alone is responsible for his act. Of all three, I feel his life is the biggest waste. He was off to a good start in life, one that many young black men in East Texas could envy. He might have become a leader in the community.

Unlike Beazley, Raymond Cobb was not a popular kid at school, though he had people around him who might have helped him if they had known him better. Perhaps he killed Margaret Owings in a panic during the scuffle when she discovered him robbing her living room. But nothing explains why he went out of his way to kill her baby by burying it alive.

So how do we measure their degrees of guilt? The men are different. Their crimes, or at least the consequences of their crimes, are not. All their victims are equally dead.

5

The Defenders

*A society should be judged not by how it treats its outstanding
citizens, but by how it treats its worst criminals.*

FYODOR DOSTOEVSKY

THE HUNTSVILLE telephone directory, a thin volume less than an inch
thick, devotes twelve of its yellow pages to ads for attorneys. One full-
page spread, announcing INJURIES in large capital letters across the
top, promotes the merits of K. S. "Gator" Dunn. Mr. Dunn's photo is
encased in a black triangle, the three sides of which are labeled "Acci-
dents," "Wrongful Death," and "Car Wrecks (& Other Selected
Cases)." Framing the page are icons of little open-jawed alligators.
Though many of the ads use the slogan "No Recovery — No Fee,"
none advertises for murder cases.

The really big lawyers, the movers and shakers with long-term con-
nections in the community and plenty of staff, usually rent office space
in the town's two largest bank buildings. Others, who have to do their
own legwork, often prefer quarters located on or near the courthouse
square.

The old stone building catty-corner from the Walker County courthouse harbors half a dozen lawyers, among them John Wright. The
building, its interior recently remodeled, dates back at least a century
and consequently has undergone numerous transformations, the latest

only weeks before the October day I met Wright there. Before the law-yers moved in, a picture-framing shop had occupied the old stone struc-ture. As if to erase those memories of the structure's commercial past, the current inhabitants have refinished the foyer's wood floor to a sub-tle shine and spread it with strategically placed oriental rugs. A polished sideboard stands against the wall as if waiting to receive engraved call-ing cards.

Having seen the prosecution's point of view on capital cases, I have asked John Wright, who has defended a client all the way to the U.S. Su-preme Court, to give me his side of the story. He is on the phone when I open the door to his office, but he waves me in and toward a chair across the desk from him. The bookcases sag slightly under the weight of his law books. The wall behind him exposes the original rock struc-ture. After he finishes his call and we introduce ourselves, I ask him to tell me how he got involved in his most famous case — defending Johnny Paul Penry.

"When I first came here, fresh out of law school in the mid-seventies," Wright says, "I was looking forward to specializing in tax law, one of the law's more lucrative branches." That made sense, since Wright was already a licensed CPA. It only took a few years, however, till he decided that numbers simply did not interest him as much as peo-ple and the messes they frequently, sometimes habitually, got them-selves into. So it was that, in 1979, John Wright landed the case that would make him, if not famous, at least well known to his legal col-leagues and to activists working to abolish the death penalty. Or per-haps more accurately, the case landed on him.

Wright was returning from appealing a case in Dallas one evening, making the three-hour drive on Interstate 45 to his home south of Huntsville. He switched on the car radio and happened to catch the end of a story about a particularly gory murder just discovered in Polk County, east of Huntsville. He remembers thinking, *Man, am I glad I don't live there.*

A couple of nights later his phone rang at home. He was surprised to hear the voice of Judge Joe Ned Dean from Livingston. "I've got a man by the name of Henry over here," the judge said. "He's charged with murder. I'd like you to come talk to him."

In a way Wright was flattered. In another way he was puzzled. Livingston had plenty of lawyers. Why call him?

"But when I get there," Wright recounts now, leaning back in his desk chair, "I find out the part the judge hadn't told me." Joe Ned Dean, it seems, had already called every lawyer in Livingston, looking for someone to take on the murder. They had all turned him down.

"Also," Wright continues, "the judge didn't tell me the charge was capital murder, just murder. Didn't say the defendant had already signed two confessions and then told the sheriff where to look for the evidence. Didn't tell me that the victim was the sister of a professional football star once named Most Valuable Player in the NFL, nor that she belonged to one of the most prominent families in deep East Texas. The judge even got the defendant's name wrong. Called him Henry instead of Penry."

"Did you have the option of turning the case down?" I ask.

"Yeah, you do, technically," Wright says, wrinkling his forehead. "But often you don't do it. And the reason is you may have an important case, say a personal injury claim where you have a fee riding on a live several hundred thousand dollars, and the same judge is sitting for that trial. You don't want to tick him off by turning him down."

And John Wright, the new kid on the block, did indeed have another case coming up soon in Judge Dean's court.

Twenty-two years have passed since that nighttime phone call. Joe Ned Dean is retired from the bench now. But John Wright is still working the appeals of Johnny Paul Penry, whose case has the distinction of having been argued twice before the U.S. Supreme Court.

"Some cases are like that," Wright says, leaning back so far he is almost horizontal. "Just like Tarbaby. Once you touch them, you can never get loose of them."

Wright prefers to take cases from surrounding counties, rather than Huntsville lawsuits. "Living in a town this size," he says, "I feel like I know too many people." He would rather not know either the plaintiffs or the defendants personally. Likewise, potential jurors.

Defense attorneys usually take cases in courts where the judges are familiar with their work, and since the neighboring judges know Wright well, he sticks with those courts. In fact, from the stories he tells me this morning, hands tucked behind his head, it appears that a good part of the justice system works that way — behind the scenes, personal contact, local milieu, and the crafty sizing up of prospects.

The fate of defendants in criminal cases, for instance, used to depend on certain local-option laws. Just as individual precincts in Texas can vote on whether or under what conditions liquor can be sold within their confines, individual counties can also decide how to fund legal counsel for defendants unable to hire their own lawyers.

"It makes sense," Wright tells me. "In a state the size of Texas, it's hard to impose a single set of requirements that will fit every county's situation. Out in West Texas, for instance, you've got Loving County with hundreds of square miles and only ninety-four people. And I doubt many of them are lawyers. So what do they do?"

"And capital cases are very expensive to try," he continues. "These rural counties without much of a tax base just can't afford them. Up in Leon County, which is in our same judicial district, they basically told the DA, don't file capital charges here. We can't afford it."

"But doesn't that put some people in the state at more risk of getting the death penalty than others?" I ask.

Wright inserts one hand into his pants pocket and jingles the keys. "Think about this story, too," he says. "Some gang members came up from Houston, just cruising down the highway. When they got to Leon County, I guess they just said, hey, this looks like a good place. Let's go rob a bank. So they did, and ended up killing people."

"So are you saying the system makes small rural towns more vulnerable to violent crime? Would a bank robber target a county they knew couldn't afford a capital case?"

"I have no idea," he says, pushing himself upright again, "but it stands to reason. In that case, what happened was the feds took over. Federal laws are much stronger than the state's on bank robbery. Since it's a federal crime to rob a bank, they all got much longer sentences than if they'd been tried under state law, though they didn't get the death penalty. And all the expense was federal, too, so Leon County was off the hook."

Wright smiles and throws up his hands. "You see how it works? San Jacinto County, which is having some real trouble with its bookkeeping right now, just recently had three people in jail over there, all charged with capital murder. It looked for a while like they were going to have to foot the bill for three capital cases right in a row." He pauses and chuckles. "But one of the guys died in jail this last weekend. Apparently, he'd saved up some medication he was on, took all the pills at once, and died of an overdose."

Thirty years ago, unless a county had a sufficiently hefty tax base, it opted not to employ a public defender. Most counties still do without one, preferring instead to farm the work out, usually to young, hungry lawyers. That decision is based partly on cost and partly on Texans' innate aversion to bureaucracy.

In 1995, however, after a flurry of bad publicity about court-appointed lawyers sleeping through their clients' trials, the state made an effort to construct a more equitable system. Counties still can decide whether or not to hire a designated public defender, but if they should choose to rely on court-appointed attorneys, they must now provide assurances that those lawyers meet at least a minimum standard. To ensure compliance, the new regulation was linked to state funding. Now court-appointed attorneys must have a specified amount of defense experience, pass a statewide exam, and take a quickie course in the details of the case. Otherwise, the county gets no state funding.

Pamela Moseley Carpenter, a Livingston housewife, had been making Halloween decorations in her kitchen when Johnny Paul Penry, on parole for a rape charge, broke into her home, raped her, stomped on her, bashed her head against a stove, and then stabbed her to death with the scissors she had just been using to cut out pumpkins and black cats.

There never was any question about Johnny Paul Penry's culpability, especially since he had twice confessed to the crime. But Wright and all his subsequent lawyers have claimed that Penry is mentally retarded. Expert witnesses for the defense estimate Penry's IQ to be less than 70, putting him in the retarded category. Prosecutors obviously dispute this, classifying him as at best only borderline. To them, the important question is whether Johnny Paul Penry knew that raping and killing Mrs. Carpenter was wrong. The prosecution contends he did. In 1979 at Penry's first trial, the Polk County jury agreed and sentenced Penry to death.

All death sentences in Texas are automatically appealed to the state's Court of Criminal Appeals. After its hearing by that court, Penry's case eventually made its way, in 1989, to the U.S. Supreme Court. The Supreme Court agreed that states had a constitutional right to execute the mentally retarded. Nevertheless, Penry's death sentence was overturned on the grounds that the district judge had not instructed the jurors to take Penry's mental deficiency into account as a mitigating circumstance.

The following year, 1990, Penry was retried, this time in Walker County. The Huntsville jury also found him guilty and again sentenced him to death. However, once again the judge did not instruct the jury to consider Penry's mental state as a mitigating factor. Not until months after the second trial did the Texas legislature pass a law requiring that mental retardation be regarded as mitigating in death penalty cases.

Again the case was appealed.

Nevertheless, as is the common practice, plans for Penry's execution proceeded apace despite the pending appeal. On November 16, 2000, the van from the Ellis unit arrived at the Walls, transferring Johnny Paul Penry from death row to the death house. Then, only four hours before his scheduled execution, a stay arrived from the U.S. Supreme Court, saying that the justices wanted to reconsider the case. So Penry was taken back to death row, where he did a number of telephone interviews with publications around the country.

After deliberating for several months, the high court found that the judge in the second trial had also failed to instruct the jurors properly regarding mitigating circumstances of mental retardation and the severe abuse Penry had suffered as a child.

Twenty-two years have now passed since Pamela Moseley Carpenter was raped and killed that October night. The children for whom she was making the Halloween decorations the night of her murder are grown now. Johnny Paul Penry is middle-aged, forty-four years old, and about to face a third trial. John Wright will be at the counsel table in Washington, along with a host of other lawyers.

"Of course, I'd love to see it settled sooner," Wright tells me now.

"And to see the court give him a life sentence?" I ask.

"Sure. But the problem this time is that Penry has already served twenty years on death row, and under the laws that existed at the time of his crime, he can now be considered for parole." Wright suddenly shoots forward from his reclining position and swivels his chair around to face me. "Now you know and I know that nobody's ever going to parole Johnny Paul Penry. But the prosecution can *pretend* that he might be. They can suggest that it's possible." He shakes his head. "And there's been some horror stories, no doubt about it. What happens to guys like Penry is that they get McDuffed."

On November 18, 1998, Kenneth McDuff, with two death sentences from two different counties hanging over his head, was finally executed at the Walls. In 1968, McDuff had been convicted of a triple homicide and sentenced to death. Then came the 1972 U.S. Supreme Court ruling halting all executions until states brought their laws into compliance with the Constitution's ban on cruel and unusual punishment. McDuff, along with the fifty-two other condemned men in Texas, had his sentence commuted to life by the governor. In 1990, having served twenty-two years, McDuff was released on parole.

He began killing again almost immediately, burying his victims' mutilated corpses all over Central Texas. In all, Texas lawmen credit Kenneth McDuff with having killed at least fifteen people, mostly women whom he first tortured and raped. He shot off their faces, slashed and stabbed them, bludgeoned them to death. An accomplice testified that McDuff told him, "Killing a woman is like killing a chicken. They both squawk."

McDuff's luck in slipping through the net of the law was prodigious. Even after being arrested, tried, and convicted of murder again, he managed to postpone his final date with the executioner by an ingenious bit of bargaining with law enforcement officials. In late September of 1998, he supposedly exchanged information about location of some of his victims' bodies for a few more weeks of life while sheriffs checked out his stories. One corpse was found near the little town of Rosebud where McDuff had spent his childhood.

Nevertheless, McDuff did finally receive his lethal injection one evening in November a few weeks after this temporary stay. And even staunch activists against the death penalty refused to protest his execution. "I really do hate the death penalty," one of them told a reporter, "but I would've done it for them if they'd asked."

Even now, McDuff's name only has to be mentioned to revive monstrous memories of a crazed killer out on parole. The story is still fresh enough in people's minds, John Wright fears, to affect the outcome of Johnny Paul Penry's third trial.

"And the escape of the Texas Seven last Christmas didn't help us any either. That story got a lot of publicity," he sighs, then adds, "Of course, those guys weren't on death row."

"But Martin Gurule was," I say, reminding him of a recent escapee from death row that TDCJ spent a week hunting.

"Yeah. That hurts us, too." He pauses a minute. "The public is always highly suspicious of manipulation of the system by the defense. But I tell people who sit on juries, look, there's three legitimate things that a defense attorney can do." He ticks them off on his fingers: "Once in a while you have a client who's not guilty of anything and you try to prove that. Second, most of the time the guy's guilty of something but not necessarily what he's charged with. And, thirdly, even if he is guilty of everything they say, he may not be deserving of a punishment as severe as the prosecution is after."

I mention the Andrea Yates case. "She was judged competent a couple of weeks ago," I say.

"You understand, though, that just means she's competent to stand trial, not that she was sane at the time of the crime," he points out. "Of course, their only defense is insanity. Still, I think that she'll be judged sane and that the Harris County DA will go for a death sentence. Now, whether she'll actually get it. . . ." He shrugs, signaling his unwillingness to predict the outcome.

"What about the law that forbids a judge to tell jurors what happens if she's found not guilty by reason of insanity?" I ask. "Her lawyers are claiming it's unconstitutional."

"Right. If she's convicted, she could be sent to a state hospital. She'd spend more time there than she'd do for a life sentence," he says.

I tell Wright I'm surprised that every lawyer I talk to thinks Andrea Yates doesn't have a chance.

"It's hard to tell," he says, holding up his palms. "Public opinion doesn't really seep into the courtroom much. There are two groups of people who get excluded from sitting on a jury hearing a capital case: the people who can't give the death sentence and the people who would give it every time. Some even for burglaries, robberies, you name it. Of course, we used to do just that — in my lifetime. But most people who show up for jury duty are honest. They just may not be fully in touch with what their attitudes and views are."

"That bothers me, this requirement for a death-qualified jury considering capital cases," I say. "It seems to exclude a certain group of people from the judicial process."

"Well," Wright says now, drawing the word out as if to temper any criticism of the legal process, "the idea is to exclude both extremes."

"Has it been your experience that it really works that way?" I ask dubiously. "Do juries actually end up coming from that middle section?"

"Like I say, I think people are pretty honest about their attitudes during jury selection. It's rare that anyone tries anything deceptive," he says. "The major complaint that I have about the way trials are conducted has to do with the way judges instruct — or don't instruct — juries at the end of the trial, especially in capital cases."

He leans forward with his elbows on the desk now. "In the Penry appeals, for instance, the first Supreme Court ruling said, Thou shalt instruct the jury as to mitigating circumstances. And the second Supreme Court ruling said, Thou hast not done this. Go back and do it again."

"What about the issue of the prisoner posing a future danger to society?" I ask. "That appears a particularly valid point to me."

"Sure," he agrees. "The jury needs to consider whether or not the person is going to be a continuing threat. But the way it's put to the jury, the question is ambiguous: Is there *a probability* that the defendant will commit crimes of violence such as to be a threat to society in the future?"

Wright sits back, mugging astonishment. "A probability? Even Mother Teresa would have offered *some* probability. Human beings are just that unpredictable. So defense lawyers have said, okay, let's make it so the judge explains to the jury that there has to be a relatively high probability this will happen. Denied.

"Then they say, all right, let's say what kind of crime we're talking about. Specify a crime this person is likely to commit. Denied.

"Well then, can you spell out how long this continuing threat is supposed to last? Denied. Okay, let us explain to the jury that under current law the offender will be in prison at least forty years. Denied."

Wright has another criticism of the process, too. He attributes much of the trouble with criminal jurisprudence in Texas to our system of electing judges. "A judge cannot make any reasonable adjustments unless the people of the state want that to happen. That means, if you're an elected judge in Texas, thou must not mess with the death penalty. Not if you want to keep your job. And those jobs pay over a hundred thousand dollars." He raises his hands toward the ceiling. "I'm sorry, but most criminal defense lawyers in Texas are not making near that much. They really want those jobs."

He sticks his hands in his pockets as if unconsciously demonstrating their emptiness.

"In Texas during recent years we have had about a 97 percent affirmance rate in capital cases. In other words, you have 3 percent chance on appeal. Our judges are scared to reverse the judgments of a lower court or to reduce the sentence. They'll find any way in the world not to do it. You can compare our numbers to Florida's. I think Florida has a 50 percent affirmance rate. Now, are our trial judges that much better than Florida's, so that they never make mistakes, or is there something else going on here?"

He frowns now, and switches to a new point. "When Johnny Paul Penry was tried the first time, a second requirement had just been added to the M'Naughton rule, which says that a defendant must have the mental capacity to understand his crime and know wrong from right."

"So what was added?" I ask.

"The jury had to decide if the defendant was unable at the time of the crime to control his impulses or conform his conduct to the requirements of law."

I raise a skeptical eyebrow. "I can see how that might be open to a good deal of interpretation."

"Well, it was revoked anyway, soon after John Hinckley tried to shoot the President," Wright says, waving one hand as if consigning the lost M'Naughton amendment to the wastebasket. "Texas will always seek the absolute constitutional minimum when it comes to the protection of the individual in criminal court. That's what they did with Johnny Paul Penry. They went for the lowest constitutional minimum." He smiles. "But those two Supreme Court rulings have been a big embarrassment to the Texas attorney general's office. They just aimed a little bit too low that time."

My hour with the attorney is up, so I thank him and stand up to leave. But just as I open the door, John Wright stops me to ask a question of his own.

"Why do people hate lawyers so much?" He looks genuinely puzzled.

———

THE VANITY license plate on the rear of Hal Ridley's black Lincoln Continental reads "AG LAW" — a reference, obvious to any Texan, that identifies the car's owner as a graduate of Texas A&M. And, indeed, Ridley graduated from that university in 1975, where he belonged to the Army Corps of Cadets, a membership that marked him in those Vietnam years as a hardcore hawk, an unquestioning patriot, and someone beyond tough on crime. Yet Ridley is the only lawyer who lists himself in the Huntsville yellow pages as a board-certified criminal attorney.

So I'm wondering, as I enter the small brick building half a block off the courthouse square that houses Ridley's law office, how this good Aggie ended up defending felons? My wonderment increases as I reach across the desk to shake hands with a very large man, going bald in front now but compensating for that frontal loss with long, auburn hair curling to his shoulders in back. Not your typical Aggie buzz-cut.

Nevertheless, the room is stocked with Aggie memorabilia, including a large framed print of tanks in tones of masculine-blue. A white A&M game ball, covered with autographs, sits on the bookcase beside him. After shaking my hand, Ridley rocks back in his office chair and spits into a sixteen-ounce Styrofoam cup. That's when I notice the round, flat can of Skoal near the phone. A chewing-tobacco addict *and* an Aggie?

I sit down and begin explaining my project, adding that I'm trying to figure out the culture of this prison town.

"Culture?" he echoes the word doubtfully. "I never thought of Huntsville that way."

I point out that, like any company town, almost every aspect of Huntsville's identity is colored by the presence of its prisons.

He shrugs a qualified acceptance of this.

"But I'm wondering," I say, "how an Aggie like you comes to be against the death penalty?"

Ridley smiles. "There can't be many of us, I admit. And when I was in the Corps at A&M, I was just like everybody else — kill all the bastards and let God sort 'em out later."

Hal Ridley grew up in Freeport, another company town down on the Texas Gulf coast. His father worked for Dow Chemical, as did everyone else in town, "except the school teachers and people who owned their own store," he tells me. But Ridley knew he wasn't a company man, so he enrolled in Texas A&M and got a degree in business. After that, he got another degree, this time in education. But after his stint of student teaching, he likewise decided that teaching in public school wasn't the life for him either.

That's when he joined the National Guard. And by the time that commitment was over, he had finally settled on law school.

He came to Huntsville twenty years ago and "took whatever fee walked in the door," he says, till his practice got on its feet. "Taxes, real estate, DWIs, misdemeanors, felonies, you name it."

The phone rings, and while he answers it, I glance at the plaque on a shelf by my chair. It reads: "Percy Formoney," a reference to the renowned Texas trial lawyer Percy Foreman, who said, "Every man is considered innocent until proven broke."

The phone call over, Ridley returns to his legal history. He opened his office in Huntsville, but, unlike John Wright, he wasn't particular about taking on local cases. And he was just in time to catch the newly reinstated capital cases. Like John Wright, he has pursued one of them all the way to the U.S. Supreme Court — *Raymond Cobb v. Texas Court of Criminal Appeals.* It was Hal Ridley who defended the teenager who had belonged to my parents' church and who, two days after Christmas 1993, had killed Margaret Owings and buried her with her sixteen-month-old baby, still alive.

That wasn't Ridley's first capital case, however. In 1988 he defended Gary Johnson, a thirty-seven-year-old ranch hand who, with his older brother, killed ranch manager James Hazelton and his brother-in-law, Peter Sparagana, both in their twenties.

This is also a murder I remember. Peter Sparagana and his wife had just started coming to my church, St. Stephen's, a few weeks before he was shot.

"Ah, yes, the Johnson clan," Ridley says with mock relish. "Clan being the operative word here."

Whatever the Johnsons' personal virtues or lack thereof, they tended to clump, if not stick, together. "All of them lived together in some trailer," Ridley recalls. "Gary and his brother Terry picked up work wherever they could find it. A little ranching here, a little welding there."

But on the night of April 30, 1986, the two brothers had been doing a little stealing. Recently employed to mend fences by the Triple Creek Ranch ten miles west of Huntsville, Gary and Terry had had ample opportunity to explore the expensive tools in the barns. The ranch belonged to Huntsville's prominent Gibbs family, but it was leased to Thomas Gee, a Fifth U.S. Circuit Court of Appeals judge. A fact the Johnson clan must have overlooked.

Evidently they also didn't know that Bill and Shannon Ferguson were out at their Diamond Rustler Ranch across the highway that night, waiting for one of their breed mares to foal and worrying about a thunderstorm that was threatening a downpour. Bill Ferguson testified at the trial two years later that he had seen a pickup truck pull into the entrance of the Triple Creek Ranch a quarter mile away and turn its lights off. A little later he heard a man scream, "Don't kill me," just about the time the thunderstorm broke.

Mrs. Ferguson testified at the trial that, although she and her husband could not make out the license plate on the truck due to the weather, she did observe the peculiar pattern of its four red brake lights. Their suspicions were sufficiently aroused to call the sheriff.

Hazelton's and Sparagana's bodies were discovered when the sheriff arrived. Hazelton had been shot in the head with a .38 and once in the mouth with a larger caliber weapon. His brother-in-law was shot twice as well, once in the head and once in the heart. But the thunderstorm had washed away any footprints or tire tracks.

AT THE TRIAL, Mrs. Ferguson also testified that the following day she noticed a truck parked in the driveway of a mobile home with the same arrangement of lights she had seen on the pickup the night before. The mobile home, as it happened, where the Johnsons lived at the time.

Under Ridley's cross-examination, however, Mrs. Ferguson admitted that a Texas Ranger had suggested she look in that particular location for those distinctive taillights. It was hardly a point sufficient to exculpate Gary Johnson, though.

Four of Gary's brothers testified against him — including Terry, his erstwhile partner in crime. Terry, it seems, had made a deal with Frank Blazek, the district attorney at the time: a prison sentence instead of a capital charge in exchange for testifying against his brother.

Not that Ridley had ever seriously expected to get Gary Johnson off entirely. The most he had hoped for was a life sentence instead of death. But during the sentencing phase of the trial the prosecution called a Dallas psychiatrist, dubbed "Dr. Death" by the press for his predictable testimony that defendants charged with murder would doubtless kill again if released. As expected, he swore that Gary Johnson would "certainly" kill again, too.

Ridley impugned the psychiatrist's procedures, noting that he had examined neither Gary Johnson nor his criminal record. Ridley, of course, produced his own psychologist who, while not venturing to predict the future likelihood of another Gary Johnson homicide, declared such prognostications were statistically insupportable and irresponsible.

The jury of seven men and five women, however, did not linger overlong studying the laws of probability, but assessed a penalty of death in thirty-five minutes flat.

When Terry Johnson was tried next, the district attorney waived the death penalty, but the jury, possibly hoping to correct his leniency, handed down a sentence of ninety-nine years.

After the trials, Hal Ridley pointed out to the press the inherent unfairness in the treatment the two brothers had received at the hands of the law. Even with a ninety-nine-year sentence, he contended, the older brother could conceivably be out on parole in eight years, while his client would be executed. The district attorney, defending his decision, said he could not justify spending any more of the county's resources on another capital case for the same crime.

"Where's the fairness in that?" Ridley demands of me now, still riled at the outcome. "It's been thirteen years and, for all I know, his sorry brother's out by now, but Gary Johnson is still sitting on death row."

Until last year, Ridley had three clients on death row — Gary Johnson, Raymond Cobb, and Ramon Mata.

The year before the Triple Creek Ranch murders, Ramon Mata, a trusty at the Ellis unit, had been working as an inmate on the cafeteria serving line. Mata had been sentenced to thirty years for killing two men in Pecos County. One night, about nine in the evening, he and three other inmate kitchen workers had been cleaning fish. With them was Minnie Houston, the TDCJ employee in charge of supervising the kitchen work on second shift.

Over the past few months, a romantic relationship had developed between Mata and Houston, one that he took so seriously he had recently written to his family announcing his intention to marry Minnie and adopt her son.

But after the other workers had left the kitchen that evening, Mata took one of the large boning knives they had been using, forced Mrs. Houston into a restroom stall, and stabbed her to death. Then he took her keys and tried to escape in her car.

Hal Ridley defended Mata, whose case he figured was unwinnable from the start. An inmate who kills a prison employee can count on receiving a death sentence. But Ramon Mata never made it to the Walls' execution chamber. He died on death row last year of "natural causes," which TDCJ records more specifically identify as "septic shock."

"What about Raymond Cobb's case?" I ask Ridley next.

He picks up the Styrofoam cup and spits. "I can't tell you anything there except what's public record. He's still got some appeals left."

"But I thought the case had already gone all the way to the Supreme Court," I say, surprised.

It had taken a little over four years for Raymond Cobb's case to wind its torturous way to the U.S. Supreme Court. Cobb, who had killed Margaret Owings and her daughter Kori Rae two days after Christmas in 1993, had confessed to Odessa police almost two years later on November 11, 1995. Almost two more years went by before a Walker County jury found Cobb guilty and sentenced him to death on April 28, 1997.

So why is Raymond Cobb still on death row almost a decade after the murders? The automatic appeal of a death sentence before the Texas Court of Criminal Appeals gained Raymond Cobb three more years. Hal Ridley once again served as Cobb's lawyer. On March 15, 2000, the Appeals Court ruled against the state and for Cobb, a rare victory, if John Wright's figures about successful death sentence appeals are right.

Indeed, Hal Ridley's appellate record is phenomenal. "I've had eight death sentences and successfully appealed all eight," he claims with some pride.

An ordinary layman may have some trouble understanding on what grounds a Texas appellate court, not known for its leniency, might overturn Cobb's death sentence. I was certainly puzzled. But that's why we have lawyers.

Ridley filed eleven points of error in his appeal and requested a new trial for his client or, failing that, a reduction of Cobb's sentence from death to life imprisonment. In his final and eleventh point, Ridley argued that Raymond Cobb "(1) was only seventeen years old at the time of the offense, (2) he had no prior history of violent conduct, (3) he had no prior convictions." Ridley also disputed the testimony of the prosecution's clinical psychologist, claiming it was "inherently unreliable" and thus inadmissible since the psychologist had not actually examined Cobb. The psychologist for the defense, who, Ridley pointed out, had examined his client, had testified that Cobb would not likely be a future danger, if imprisoned for life.

This was a shaky argument, however, considering that Texas has no life-without-parole option, and indeed the court found for the prosecution on that eleventh point. Raymond Cobb, they believed, had "a dangerous personality disorder and lack[ed] any regard for the welfare of others" and the jury had acted rationally in finding him "beyond a reasonable doubt . . . dangerous and incorrigible."

The court did not rule on any of the other points, except for the fourth, in which Ridley contended that his client's Sixth Amendment rights had been violated.

The Sixth Amendment to the U.S. Constitution declares, among other things, that in "all criminal prosecutions, the accused shall enjoy the right . . . to have the assistance of counsel." His client, Ridley said, had been deprived of that right when the Odessa police had questioned him without Ridley being present. True, the Odessa police had read Raymond Cobb his Miranda rights when they brought him in after his father had relayed his son's confession to them. And they had informed the Walker County authorities that they were questioning Raymond Cobb. However, the Walker County sheriff's department had never mentioned to their Odessa counterparts that Cobb had an attorney defending him on the burglary of the Owings home. Thus, Ridley argued, his client had been effectually denied counsel, and the confession Raymond signed later that day in Odessa was not valid and could not be admitted as evidence.

Against this line of reasoning, the state countered that when Cobb had been read his Miranda rights by the Odessa police he had not requested counsel. Furthermore, Ridley had been his counsel for the charge of burglary, not murder. Thus, the police were under no obligation to contact him for his permission before questioning his client about the murders. Also, the Walker County authorities said they had asked Ridley twice before if they could question his client without his presence, and both times Ridley had agreed.

On this fourth point, the Texas Court of Criminal Appeals came down on Ridley's side. Six of the nine justices concurred that Cobb's constitutional right to counsel had been violated. It was up to the state, the court said, to prove "a voluntary, knowing, and intelligent waiver" of that right. As for the state's contention that the two crimes — burglary and murder — were unrelated, the court found that a specious argument. The murder had obviously happened during, and possibly as a result of, the burglary. Thus, the two crimes were "factually interwoven." While it was true that Ridley had twice granted permission for his client to be questioned, he had first made certain that his client was not then a suspect in the murder investigation.

The court thus reversed the district court's decision and, on March 15, 2000, remanded the case for a new trial. It did not rule on the other nine counts in Ridley's petition.

What happened next, however, was not a new trial, but another appeal to the U.S. Supreme Court, filed this time by the state. The suit was scheduled for argument in December 2000. But the high court found itself otherwise engaged during that month, settling the Florida recount of the 2000 presidential election. Cobb's hearing was postponed till January, but not until April 2, 2001, did the nine justices issue a ruling. This time they split along their customary line, overturning the Texas Court of Criminal Appeals' second ruling by a five-to-four vote.

The questions to consider, the Supreme Court said, were these: "(1) May an accused make an effective waiver of his Sixth Amendment right to counsel when his only previous 'assertion' of right to counsel consisted of accepting appointment of his attorney following his indictment on a different, but related, crime nearly one and one-half years earlier? (2) When an accused has been indicted for burglary, does his Sixth Amendment right to counsel attach to questioning about a factually related capital murder?"

The majority of five overturned the state appellate court's ruling, claiming that "any harm done to due process by the admission of Raymond Cobb's confession was negated by Charles Cobb's testimony that Raymond had admitted the killings to him."

Also, the right to counsel guaranteed by the Sixth Amendment, the majority opinion said, "is personal to the defendant and specific to the offense." Thus, the Odessa police had not violated Raymond Cobb's right to counsel by questioning him without a lawyer, even if that lawyer was his counsel for a related charge. "The Constitution does not negate society's interest in the ability of police to talk to witnesses and suspects, even those who have been charged with other offenses."

For once, the U.S. Supreme Court had proved more conservative than the Texas jurists.

Almost another year has passed since that ruling, but if you think that the white TDCJ van is anywhere near ready to take Raymond Cobb on his last ride to the Walls, guess again. Eight years after the murders of Margaret and Kori Rae Owings, Cobb probably has several more years to go on death row, waiting for the Texas Court of Criminal Appeals to consider the other nine of Hal Ridley's original eleven objections.

After explaining this complex history of the Cobb case to me, Ridley reaches again for the Styrofoam cup before rocking back wearily in his chair. "I'm not gonna handle it anymore, though," he says.

"Really?" Hal Ridley does not strike me as a man to give up easily. He has several times spoken like a crusader against the death penalty this morning, calling it "not justice, but revenge."

"Yep. In fact, I'm not gonna be taking any more murder cases at all."

"You mean the court-appointed capital cases?" I ask, thinking maybe it's the low pay he doesn't like.

He barks out a laugh. "They're all court-appointed, every murder case I've ever tried. We don't have that many rich people around here — at least not that get caught. They say it's a deterrent," he scoffs, "but if they really thought that, they wouldn't sneak around to do it in the dead of night."

Before I can point out that executions now take place at six in the evening, he waves the correction away.

"Oh, I know they've moved the executions from midnight to six in the evening. But you know what their reason is for that? It's so the fraternity boys don't have time to get all liquored up and come down there to make asses of themselves on national TV. No, if they really thought it was a deterrent — which it's not, by the way — they'd do it in broad daylight right out on the high school football field with all the kids in the stands. Draw and quarter 'em and stick their heads up on poles like they used to. But that didn't stop crime then and it doesn't now. And they know it. That's just an excuse. What it is, is revenge, pure and simple. That and making these dadburned victims' rights organizations happy come the next election. There's not a judge or a DA in Texas with the balls to stand up to MADD."

Then veering off to another personal vexation, he leans forward to ask me if I know the only crime in Texas with a mandatory jail sentence.

I shrug my ignorance.

"DWI," he says, slamming his palm on the desk. "Get caught with an open can of beer in your vehicle and you can get a five-year mandatory sentence. But if I was to jump across this desk and rape you right now, I could probably get off on a probated sentence. Now," he throws himself back in the chair again, "tell me where's the justice in that?"

After a moment he adds in a quieter tone, "Every one of those eight men I've defended, I've gotten to know them. Maybe I wouldn't want them out on the streets either, but they're, you know," his shoulders give a twitch, "people."

I repeat my earlier question. "So why aren't you taking any more capital cases?"

He heaves a heavy sigh and reaches for the Styrofoam cup. "Just don't have the stomach for it anymore," he says. And spits.

As I DRIVE home, I ponder the differences between the two attorneys, John Wright and Hal Ridley, one a fairly button-down former CPA, the other a candidate for a Dickens novel set in East Texas. Yet neither of them appears to be under any illusions about the clients he has defended. John Wright knows that Johnny Paul Penry did indeed kill Pamela Moseley Carpenter. Hal Ridley realizes that Raymond Cobb murdered Margaret and Kori Rae Owings. Both of them have taken these cases all the way to the U.S. Supreme Court. However, neither man believes his client should be executed by the state of Texas. In fact, they don't think anybody should be executed.

And to keep that from happening, they must base their cases not on their beliefs, but on whatever point of law presents itself as a likely and effective device for forestalling the defendant's death. Does Johnny Paul Penry have sufficient intelligence to know that it's wrong to kill people? Should Raymond Cobb's conviction be overturned for lack of counsel, even though he was read his Miranda rights? Or because he was seventeen when he committed murder?

Once guilt or innocence is established, most people become impatient with considerations of mitigating circumstances. The legal process comes to seem like a swindle, the various angles of argument like verbal shenanigans. Yet, in our judicial system, defense attorneys are obligated to use them, especially if they are to save their client from death.

Even the fact that lawyers can so thoroughly detach their beliefs from their legal duty seems unnatural to the rest of us. Personally, whether they argue for the defense or the prosecution, they maintain a professional camaraderie, like pro football players on opposing teams. But capital murder is not, after all, a game.

Between these two cases, three lives have already been lost, and two more hang in the balance. We don't like to see matters of life and death treated like a game, even a chess game. To us outside the judicial system, a lawyer's practical detachment looks like a disregard for the truth.

"Most people operate by common sense," John Wright told me, "but common sense isn't the law."

Maybe that's part of the answer to his question about why people hate lawyers.

6

Working on the Inside

The mission of the Texas Department of Criminal Justice is to provide public safety, promote positive change in offender behavior, reintegrate offenders into society, and assist victims of crime.

TDCJ WEB SITE

IN THE MID-1960s, when Truman Capote wrote the best-selling book *In Cold Blood* about the murder of the Clutter family in Kansas, the mean time convicted murderers spent on death row was seventeen months. Today, in Texas, the average time has stretched to 10.58 years. Many marriages today don't last that long.

But whether or not they are headed for the death chamber, all prisoners begin their incarceration at the Byrd unit northeast of town, near Huntsville High School, where they are processed into the system. The local population, however, has always called the Byrd unit by its original designation, Diagnostic. In that facility, all incoming prisoners have sociological interviews, medical and psychological evaluations, special needs assessments, and finally receive a classification that determines which unit they are sent to. This intensive process can take up to twenty-four months because of the ever-growing influx of felons.

Originally, Diagnostic had plenty of room to accommodate incoming prisoners. But now two other facilities have had to be turned into way stations to catch Diagnostic's overflow. On the north end of town, a relatively new unit, Holliday, named for a former TDCJ official and not intended as a dark joke, was designed originally to house young offenders but has since become primarily a transfer facility, as has the old Goree unit south of town.

In the early 1950s, my school bus stopped at a red brick house just inside the entrance to Goree to pick up two little boys. At that time, Goree was the state's sole prison for women. Its warden, a woman, a rarity in those days, was Velda Dobbs, a longtime friend of my mother. The two little boys were hers. I would look at the boys with furtive awe every morning as they climbed aboard the school bus, wondering what it was like to live inside a prison compound and have convicted criminals cooking your meals and cleaning your room.

In those days, Goree was outside the city limits, but, owing to Huntsville's minor version of urban sprawl, the town has lately encapsulated the unit. Today, the grounds are still as well groomed as if Goree were the headquarters for some light industry — say, Honeywell or Hallmark. Crepe myrtles line the low fence, and, in the spring, I watch for new foals, the product of the prison's horse breeding program. They caper about the seven hundred green acres that stretch out on either side of the main prison building.

Some mornings, on my way into town, I also see men in loose white pants and shirts, picking up trash along the highway. At other times, a flatbed trailer, hitched to a tractor, hauls a work detail to their day's assignment. I scan the faces of those men as closely as I can at fifty miles an hour, looking for clues to criminality. But their faces are a blur, and, except for the loose white clothes, they might be migrant laborers or a small-college football team on their way to practice.

Years after I had left home, my mother took a job as the warden's administrative assistant at Goree. The uniform she wore to work looked like a Girl Scout outfit in primary colors. The dress was royal blue polyester, the detachable collar white, and the neckerchief a bright red. I was disappointed when prison policy mandated a change to the dull gray twill.

The Goree staff was small then, and my mother wore many hats over the years, including personnel director in charge of records and training new employees, switchboard operator, and group counselor. One woman, who had received a life sentence for killing a sheriff, had been separated from her children for twenty years when she became especially attached to my mother. Her husband, the actual shooter in the murder, had been paroled years ago, but the woman had been denied release. When, after forty years, she was finally paroled, she continued to write my mother regularly. They even exchanged small gifts at Christmas, though such contacts were against the rules, I believe.

In 1973, one of the new employees my mother trained was Dessie Cherry, a young African American woman fresh out of college with a sociology degree. After three years at Goree, she transferred to Mountain View, a facility that had first belonged to the Texas Youth Commission but later had become Texas's second women's prison. In 1991, Cherry returned to Goree as warden.

The unit Warden Cherry returned to was much different from the one she had left some fifteen years earlier. It was now a catchall facility, housing the system's psychiatric patients, a boot camp for young offenders, overflow from Diagnostic, a Sex Offenders Treatment Program, and inmates being transferred to other units. Today, it also has a wing with 136 beds for women inmates en route to the system's main medical facility in Galveston, making it Texas's first coed prison. Out front, between the old administration building and the highway, is a new structure built for the Immigration and Naturalization Service and housing a federal judge's courtroom.

Warden Cherry recently retired from TDCJ, and I was interested to hear her views on the changes that had occurred over the years.

"Everything in those early days was smaller," she tells me. "We only had about four hundred inmates then, and now Goree has that many employees. On my last day, Goree had 1325 offenders. And during my first years there, we never turned out more than two security officers on a shift."

She also confirms that the sole firearm on the unit, a pistol, was kept locked in the warden's safe. Periodically, all the employees, including my mother, had to qualify on the prison's shooting range, even though the gun at Goree was never taken out of the safe except for periodic cleaning.

In the fifteen years my mother worked there, I only went inside the prison two or three times, mostly to attend special performances by the inmate choir at Christmas. "We put on a Christmas pageant that we took to all the units around here," Warden Cherry recalls. "All the parts were played by our women." She smiles and shakes her head. "We operated as a family then."

Inmates so inclined could take courses like cosmetology, floral arrangement, horticulture, home economics, and secretarial skills, aimed at equipping them with what were then marketable trades for women so they could get jobs upon release. A friend of mine, who taught art in prison units, also served in Goree's pre-release program. She sometimes took women who were scheduled for release soon on excursions to fast-food restaurants or parks or grocery stores, reintroducing them to the free world. She has told me that women behave differently from men in prison. "They like to joke and sing. I guess you'd say they have more social skills, generally speaking."

But my friend retired from the system long ago, and women are no longer as biddable as they once were, according to Warden Cherry. Also, there are a lot more of them. In the last decade the number of women in U.S. prisons has doubled — to 87,000 in 1999.

"Working with males is easier than working with females now," Warden Cherry says. "A lot easier."

Her response surprises me. "In what way?"

"Women are mouthier," she says, "disrespectful. They always have to have the last word. And women have more issues. Not that men don't. But men can accept a response, yea or nay. Maybe they'll ask once for you to reconsider a decision. But females keep on and plead and beg."

This is only one manifestation of a broader societal change Warden Cherry has observed in prisons during the past quarter century. "People's morality and ethics have altered," she says. "You see this in the system's employees as well as in the offenders. We used to be proud of our attendance record, for instance. Now there's not much of a work ethic." She sighs. "Society has changed so much. It's hard to see a fourteen- or fifteen-year-old coming in, being processed. You think, that's going to be their life from now on. They'll never know what normal life is."

Sheer numbers have all but overwhelmed the justice system. In 1980, TDCJ's entire inmate population numbered only 22,000 and lived in a half-dozen units, almost all in Walker County. Now it takes 107 prisons, plus a number of state jails, to hold the 163,190 people who are living behind bars in Texas, a figure that includes federal as well as state facilities, and a total that exceeds that of any other state.* Obviously, a system of that size can no longer function like the "family" that Warden Cherry recalls from the early seventies.

In most units now, a prisoner's day starts at 4:30 a.m. so that a thousand or more inmates can be fed and transported to their work assignments, which may be at other facilities. Most inmates work at jobs aimed at maintaining the units — doing the necessary cooking, cleaning, laundry. About ten thousand inmates work the 139,000 agricultural acres of the several farm units, growing the food they and their fellow prisoners will eat, tending livestock, and chopping cotton, crops whose worth TDCJ estimates to be $50 million a year.

In addition to agriculture, TDCJ runs a number of factories. Scott Watson, who came to TDCJ from the lumber company Louisiana Pacific, serves as plant manager at the woodshop on the Ellis unit, which until a year ago housed Texas's death row. Watson's position gives him the rank of major, though, as a quasi-civilian, he is not required to wear the standard gray uniform. He started at TDCJ, however, like almost everyone who works for the prison system, as a security officer.

David and I are sitting on Watson's screened-in porch on a warm October afternoon, drinking the dark roast coffee he has just made. "TDCJ likes to hire from within," he explains, taking a seat in the porch swing. "Even though I'd worked in the same position in the free world, I was never seriously considered for the job of plant manager until I

---

* It is reasonable to think that California, the country's most populous state, with a reputation for being as tough as Texas on crime, would have the largest prison population. But, as a California ABC TV station reported recently on its Web site, "In 1994, the state predicted a prison population of 260,000 in the year 2000. It didn't happen. Right now, there are less than 150,000 inmates in the state" ("Prison Population Down," *ABC-30* KFSN-Central Valley Homepage, March 9, 2002: http://abclocal.go.com/kfsn/news/081501_nw_prisons.html).

agreed to serve as a guard first. It's how you earn your spurs in the system, so to speak, though they'd never say that on the record."

Watson's woodshop makes desks and other office furniture for state agencies, though by now they have pretty much saturated that market. Two hundred inmates work in the shop, supervised by about twenty-five security officers.

"Supposedly my mission is to train the inmates for this kind of work in the free world," he explains, "but that part of the job gets lost in the production end of it." He frowns. "If I were running a plant in the free world, I wouldn't need two hundred employees for this size operation, probably not even a quarter of that. But in the free world, employees have a reason to work. You don't want to lose your job. You want to be able to eat, have a place to stay, take care of your family. That's not exactly a factor here."

To at least partially remedy that lack of motivation, Watson believes inmates should be paid for their work, even if the amount is small. However, state law forbids compensating prisoners for their labor.

"Everybody's got to have some incentive, though, you know? I understand that working in the prison industries is supposed to be the way inmates repay the state for their upkeep. But the way it is now, they don't see it that way. Even if we paid them something — it wouldn't have to be much — and then charged them back for their board and room, a set-up like that would give them a little more incentive, besides preparing them to be self-supporting in the free world. I'd like to be able to pay the guys who work for me on a graduated scale, so the ones who really have an aptitude for this kind of work would be rewarded, just like in a regular shop. Something to give them a reason to show up."

"Without that, how do you get cooperation from them then?" I ask.

"They know I'll go to bat for them when they get into trouble," he says simply and without a trace of bravado in his voice. The porch swing creaks as he rocks back and forth a couple of times. "I had this one guy in my shop who got fifty-five years for stealing a microwave oven — can you believe it? When he came up for a parole hearing, I went before the parole board and tried to convince them that this was not a violent criminal they're dealing with. After all, he's been driving an eighteen-wheeler, had access every day to all kinds of tools that could be deadly weapons, yet he's never hurt anyone. So why not parole him?" The swing stops abruptly. "So what happens? That gets me the reputation of being a convict-lover."

Like Warden Cherry, Watson believes that the system has changed over the last ten years or so. "TDCJ went from having the highest release rate in the nation to having the lowest rate. When I first came here, it truly was a revolving door. People with a twenty-year sentence were getting out after serving a year or two. We just didn't have any place left to put them. Then, the voters got upset with that situation and wanted to lock 'em all up and throw away the key."

The porch swing begins to squeak again. "It's gotten beyond all reason," he adds. "That guy in my shop who got fifty-five years for stealing a microwave? Just think, he'll be — what?" He calculates quickly. "Eighty years old when he gets out, if he lives that long. What does he care about improving his chances of getting a job when he gets out?"

In addition to their work assignments, prisoners can take classes under the auspices of the Windham School District, the only fully accredited in-prison school system in the nation. It supervises the education of more than 60,000 inmates at all academic levels, as well as 16,000 more who receive vocational training in areas like computer repair and automobile mechanics. About 9000 inmates earn their GED's under Windham's tutelage every year.

Both the work programs and the learning opportunities fit the system's avowed purpose found on TDCJ's Web site: "The mission of the TDCJ is to provide public safety, to promote positive change in offender behavior, reintegrate offenders into society, and assist victims of crime." However, these goals are curiously at odds with certain get-tough-on-crime laws enacted during the 1990s under both the Democratic administration of Ann Richards and the Republican administration of George Bush. Suspicion of being soft on crime can undercut any politician's chances for election in Texas.

During the past decade, by passing laws allowing stiffer penalties for violent crimes as well as tightening up parole regulations, Texas has increased its number of prison inmates by 173 percent — more than twice the national rate. In fact, the national trend has been in the opposite direction. Starting in 1998, the U.S. as a whole began experiencing its slowest rate of prison population growth in twenty years. But as Larry Todd, the information officer for TDCJ, told a reporter, Texas voters intend to fight crime with stricter laws and longer prison sentences.

Texas's anti-crime strategy comes at a price — $2 billion for new prison construction, a figure that does not include the salaries and training expenses for the additional security personnel needed at those new facilities. The sum seems especially hefty considering that the plan has proved so ineffective.

But few people in Huntsville would complain about the cost. Huntsville is a company town. The gray twill unisex uniforms of prison guards thread like warp through our town's fabric, holding its economy together and providing the texture of its identity.

ANOTHER DAY and David and I are once more drinking coffee, this time with Rusty Murcheson at a local pancake house. Murcheson, a guard at the education building in the Walls unit, agrees with Watson that incarcerated workers should be paid for their labor. He points out that Texas is one of the few states that do not do so.

"I'm not talking about big wages," Murcheson says. "Other states pay, like, from a dime up to a dollar an hour. The official line used to be that the inmates were being paid in good-time, and when their time served plus good-time equaled half their sentence, the parole board would wave goodbye to them. But that's all changed. Now the parole board just says they'll think about it. Not having that incentive makes for a feeling of hopelessness in many of the inmates. And having a bunch of unmotivated workers to corral doesn't help the guards, I can tell you."

A former Air Force pilot, Murcheson retired from the Air Force early in 1985 and moved to Huntsville with his wife. In his mid-forties then, he planned to work at TDCJ for fifteen years, and thereby add a tidy state pension to his Air Force retirement pay. Initially, Murcheson felt dissatisfied with being a TDCJ guard. The job requires only a high school diploma or GED. He was a graduate of the Air Force Academy and, as a commissioned officer and pilot, had flown cargo planes into Vietnam. Prison guard ranks a good bit lower on the prestige scale than pilot. So he returned to his native Nebraska, where he worked at a youth detention center. After a year, he decided he might as well go back to prison.

Clearly, Murcheson is not your ordinary prison guard, and not just because of his education level and former career. He is also older than the average security officer. And, perhaps most extraordinarily of all, he doesn't believe in capital punishment. In fact, he's not so sure that punishment should be the primary aim of incarceration.

"As I remember," he says, "TDCJ's first job is to keep the public safe. After that, it's supposed to 'promote positive change in offenders' behavior' and eventually send them back into the community rehabilitated. If you'll notice, there's nothing in there about punishment."

In Murcheson's opinion, however, not enough of the security personnel subscribe to this stated mission of rehabilitating inmates. "They think of inmates as the scum of the earth. But, at the same time," he pauses to shake his head, "some of the guards are actually jealous of the prisoners."

"Jealous?" I repeat. "Whatever for?"

"The education program. They complain that no one ever offered to pay their way through college."

Ultimately, though, the state does not pay for inmates' education above the secondary level. All inmates, Murcheson tells us, following their release on parole, must repay the state for any college courses they took while in prison.

Murcheson is currently assigned to the Standley-Beseda Educational Building at the Walls. He patrols the afternoon session of classes and the law library, one that is as up to date, he claims, as that of any big law firm in Houston. He believes that most of the inmates at the Walls tend to be more highly motivated than those on the prison farms.

"The teachers, too," he says, noting that many of the instructors at the Walls previously worked in public schools. "Now they wouldn't go back there for all the tea in China. In prison, their students are better behaved and show them more respect than in public high schools. And they don't have to mess with cafeteria duty or parent-teacher conferences.

"Of course, you do get the occasional oddball," he admits. "Like last week, we had a student who began to get a little too argumentative with the teacher — more than just ardent discussing. So, one of the other inmates stood up and put him in his place. I didn't have to do anything. In fact, most of the time when a guy gets out of line, I end up having to pull a bunch of other inmates off him."

When Murcheson first went to work at the Walls, he worked the cell blocks. "Not in the cell block, though. Back then, bosses didn't go inside the blocks. You probably remember when the courts made TDCJ get rid of building tenders. A building tender was an inmate who took care of the cell block for the guards, a lot of the time by what I would call the brutality method. Anyway, we were still too shorthanded in 1985 to put bosses inside the cell blocks."

Prohibiting the use of inmates as building tenders was only one of the prison reform rulings that made Judge William Wayne Justice one of the most reviled men in the state. But since many of these rulings were aimed at reducing the overcrowded conditions in the Texas prisons, they also kicked off a prison building boom across the state. Tiny towns on the verge of dying, from Spur and Fort Stockton in West Texas to Diboll and Dayton in East Texas, were saved from extinction when the legislature decided to spread the units to every corner of the state. Not only did the new prison construction bring jobs to these areas, but the infusion of TDCJ payrolls resuscitated their moribund economies.

Despite the decentralization of the state's network of prisons, the Walls unit in Huntsville continues to be the symbolic center of TDCJ. Murcheson describes the Walls as a "laid-back" unit under the supervision of Jim Willett, the warden who retired from that position a few months ago. "Things have changed under the new administration," Murcheson tells us now. "They're trying to turn the Walls into a hard-nosed facility."

Besides housing the death chamber, the Walls also serves as the single discharge point for the entire prison system. It is from the Walls that the gates to freedom swing open for those who have served their time. If, for instance, an inmate is released from an Amarillo prison, he is first brought five hundred miles by bus to Huntsville, housed at the Walls until he is processed out, then released through the unit's gates. Afterwards, he walks two blocks up the street to the Greyhound station where he catches a bus back to his home in Amarillo. Thus, the Walls is a symbol with multiple meanings for the state's offenders.

David asks Murcheson if he has any positive interactions with the inmates in the course of his work.

Murcheson nods. "Generally, yes. I think most of the guards who have had previous careers usually get along well with the inmates. They've learned how to deal with people. For instance, it's a whole lot easier just to say, 'Hey, would you take care of that?' instead of 'Do that!' The younger bosses without much experience or education like to give orders ending with 'Because I said so!' The inmates already know that they've got to do whatever I tell them to, but it creates a different atmosphere if I ask. It just makes anyone feel more like a human being."

He raises his coffee cup, then sets it down again, as if not totally satisfied with his answer. "The public has the general perception that all those guys wearing white are foaming-at-the-mouth homicidal maniacs looking to rape, pillage, and plunder. Quite frankly, there are a few that probably fit that description. But the vast majority of them aren't a whole lot different than the people we see in church every Sunday. They just made mistakes."

The waitress appears and refills our cups. When she's gone, Murcheson asks if we've seen the story in this morning's newspaper about the shortage of officers and how much the shortage is costing the state in overtime pay — $3.3 million a month.

"I can understand that, though," he says. "At least financially. It's cheaper paying overtime to people already on the payroll than paying benefits to new employees."

I tell him I've heard that the Walls is operating with less than 60 percent of its full complement of security personnel.

"The rate of turnover is accelerating," Murcheson confirms, "though, of course, with so many people being laid off in business and industry now, we may pick up some of those workers."

"Switching gears a little," David says, "let me ask you about execution days. Do you detect any change in mood or atmosphere at the Walls when they bring the prisoner in from death row?"

Murcheson studies this for a minute. "Back when they first restarted the executions," he says, "it would get real quiet around there on execution day. But no longer. Now the only difference is a slight interruption in schedules. They shut down some of the activities those days, especially in the recreation yard, because there can be no contact between the one they're bringing to the death house and our guys. Those on the inside don't see anything of it. Not even the reserved parking space for the van from Terrell." He pauses, then adds, "That day they executed the guy there was so much fuss about — what was his name?"

"Gary Graham?" David prompts.

"Yes. It was sort of funny, but all the other units around here were in lock-down because they had to bring in a lot of extra guards off the units to patrol the streets around the Walls. The biggest job was keeping the opposing protesters apart. But at the Walls we weren't in lock-down mode. Our prisoners even had yard time that day."

"So the other prisoners don't feel affected when an execution takes place right in the unit?"

"Not really. To most of them it's just a curiosity. They're more interested in what's going on outside — the people gathered out there, the reporters and TV vans."

Murcheson shakes his head before continuing, and what he says next is not about the inmates but about the citizens of Huntsville. "You assume that people who live here would be more knowledgeable about how the system works, but I've had people ask me what kind of gun I carry when I'm on duty." He shrugs, turning his palms up to indicate their emptiness. "Only the pickets up in the guard towers have guns — a rifle and .38."

He chuckles. "Of course, years ago, long before my time, the pickets all had the old Thompson submachine guns. Can you imagine? If someone cut loose with one of those things — ?" He breaks off, shaking his head, still laughing.

"What about training?" I ask.

"Before you start on the units, you have to spend three weeks at the pre-service training academy in Beeville. Recently, though, they've had to offer training classes here in Huntsville, too, just to keep up with the numbers."

David mentions that he has noticed classrooms filled with gray uniforms in the College of Criminal Justice Building on campus.

"In general, what they teach you is how to deal with the worst types of inmates," Murcheson says. "You learn a little bit about how to take care of things and not violate. But they don't emphasize that enough in my opinion. Of course, they have to teach you how to deal with hard cases, but that's only a small percentage of the job. I don't think they give enough training on how to deal with the average prisoner. And then, of course, you do have to qualify with a semi-automatic rifle, basically a modified old M16, as well as with the pistol. It's a .357, but it fires .38 ammo. They also teach you defensive tactics. At least I think that's what it's called now."

He frowns and twists his cup back and forth on the table, making patterns on the Formica with the condensation rings. "But they've changed their attitude recently. You can now take more offensive action at the beginning of a problem to subdue the prisoner. But still, the rule is that once you've subdued him, that's it. You've got to quit."

Murcheson looks up. "You know that guy out in California, Rodney King? The police had that guy subdued. There was no question that they went too far. But the problem at the trial was with the judge's instructions to the jury. He told them they all had to agree on the exact moment when the cops' force became excessive. Maybe one juror thought hitting him once was enough, but the next juror thought it took two blows to subdue him. The question was not if they should have stopped but when. That's what they couldn't agree on."

"What about your fellow guards and their attitude toward the prison system?" David asks.

Murcheson shrugs. "On the one hand, they think that the rich buy their way out of everything. But on the other hand, the younger ones especially tend to treat the inmates like they are the lowest form of life. In fact, there's one guy who writes letters to the newspaper regularly and calls them 'the feces of society.' Not a lot of guards seem very concerned about the end product, though. That doesn't make sense to me. After all, most inmates are going to be out on the streets again. It seems like we ought to be working with them so they don't get out and do the same thing again."

"Are prisoners different now than when you first started?" I ask.

Murcheson nods. "It's true that we're getting some that are rougher than we used to get. Again, this is just personal opinion, but I believe our legislature is a big part of the problem. Some of the sentences being handed down, mandated by law, just don't make sense. I mean, can you imagine a twenty-five-year-old coming in with an eighty-year sentence, and he's got to serve at least 50 percent of it before he can even be considered for parole? He'll be sixty-five by then. That kid can't even imagine being that old. What kind of incentive does he have to do better? Say he's out on one of the farms, it's ninety-five degrees with 90 percent humidity, and some eighteen-year-old boss tells him to get his blankety-blank rear end out in the field. If I were him, I'd tell the young gentleman where to stick it. What can they do, after all?" he laughs without mirth and adds, "Lock you up?"

"Tell me about good-time," I say. "How does a prisoner accumulate it?"

"Certain work assignments they get extra credit for, plus taking classes in the education program," Murcheson says. "And staying out of trouble, not fighting."

"What brought about the change in good-time policy?" David asks.

Murcheson raises his eyebrows and sighs. "As far as I can tell, this hard-nosed attitude was a reaction to conditions in the late '80s and early '90s when prisons really did seem to have a revolving door. A lot of sentences were cut much too short just to take care of overcrowding. Some inmates were serving as little as 10 percent of their sentence. DAs had plea-bargained in good faith, maybe convinced an offender to cop for twenty years, believing he would only serve two. But while they were inside, the laws changed. The legislature tightened the parole requirements. So we've just traded one problem for another."

"And you've got female guards," David says. "How do the men get along with the women? Guards, I mean."

Murcheson hesitates momentarily, then says, "The number of female guards is quickly approaching 50 percent. Some good, some bad. Sometimes it just makes things difficult. And quite frankly, if there's ever a problem with the prisoners, some of the women I wouldn't want around. On the other hand, there are a few females I would just as soon have as a guy."

"What about the inmates?" David asks. "How do they feel about the women guards?"

"A lot of inmates, they don't respect the women who work there. A lot of them come from an environment where women are definitely subservient to men, so they resent a woman telling them what to do. I just tell the guys, 'Hey, that's what the federal law says. Get over it.'"

"What about working in a women's prison?" I ask.

"I just hope I never have to work there," he says, laughing and shaking his head. "For one thing, in most cases a woman just gets a slap on the hand for the same crime a man would get sent to prison for. Therefore, the women who do end up in prison are pretty bad."

"What about Karla Faye Tucker?"

Murcheson looks off into the distance now. "I was working the gate the day they brought her in for the execution. In fact, I opened the gate to let her in. There's no doubt in my mind they killed a different woman from the one that buried that pickax in her victim's chest. Karla Faye was a totally changed woman, truly a born-again Christian, and she's going to be in heaven just like we are."

His gaze comes back to the table. "On the other hand, the death penalty is the law. The fact that she was a woman is totally irrelevant. And the fact that she was a Christian is, too. Like they say, you do the crime, you do the time."

I FIRST met Gabrielle Headley at the local health club where I go to swim three times a week. I do my laps early, around six o'clock, to avoid the water-aerobics crowd that begins to arrive around seven-thirty. Gabrielle gets there before seven, coming straight from her night shift at the Ferguson farm unit northeast of town. She strips out of the gray uniform and heavy boots of a TDCJ correctional officer and reemerges in workout clothes.

Small and perfectly proportioned — and Lycra doesn't lie — she stays in shape riding the stationary bike and lifting weights. At thirty-one, she has formidable muscles. With her long, dark, corkscrew hair drawn back and up in an enormous pompom, she scrubs the showers in the dressing rooms Wednesday mornings and checks out the pool's temperature and chlorine level before taking charge of the front desk. These duties give her a break on her membership at the club.

During months of locker room chit-chat, I've learned that Gabrielle and her husband both work for TDCJ, and that she has chosen the night shift so she can work while her nine-year-old son is asleep and then be at home when he gets out of school in the afternoon. Her devotion to her son is plain, of a piece with her earnest approach to life in general.

She has agreed to tell me about her work at TDCJ, but when I show up at her home on the Saturday morning we arranged, I apologize for taking up part of one of her rare weekends off.

"No problem," she says, inviting me into the two-story suburban house and asking me to excuse the messy house. "The clothes never make it back into the dresser drawers," she says, gesturing toward a basket of laundry. We sit down on sofas arranged at right angles in front of the fireplace and she tucks her ankles up onto the sofa, Indian-style.

Gabrielle's father is Scott Watson, the supervisor of the Ellis wood shop. "I've already talked to your dad about the effect that Martin Gurule's escape from Ellis had on that unit," I tell her. Gabrielle works at the Ferguson unit, about twenty miles northwest of Huntsville in the next county. "But what about Ferguson?"

"That escape at Ellis wasn't the only one," she reminds me. "There were several incidents fairly close together. Remember that officer at Holliday who was held at gunpoint, and then the Texas Seven last Christmas? All those really tightened up security at all the units."

"How did they handle that at Ferguson?"

"They put a man outside the perimeter, just to check IDs. When employees came to work they had to send their IDs up in a bucket to the picket on the tower. He had to physically hold it and examine it to make sure it wasn't fake. Then at the control center at the building entrance, we have to go through the same rigmarole again. That took several people off of their regular assignments inside, which meant that the people working inside had to cover their area, too."

"But weren't you already understaffed?" I ask. Recent reports in the media have claimed that TDCJ needs over three thousand more security officers to adequately cover all the units.

Gabrielle confirms the figure. "What that means is, we all have to work longer hours and be responsible for more area."

"There's speculation that the system is saving money by not hiring more guards," I say. "By using compulsory overtime, they don't have to pay expensive benefits to additional employees."

"I wouldn't doubt it," Gabrielle says and shrugs, but doesn't take advantage of the opportunity to complain. Instead, she explains the different security jobs inside: pickets, blocks, and "ad seg" — a shortening of "administrative segregation," the official term for solitary confinement. "Pickets are up in the towers or in control spots like the keys. The blocks, they're just those ordinary rows of cells in tiers. I'm working seg right now."

"How many prisoners does that mean you have in your charge?"

"Anywhere from one to sixty. It varies from day to day and unit to unit."

"What about the blocks? How many do they hold?"

Gabrielle's husband Jim has just joined us, holding what looks like his first cup of coffee for the day. Jim is a supervisor, with the rank of captain, at the Holliday unit. Gabrielle turns to check with him now. "Seventy-eight?" she says, making it a question.

Jim sits down on the sofa beside Gabrielle. He's tall and lanky, wearing shorts and a T-shirt on this rare shared day off. "There's twenty-six cells on a run. So that's twenty-six times three. Yeah, seventy-eight."

"What's a run?"

"There's three different runs," Jim answers. You know, like at Motel 6? All those rows of rooms, each one facing out? We call those runs."

Gabrielle adds that the lighting, though recently improved, is dim and "real gloomy."

The couple take their work with a degree of seriousness that is probably rare among the younger guards. Their wild oats, if they've sown any, are behind them now. They are homeowners, parents of a child in grade school, determined to keep the stable jobs that insure their stable home. They perform their duties by the book.

"So you get there," I say to Gabrielle, "for the third shift at . . . ?"

"Ten o'clock at night. That's when we have our turnout, just a briefing on what's been going on that day and any policy changes, safety stuff."

"And what's your regular routine?"

"When I first get there, the person I'm relieving tells me the count and any problems they've had with inmates in my area. I usually do my own count, too, just to make sure my number matches theirs. If it doesn't, I call the office and tell them I've got, say, seventy-four and they told me seventy-six. They'll check the move-book and see if anyone's been moved and they haven't informed me."

"I guess the inmates are asleep most of the time you're there."

She gives a little laugh. "The ones you want asleep aren't. The rambunctious ones stay up all night. It can be real noisy."

"So, after you've done the count, what comes next?"

"I do a security check every fifteen minutes to make sure everybody is still alive, that no one's escaped yet, and that there's no maintenance problems I need to report. Then we feed chow — breakfast — at three in the morning."

"Why so early?"

"I never understood that myself," Gabrielle says, turning to Jim.

"Because the schedule was designed so that each shift feeds one meal," Jim says, gaining interest in explaining the mechanics of the job. "It takes a couple of hours to feed 'em all. We start at that time so they can be done and ready for their job assignment. Then you can just turn 'em in at the half, they can eat their lunch, and you can turn 'em back out for work again. Lunch is about ten, ten-thirty. Your dinner meal, you're looking at like three o'clock in the afternoon."

"Everything in a prison is a routine," Gabrielle emphasizes. "It all fits in a time slot — usually thirty-minute slots and hour slots. With the exception of the count. We do six different counts on the third shift, which is more counting than any other shift."

"Because they're all in their cells at night?"

"That, plus they've proven statistically that the majority of all escapes happen on third shift."

"So, you like working seg?" I ask.

"I like seg a lot better than GP — general population — simply because I feel more secure."

"More secure?" I repeat, surprised.

"Oh, yes. The inmates are always handcuffed and have two officers escorting them when they're out of the cell."

"Escorting where?"

Jim leans forward to explain again. "Any out-of-cell time. In seg, that only means showers or the rec yard."

"With the recent escapes and hostage situations," I say, "don't you ever worry about being taken hostage? The official policy, as I understand it, is that the prison system recognizes no hostages."

"We go over that every year in training, but I've forgotten just how the policy's worded," she says. "They do teach us, though, that anyone taken hostage immediately loses their rank."

"I think I'd have more immediate worries than losing my rank," I say. "Why is that important?"

"Because ordinarily I have to do whatever my supervisor tells me to," Gabrielle says, "but, if he's taken hostage, he immediately loses all his rank. That means if he has a weapon in his back and tells me to open the door, I don't have to."

"Has your attitude toward the job changed any?" I ask Gabrielle. "You've been working for TDCJ for about eight years now, haven't you?"

"Yes," she says. "I was twenty-three when I started. And I hated it."

"So why did you do it?"

"I needed the insurance. TDCJ has really good benefits. I was a single mother then with a child, and it was the only job in the area that started medical coverage immediately. The pay was pretty good for around here, especially for someone with just a high school education. Really, the work isn't that hard, even if it is dangerous. On the one hand, everything is routine, but then it's never routine. There's always something happening. You have self-mutilations, you have hangings — we had one yesterday."

"A hanging? Do the inmates get so depressed they . . . ?"

"Different things," she says with imperturbable sincerity. "Some of them are psych patients."

"Are those inmates designated in some way so that you know you should keep especially close watch on them?"

"No. But after being there for a while, you know which inmates to keep an eye on more than the others. And they'll tell you. That's the odd thing about it. A lot of times they'll tell you that they're having a bad time."

"Have you ever been in a really dangerous situation?"

"There's always potential. Sometimes when you get home, you're thinking, gosh, what could have happened, maybe in a situation that kinda got heated."

"What do you do when inmates get into fights?"

She hesitates, and I start to amend my question, but she interrupts. "Oh, that does happen. Sometimes, for instance, the picket rolls two doors at once by mistake and lets two inmates out at once."

"Rolls the doors?" I repeat.

"You've seen like in the movies," Jim steps in to clarify, "the way the doors slide sideways? There's this mechanism that controls the barred doors, like a crank on a big wheel. You set these sort of prongs for the doors you want to open, then turn it. That's why we call it rolling the doors."

"Another problem is, all the communication is verbal," Gabrielle adds, "so that the picket might not hear the number of the door right. Or, like I say, he might open more than one at a time."

"That's not so likely to happen on seg," Jim says. "But in the GP, it can happen pretty easy because you have more in-and-outs. In seg, they just stay in their cells except for their shower and yard time."

"I haven't really had anything dangerous happen to me since I've been at Ferguson," Gabrielle says, as if reassuring me.

Gabrielle started her career with TDCJ at the Terrell unit in Livingston, about forty miles east of Huntsville. Except for the longer drive, she says, she liked Terrell better because it is a maximum security unit. "I just felt more secure," she says.

Gabrielle says that the drive to Ferguson, only twenty miles north of town, doesn't seem so bad after Terrell, though the roads to Ferguson are bad. "But if something happens at work that aggravates me, I have that whole drive to get it out of my system, so that by the time I get home I'm not still fuming. Then I can talk to Jim about it and not be real emotional."

"What about the way women are accepted, either by the prisoners or by the other employees?"

"It's a lot easier now than it used to be," she says. "Of course, there's men at the prison that think it's no place for women. As for prisoners, I think it's actually easier for women security officers. There's less conflict — a female talking to a male offender. They may not respect my orders, but they're not going to challenge them like they would a male's orders." She pauses to consider a moment. "At least most of the time, though you do have your ones that will. But I'm not a big threat to them, so usually they'll just go ahead and do what I say instead of challenging me. Whereas a male, with their height and their weight . . . well, there'd be more trouble between them."

"How do you feel about Gabrielle working there?" I ask Jim.

"It's got its days," he says, looking up from his coffee mug. "I know the potential for danger is always there. We got folks that've done in their own family and it didn't mean nothing to them, so I doubt they'd hesitate with her. But I just tell her to be extra careful and not let things get out of hand — if there's a situation, to call for some assistance to handle it, get her supervisor down there, stuff like that. I'm a supervisor and that's what I tell my folks, so we can manage it before it gets out of hand. But you know what? She likes it, especially in seg."

"Have you ever had anybody threaten you?" I ask Gabrielle.

"I've been threatened a few times. I've had urine thrown at me. Not feces yet, but urine."

"I asked your father how he felt about your working in prison, and he was pretty positive about it. He said he thought it had given you a lot of confidence."

"Dad was already in TDCJ, so he knew what I could expect. He never made a negative comment. Now my mother," she adds, rolling her eyes, "who's never set foot in a penitentiary, she's the one that's leery about it."

"Have your attitudes changed over the eight years you've worked there?"

"I want to say I'm a lot more," she pauses, hunting for the right word, "not hot-headed, but I look into things that before I would have just dismissed. I'm more conscious of people doing things and I read more into what people say than I used to. I am more cautious in meeting someone new than I would have been. But I don't think it's really affected me as far as how I treat people."

"Have you always worked the third shift?"

"Third shift fits into our schedule so that I really don't miss school functions or anything that my son's into. I'm at work when he's asleep and I'm home when he's awake."

Jim, on the other hand, works the first shift. But, as a security captain, his schedule is more liable to change than Gabrielle's. "I get all the phone calls at home," he says.

"What about your attitude toward the inmates?" I ask Gabrielle. "I guess you were scared at first."

"To me, they're like small kids," she says. "They'll only get away with what you'll let them get away with. But if you let them know where you are, and there's no gray area for them to guess, then you have less trouble. There's no room for them to say, 'Well, today she's just moody.' They've got to know what to expect. I try not to get personal with them, because, really, there's no need for them to know anything about me or my family — how many kids I have or where I live."

"As a supervisor," I ask Jim, "do you find that to be a problem — guards establishing a relationship with prisoners?"

"I warn the younger guards that if they get personal, they might get drawn into a con. With the older ones, the ones that've been there a long time, they might get a little complacent, too.

"You can say that they're inmates and that's why they're locked up, so keep your distance. But would I say that they're all bad? No, though there's a certain percentage. Some'll never give you any problem, just do what's expected of them. Then you have a bunch that have been in prison a few times, or a number of years. They can try to establish a relationship to be on a personal level and then take it to another level. They try to suck an employee in. We just tell the officers to stay professional. No need to socialize with any of the offenders, because they'll use it against you. They'll threaten to come get you, that they'll kill you and your family. They'll tell you, I know where your family's at, I know your family's from Houston, I can look 'em up. I want you to start doing such-and-such for me or I'm gonna send word out there and hurt your family. Then the employee doesn't know what to do. They're between a rock and a hard place."

"There's documentation of some stories like this that are actually true," Gabrielle adds.

"I understand prisons were different back, say, in the seventies."

"Back then," Jim says gravely, "you're talking about building tenders and turnkeys. You had inmates running the facility. At Ferguson out there, you'd have nine or ten officers who'd show up and just kind of supervise the inmates that were actually running the unit. Then, in the mid-eighties, TDCJ had the big killing sprees, inmate on inmate. That's when gangs were getting into TDCJ. A lot of drug wars started and stuff like that. That's when they began to use ad seg, so they could separate out those people."

"That's when they also started giving long sentences for drug offenses, wasn't it?" I ask. "That really filled up the prisons, didn't it?"

"You can find offenders doing more time for drugs than others do for murder," he agrees. "Depending on what county they were tried in and stuff like that. Some places have a zero-tolerance policy for drugs. And now those offenders have to do a bigger percentage of their time than they used to. When I first hired on, you could take an inmate's sentence, cut it in half, and then cut it in half again, and that would give you a ballpark figure of how long he actually stayed in TDCJ. Now, if they violate parole, they're actually having to come back and do some time on it."

"How has working in the prisons affected your family life?"

"As far as how it affects me," Gabrielle says, "I look at the worst of the worst every day. So, when I come home, it makes me really conscious of what I've got. We're not promised another day, you know, so I'm real thankful.

"We're real family oriented," she goes on. "I'm in a situation where I see child molesters, and the results. So, we're really involved in Jared's education, where he is, who he's with. It's made me more cautious about him. I feel more leery of just letting him go outside and play. I mean, we all go outside and play now. He doesn't go to the restroom by himself when we're out somewhere. He goes with Jim. It's just made me more protective of him."

"If there was just one of us in this line of work," Jim says, "we wouldn't be living in this kind of house. And if she didn't work for

TDCJ too, she wouldn't understand the kinds of problems we have there."

"For me," Gabrielle puts in, "with him being a supervisor and me being a CO [corrections officer], I understand the supervisor's point of view better."

"Are there things in the system that you can see could be better?"

"Other than hiring another thousand people?" she laughs. "The quality of staffing, too. We need higher standards."

"Some people don't think the pay is too good," Jim says. "Entry level is like $25,000 now, and it maxes out up around $28,000."

"So what position do you see yourself working up to? Warden?"

"I'd like to," he says. "I don't want to be just a correctional officer for the rest of my tenure with the state. If I ever decided to quit and go somewhere else, I'd like to have something better on my resume."

"What about you, Gabrielle?"

"Me personally, with Jared, I don't want to come home and have the phone calls and all that. My schedule is pretty much set. But I would like eventually to go back to school."

"In what? Criminal justice?"

"No. A whole different field." She tilts her small, neat head to one side as she speculates. "Maybe physical fitness."

7

The Death House

*It just couldn't be done, boys. A Warden can't be a Warden and
a killer too. The penitentiary is a place to reform a man, not to
kill him.*

R. F. COLEMAN*

THE LONG LOW rectangles of the Ellis unit hunker down among the
piney woods where county road 980 arches along a bend in Lake
Livingston about fifteen miles northeast of Huntsville. It's the kind of
place, as we say here, you have to be going to to get there.

The Ellis unit has housed death row since 1965. The number of condemned prisoners had grown far beyond the capacity of the eight cells
at the Walls originally allocated to condemned men awaiting execution. At Ellis, men on death row were allowed to participate in the work
program, which meant they got out of their cells and mingled with the
rest of the prison population every day.

Martin Gurule changed all that.

Convicted for shooting two men while robbing a Corpus Christi
restaurant in 1992 and sentenced to death, Martin Gurule was determined to cheat the executioner one way or another. On Thanksgiving

---

* R. F. Coleman, following his resignation as warden at the Walls unit when the
Texas legislature designated him the state's executioner.

night in 1998, he led six other death row inmates over the roof of the main building at Ellis and through a hole they had earlier cut with a hacksaw in the fence of the recreation yard. A guard finally spotted them from a tower, and, before they could all reach the perimeter fence, a barrage of gunfire was raining down on the seven escapees.

Gurule's six cohorts surrendered then, but he kept going. He had strapped cardboard beneath his clothing and thus managed to make it over two electrified chain-link fences topped with razor wire. Then he disappeared into the foggy bottomland beyond the prison perimeter.

The hunt for Gurule went on for a week. The state patrol set up checkpoints on all the roads in the area. Search teams with tracking dogs combed the thick woods for miles around. Helicopters with heat-seeking scanners hovered over the pine thickets like bees around clover. Rumors abounded that Gurule had been spotted as far away as San Antonio, as near as the closest convenience store. The prisoner appeared to have vanished without a trace.

The first week in December, a couple of off-duty TDCJ guards were fishing in a nearby creek about a mile from Ellis when they noticed what looked like a bundle of floating rags. The water was deep and murky, and not until they brought their boat closer did they recognize the bundle of rags as Gurule's bloated body. When a retrieval team arrived from the prison, they discovered that the body was too badly decomposed to tell if Gurule had been hit by gunfire. TDCJ records state that his cause of death was drowning.

Gurule was the only prisoner to have made an even partially successful escape from Texas's death row since 1934, when Bonnie Parker and Clyde Barrow shot up the Eastham unit to rescue a cousin.

Gustavo Garcia, one of the failed escapees from death row, told reporters he had hoped Gurule had made it to freedom: "It would have made everything worthwhile for me."

Gurule's escape, especially as the hunt went on for so long, gave TDCJ in general and the Ellis unit in particular a considerable black eye. In the general shakeup of the prison's administration, the warden was demoted and transferred to another unit, as were two assistant wardens. Scott Watson, the plant manager for the Ellis woodshop, remembers that Gurule's escape put considerable pressure on officials throughout the prison system. "The word went out to all the units' wardens," Watson told us. "One [prisoner] leaves, and you're looking for a job."

The configuration of the Ellis unit itself was also blamed for the escape. It allowed too much access to other prisoners, the state prison board concluded. Almost immediately they began planning to move death row to a new location.

By 2001, 460 condemned men had been transferred from Ellis to the Terrell unit, about forty miles east of Huntsville. Terrell already had a reputation among TDCJ inmates. In 1994, guards had stood by for two hours while a twenty-three-year-old inmate was beaten to death by other prisoners for refusing their sexual demands. In another episode, two guards had beaten a prisoner to death for spitting on them.

Conditions on death row at Terrell proved considerably less agreeable than those the inmates had previously known at Ellis. Each man still has his own cell, measuring sixty square feet, about the size of an ordinary bathroom. But unlike Ellis, where the front of the cell was barred, at Terrell the cells have solid steel doors, with only a small aperture for observing the inmates and delivering food trays. The men only leave their cells to shower and for an hour each day in the recreation yard — alone.

Also, death row inmates are no longer allowed to participate in the work program. Previously, TDCJ had been proud of having the only work program in the nation for death row inmates. Qualifying for the program was one of the few incentives motivating condemned men to cooperate with their guards. Scott Watson's woodshop at Ellis, for instance, had had a two-year waiting list. But state authorities blamed the work program for providing men on death row with contacts to the general population, thus making Gurule's escape possible. The chairman of Texas's prison board, Allan Polunsky, told reporters that, given that the work program was set up to provide job skills, it would be wasted on the death row prisoners, "since all the participants are obviously terminally disadvantaged."

At their new location, death row prisoners are still allowed books, writing materials, and legal documents. With good behavior, they may also get a radio. But other than the guards who escort each inmate to and from the shower and the rec yard, they have little human communication. In their new habitat, death row inmates face years of virtual isolation.

Trouble began on death row at the Terrell unit even before the entire complement of condemned inmates was transferred there. On New Year's Day of 2000, some of the men on death row began a short-lived hunger strike. TDCJ spokesman Larry Todd dismissed the effort, noting that the last time a prisoner supposedly went on a hunger strike, he gained weight from the candy bars he had sequestered in his cell.

The next incident was more serious. In February, fifty-seven-year-old Jeannette Bledsoe, who had worked as a guard for a little more than three years, was escorting Howard Guidry, one of the failed escapees from Ellis, back to his cell after his hour in the recreation yard one afternoon. As they passed the cell of Ponchai Wilkerson, another of the six erstwhile escapees, he flung open his cell door. He was armed with a "bean-slot tool," a bar used to open the narrow aperture through which food trays are slid.

Both men grabbed Bledsoe and dragged her into a small room adjacent to death row. There they handcuffed her and shackled her leg to the floor. Then they issued their protest to conditions on death row at Terrell. They demanded more than the hour a day outside their cells that death row inmates are currently allowed.

Wilkerson, the son of a retired deputy sheriff, was scheduled to be executed in three weeks. He obviously had little to lose at this point. This time Larry Todd, the TDCJ spokesman, was somber as he told the press he was not optimistic about the outcome of this incident. However, to everyone's surprise, Jeannette Bledsoe was released unharmed after being held for thirteen hours. Prison officials' only concession was an agreement to let the two inmates speak to a representative of an abolitionist group. Wilkerson's execution was carried out as scheduled, though he had to be extracted from his cell at Polunsky (then known as Terrell) for the ride into Huntsville and again from the cell at the Walls where he waited for his execution. Guards used extra straps to hold him on the gurney in the death chamber. Just before he took his last breath, Wilkerson spat out the universal handcuff key he had hidden in his mouth — his final act of defiance.

Less dramatic criticism of death row's move to Terrell came from other quarters as well, one of them quite unexpected. Prisons are traditionally named for emeritus members of the state's prison board. Charles Terrell, a Dallas insurance executive for whom the unit had been named, suddenly requested that his name be removed from the facility. Though previously chairman of the prison board and renowned for his hard-nosed approach to crime, Terrell said he felt "ambivalent" about the manner in which the death penalty is currently imposed in Texas. On July 20, 2001, the TDCJ board voted quietly and unanimously to change the prison's name to the Allan B. Polunsky unit, in honor of the most recent board chairman.

THE DEATH HOUSE itself, the location of the actual executions, remains at the Walls, only two blocks east of Huntsville's courthouse square, where it has been since the state took over executions from county authorities in 1924. A minimum security facility, the Walls now houses about 1500 inmates, give or take a couple hundred who may be in transit to other prisons or who are scheduled for release. In the 1970s, the facility housed most of the prison system's educational programs, of which it was justly proud.

The school at the Walls had adopted the open-classroom configuration popular among education theorists during that era. The school, its library, and administrative offices took up the third floor of the prison compound's west side, right above the inmate cafeteria. The library and teaching area occupied opposite ends of the floor. Between those two areas the only enclosed spaces were the staff offices, a reading room, and supply closets.

In the summer of 1974, Fred Carrasco and two accomplices commandeered the third floor and took twelve prison personnel and a number of student inmates hostage. Sylvia Weathers, who later worked with my mother at the Goree unit, narrowly escaped being one of the hostages.

Sylvia had been familiar with the big red brick fortress called the Walls since childhood. When she was still in grade school, her father and mother would take her on Friday evenings to the prison auditorium to watch inmates perform for a radio program regularly broadcast from there. She remembers those shows as filled with lively music. Thus the big complex was not a scary place for her when she reentered it in 1973 as an art teacher.

Sylvia's best friend, Judy Standley, joined her the following year as the school's librarian. The two women had grown up together, gone to high school together, and then on to college. But Judy's life had taken a different direction when she dropped out of school to marry. Now she was a single mother with five children. Sylvia was particularly glad that, after so many years, she and Judy were together again, working at the same place. In fact, Sylvia's son was engaged to be married to Judy's daughter.

On the morning of July 24, 1974, Sylvia went to work at the Walls as usual. Before her students arrived, she set out the art supplies they would need that day. Classes at the Walls were divided into morning and afternoon shifts. She would be through teaching by noon. With her inmate assistant's help, she would put away the day's work materials, tidy up for the afternoon shift, and still have time to make her appointment at the beauty shop.

On a wet November morning we drink tea in Sylvia's breakfast room, full of family antiques, as she recounts the events of that day twenty-seven years ago. One of her students was late for class that morning, and when he did arrive, she noticed he seemed agitated. He would draw a little on his sketchpad, then wad up the sheet and toss it in the wastebasket. She wandered among the students, observing their work, until she reached his table. He had put down his pencil and was staring glumly at nothing. Sylvia asked him what was troubling him.

At first he just shook his head, but after a little prodding, he mumbled, "I walked up on these dudes this morning, and they wanted me to go in with them on something." He kept his head down, avoiding her eyes. "I told them I didn't want no part of their action." The student glanced up at her quickly and then back at his hands.

When Sylvia tried to reconstruct the conversation later that day, she thought he might have also added that the name of one of the dudes was Carrasco.

Inmates, she knew, could be moody at times, like anyone else. But Sylvia also knew that agitation is contagious within a prison, and she didn't want him disturbing the other students, so she merely pointed to the sketchpad. "Just put all that behind you now. You're here to learn, so let's get on with it."

She would be sorry later that she hadn't paid more attention to the incident.

After class, as she and her assistant put away the art supplies, students began filtering in for the afternoon session. When the tables were cleared, Sylvia stepped out into the hall and waved to Bill, another teacher who was chatting with one of the guards. Prison regulations required that a male employee escort all female teachers into and out of the prison.

"I'm ready, Bill," she called. "I've got to get going. I have to be at the beauty shop in ten minutes."

Bill pushed himself away from the wall where he'd been leaning. "Guess I better be going," he said to the guard, jerking his thumb toward Sylvia and grinning. "You know how impatient women are."

She was at the beauty shop, her hair still wet, when the phone rang. "It's for you," the receptionist called to her.

Puzzled, Sylvia heard the school secretary's voice when she took the receiver. "Do you remember who was at school today?" the woman asked.

"Sure." Sylvia began naming over the personnel she had seen.

"What about Judy?" the secretary asked. "Was Judy Standley there?"

The night before the two friends had gone to dinner together and then to see a movie — "The Way We Were." Sylvia told the secretary she'd seen Judy in the teachers' lounge that morning. "She said that all the librarians were planning on going out to lunch today. But they should be back by now," Sylvia said.

"Thanks," the woman said and hung up with no further explanation.

Sylvia stood staring for a moment at the phone in her hand, bewildered. Later, on her way home, the strange, abrupt conversation continued to bother her. As soon as she unlocked her front door, she went to the phone intending to call the library to find out why were they checking up on the school staff. But just as she reached for the phone, it rang.

"Thank heavens I got you," her sister said. "Are you all right?"

"Of course. What's the matter?"

"They've taken hostages at the Walls."

Stunned, Sylvia put the phone down. Immediately it rang again. This time it was Judy herself.

"Judy, where are you?" Sylvia cried.

"I'm here in the library," Judy answered, her voice surprisingly steady. "There's a bunch of us. I'm okay, but I need you to do something. Go find my daughter and stay with her."

It would not be till later that night that Sylvia realized she herself had missed being taken hostage by no more than five minutes. She must have been crossing the street to the parking lot on her way to the beauty shop at the moment when Fred Carrasco had burst into the typing class, pointed a pistol at assistant principal Novella Pollard, and threatened to shoot her if she moved.

About seventy inmate students filled the classroom area and library, along with a guard, the librarians, and the teachers, when Carrasco and his accomplices, Rudy Dominguez and Ignacio Cuevas, all brandishing guns, took over the third floor. They herded the employees into the front corner of the library and, over the next few hours, released all but four of the inmates in groups of ten after using them to move metal filing cabinets and bookcases to form a barricade in front of the library's glass doors.

Meanwhile, Rev. Carroll Pickett's phone rang at the Presbyterian manse across town. Pickett was the minister at Huntsville's First Presbyterian Church, and Jim Estelle, Director of the Texas Department of Corrections, was one of his parishioners.

"I've got a situation I need you to help out with," Estelle told Pickett. "They've taken hostages at the Walls. I've got a room set up for their families here in the administration building. They're going to need somebody with them. I don't think they're going to respond too well to our institutional chaplains. They aren't very happy with the whole prison system right now. I need somebody from the outside, someone local, to be my personal representative to the families."

Pickett was silent a moment, taking in the shocking news.

"One other thing," Estelle said. "Two of the hostages are members of your flock."

"Who's that?"

"Judy Standley and Von Beseda."

For the next eleven days, family members would spend tormented hours in the administration building as the fate of the hostages unfolded. They knew all too well the prison system policy about hostages: the Department of Corrections recognizes no hostages. It will not negotiate for the release of hostages. No hostages will leave the facility. In one of her last phone calls as hostage, Judy Standley gave Sylvia Weathers instructions for her own funeral.

When Carroll Pickett first came to Huntsville in 1967 as pastor of First Presbyterian Church, he had no idea that the town was home to the state's prison system. No one on the search committee had so much as mentioned the prison.

"There were basically four groups in the church at that time," he tells me as I sit across the desk from him in his office at Jump Rope America, an organization that sponsors, as the name indicates, jump rope competitions across the country. "There was the college group, students and faculty. Then the newcomers to Huntsville. And the ones I called the old-timers. They weren't necessarily old; they'd just lived here all their lives. And finally there were the prison people. In my congregation I had Jim Estelle, who was the director of the whole system. I also had the Director of Treatment and a warden. These groups pretty much kept to themselves. They all had their own idea about things."

"Including the prisons?"

"That was never an issue. It just never came up."

"What about during the hostage crisis in 1974?" I ask.

"Well, of course, that was hard on everyone," he says, clasping his hands behind his head as he rocks back in his chair. "I was there at the Walls from six every morning to midnight. I'd get on the phone in the evening and Carrasco would tell me which of the hostages could talk to their family that day. He was a real dictator."

Fred Gomez Carrasco was not your ordinary inmate. A major player in San Antonio's drug business, he was wealthy enough to send his daughter to a private school in Connecticut and to hire an expensive lawyer, Ruben Montemayor, who he insisted join the team of official prison negotiators. He was also intelligent. On the run from both U.S. and Mexican police after escaping via helicopter from a prison in

Guadalajara, Carrasco had been captured only through the efforts of a
determined San Antonio detective following a gun battle at a motel. He
was now serving a life sentence, assigned to the Walls instead of a maximum security unit because crippling injuries sustained in the shootout
had supposedly made him less of a threat.

Father Joseph O'Brien, the Catholic chaplain at the Walls, got
Carrasco assigned to him as his inmate assistant. "Joe thought that he
could convert Fred," Pickett recalls. "He thought he could take this guy
who had already been convicted of killing fifty-five people in the drug
business and do something with him."

As it turned out, however, Carrasco used his work assignment in the
chapel to smuggle in ammunition for his planned escape. Inmate mail
was censored, but letters or packages sent to a prison chaplain were
not. Carrasco made sure he was at his post every day in order to inter-
cept and sort O'Brien's incoming mail, especially the packages. The up-
per shelves of a supply closet in the chapel slowly filled with peculiarly
heavy boxes supposedly containing sports equipment for the inmates.

The takeover of the classrooms and library was timed to coincide
with the one o'clock whistle so that it would mask the noise of shots
fired to intimidate the teachers and student inmates.

Carrasco had also picked his accomplices carefully. Neither was as
bright as he was. Both had been born to poverty and never known the
affluence to which Carrasco was accustomed. Ignacio Cuevas was serving a forty-five-year sentence for murdering a man in a barroom brawl.
The sheriff who arrested him, however, doubted that Cuevas was his
real name. He suspected that the criminal had stolen identification off
an earlier murder victim outside of Pecos. The other accomplice,
Rudolfo Dominguez, had a reputation for unpredictable violence and
was quite possibly schizophrenic. Of their three captors, he was the
one the hostages most feared.

As the siege continued, Huntsville held its collective breath. "Everyone in the town wanted to help out some way," Pickett says. "Churches
brought in food and bedding. I just had to pick up the phone and we got
whatever we needed."

National news teams set up shop across from the Walls. State officials, including the governor, converged on the town.

Early on, Carrasco insisted that supplies — medicine and food for the hostages, bedding and towels for them all, and street clothes for him and his cohorts — be brought to him by Father O'Brien. He seemed to take particular pleasure in reversing their previous positions, making the chaplain perform the kind of menial chores earlier required of him as an inmate. Finally, Carrasco sent him out with a typed list of the weapons and body armor he wanted. When the chaplain returned around three in the morning with the prison officials' reply, Carrasco told him he was free to leave, but if he came back again, he too would become a hostage. O'Brien volunteered to stay with the others, hoping he might be a comfort to the hostages and a moderating force with their captors.

The prison siege, the longest one in U.S. history, dragged on for a week, then went into a second week while the prison metal shop fashioned steel helmets to Carrasco's specifications. Across the courtyard, nerves were frayed. Prison personnel, Texas Rangers, the FBI, and state officials had trouble agreeing to a single game plan. Carrasco's lawyer, Ruben Montemayor, sat in on the meetings, making notes on a legal pad. Assault teams were readied for storming the building. Explosives were set at the rear of the library.

The families, kept in a separate area where they were given periodic updates and allowed to talk by phone to their hostage, grew increasingly impatient with the prison officials. Eighty members of the press milled about outside, eager for more information. Instead, what they got was a media blackout.

Pickett does not second-guess the negotiations, even from a distance of twenty-seven years. "The officials figured that for every day they could hold out, they would save at least one person. And that pretty much proved true."

A prototype of a bulletproof helmet he had demanded was sent in to Carrasco. He field-tested it by firing shots at it, then angrily reported to the officials that it had failed the test. He threatened harm to the hostages if the prison didn't come up with something better. A request for bulletproof vests was denied, as was Carrasco's offer to exchange the hostages for Jim Estelle and other prison officers.

Both sides refused to budge. The press was shut out completely. Communications began to break down between the prison officials and the families of the hostages. Finally, a daughter of one of the hostages held a press conference herself, revealing to the press the messages from Carrasco.

Meanwhile, inside the education building, one of the teachers suffered an apparent heart attack. An ambulance arrived, and Carrasco allowed her to be taken out. He was a gentleman, he said, and knew how to be chivalrous to women.

When the new helmets arrived and proved to meet Carrasco's specifications, everyone began to feel that the end was drawing near.

Carrasco's final demand was for an armored car to be parked just outside the entry ramp to the third floor, its gas tank filled. On Friday, August 2, the tenth day of the siege, a thunderstorm hit Huntsville in the early morning hours, knocking out electric power to the city, including the Walls.

That evening, another of the teachers was released to hand-carry Carrasco's final plan of escape to the authorities. He and his accomplices would be inside a contraption made of blackboards to which heavy law books were fastened with duct tape. Inside this moveable shield, variously named the "piñata" and the "Trojan horse" by the media, each of the three escapees would be handcuffed to one or more of their hostages. If any attempt was made to interfere with the escape, the inmate trio swore to shoot their hostages.

"How could Carrasco have possibly believed they would allow him to get away?" I ask Pickett.

He shrugs and shakes his head.

"As I understand it," I say, "the blackboard contraption got hung up trying to negotiate the turn halfway down the ramp."

"That was one problem," Pickett agrees, leaning forward over his desk now. "But what really caused the shootout was the fire hoses."

With the armored car in position, Carrasco had herded some of the hostages inside their unwieldy contrivance and shackled others to the outside. Sharpshooters, Texas Rangers, sheriff's deputies, city police — every arm of law enforcement available were waiting for them. The hostages shuffling along inside that flimsy screen must have known how this would end.

"The last thing Judy told me when I talked to her on the phone the night before," Pickett says, "was, 'Whatever you do, don't postpone the wedding.' I figure she knew she was going to die."

About nine in the evening, the three inmates and their captives began their cautious descent of the ramp. When the awkward shield reached the ninety-degree turn in the ramp, halfway down, they tried to force the clumsy contraption through the narrow space. The shield buckled, began to come apart. Taking advantage of this moment of confusion, Texas Rangers ordered fire hoses turned on the flimsy shield.

"The plan was to knock the Trojan horse over and the people inside off their feet," Pickett explains. "They were hoping their sharpshooters could pick off Carrasco and his bunch before they could kill many — maybe any — of the hostages. But they'd neglected to bleed the air out of the fire hose. So when they turned on the water, it just spurted and dribbled, like a faucet that hasn't been used in a long time."

Instantly shots rang out from within the disintegrating box, and the waiting assault team opened fire. When the melee was over, Carrasco was lying dead from a self-inflicted bullet wound. Dominguez was killed resisting arrest. Cuevas surrendered. But two teachers, Judy Standley and Yvonne Beseda, were dead as well. Father O'Brien, the prison chaplain, was critically wounded.

"That hostage situation really got to Joe," Pickett says now. "He never got over it. It affected him so badly that they eventually had to ask him to resign." He shakes his head again. "He was a good guy."

"The fact that Carrasco had been using him must have added to his distress," I say.

"He felt really guilty. He felt like he had done his best and his best wasn't good enough. And then he got betrayed."

I know from my mother's experience working in the prison system that it is a point of pride, among both the prison personnel and the inmates, not to be taken in, to avoid being conned.

When Pickett became a prison chaplain years later, his own inmate assistant was called Blue. "Of course that wasn't his real name. They all had convict names that they called one another. But Blue never burned me. He was an old-time convict. He knew the ropes. He learned how to get things done for the chapel and for me. He knew how to protect me.

He kept his ear to the ground and, if somebody didn't like what I did, he handled it the prison way. That wasn't by using guards and the wardens either. I think O'Brien had the same trust in Fred, but Fred let him down."

He leans back in his chair again. "Joe got a new clerk after that, one that was Jewish. Now he was super. Fastest typist I ever saw in my life."

Pickett sits forward, fiddling with a paper clip. "When I left that last night of the siege, after I'd broken the news to Von and Judy's families, I told Jim Estelle, 'You know what? I'm never ever coming back inside this prison again. Never.'" He looks up at me now and smiles. "Don't ever say never."

"So when did you come back?"

"Six years later, 1980. I didn't even know they had executions at the Walls when I went to work there. There hadn't been one since 1964, and I guess we'd all forgotten about it. I know I hadn't thought about executions in all my life," Pickett says, his voice heavy with the wonder of it. "Neither had anyone else. Nobody talked about it. It wasn't in the papers. Old Sparky had been crated up and moved off to some closet somewhere."

In 1982, eighteen years after the last condemned man had been buckled into Old Sparky, the state of Texas began executing capital offenders once more, not with electricity this time, but by lethal injection.

"Nobody working at the Walls in '82 had been there in '64. When they set the date for Charlie Brooks, nobody knew anything about doing an execution. Nobody in the world had ever done an execution by lethal injection. Nobody."

As a matter of policy, Pickett never saw the man to be executed until the day he was brought in from death row at Ellis to the Walls. "Jim Estelle's philosophy was that the chaplain out at Ellis should be with him until they brought him in. Then I was to be — I didn't like this term, but this is what he called it — the death chaplain." He pauses for a moment, then continues. "I never went to death row. Never. I didn't even know what death row looked like. I knew what the inmates told me it was like, because they all wanted to talk about it."

"By the time they got to you, they were probably wishing they were back there," I offer.

"Not really. They had waited so long, most of them were ready to get it over with. I guess I got to understand how they felt. Death row is loud and vulgar and noisy. People are hollering and yelling all the time. TVs are blaring. But when they came into the death house, there would just be me and two guards. It would be the first quiet any of them had had in fifteen, eighteen, twenty years. Many of them realized that prison was all they had to look forward to for the rest of their lives." He pauses again. "They were ready to die. Let's just put it that way."

Even so, Pickett's duties sometimes got complicated. A prisoner would come in to the Walls, and Pickett would spend a whole day with him. Then the prisoner would get a last-minute stay of execution. "So they took him back out to Ellis. Stays and commutations were more frequent than you might think."

In addition to the ninety-five executions he witnessed during almost sixteen years at the Walls, Pickett estimates another forty-five or fifty men got stays or commutations. "Of course, when they went back to Ellis, they told all the others what it was like."

"What was it like?" I ask. "I mean for you."

He laces his fingers together as he considers. "Estelle told me when I first went to work there, 'Never promise what you can't deliver, and always deliver what you promise.' That's what I tried to do. I just talked to them straight. I had no prior history with them. I had nothing to do with the law. I didn't sit on the jury. I didn't pronounce their sentence. So I thought of it as a ministry to a dying person, the same way I would with a terminally ill person in the hospital. You see, I was also chaplain for the prisoners they brought in to the Huntsville hospital, including the ones who were sick and dying. So I had me a death row already. Men who were dying of diseases — and stabbings and hangings in prison, too."

Then he looks up again before he continues. "The warden said my job was to 'seduce their emotions,' so they'd get up on the table without causing a ruckus." He smiles now. "And I never had one to resist."

Perhaps Pickett's strangest experience as "death chaplain" was when Ignacio Cuevas, who had survived the escape attempt of 1974, was brought to the Walls for execution eighteen years after the hostage-taking.

"He didn't know me from Adam, of course," Pickett says. "He never saw me during the siege. But I sure remembered him."

Twice the decisions in the Standley murder case were reversed. The trials cost the state half a million dollars. But the third jury sentenced Ignacio Cuevas to death for murdering Judy Standley. Although he did not fire any shots during the melee, he was charged under the Texas law of parties, which holds that a participant in a felony that results in death shares the guilt for the murder.

Cuevas spent his seventeen years on death row working as its barber. In his spare time he painted, made matchstick crafts, and did needlework.

The Reeves County sheriff who arrested Cuevas in Pecos had always suspected that Cuevas was not his real name. And, as it turned out, the prisoner had two wives, one in Mexico, one in the U.S.

The condemned man's middle-aged son, whose name was Martinez, showed up with his wife before the execution. Afterward, the coroner released the dead man's corpse to the couple. They put the body in the back of their pickup and drove away.

"How did your prison ministry compare to pastoring a church congregation?" I ask Pickett.

He frowns. "In a way, not much different. You have to treat people like people. A lot of the inmates changed their lives in prison. I'm going to a reunion soon over in San Marcos with some of them."

"Is the reunion sponsored by a particular prison ministry?"

"No. Just a bunch of individuals I've stayed in touch with over the years. One plays the organ in the church over in Shiro. You know I'm still pastor there? Sometimes I have one of them come preach for me when I have to be away. I still do convict funerals. I don't want to say I had a good time, but I had a good ministry in prison."

He seems particularly proud of the four choirs he organized in prison. "We had a Spanish choir, a Catholic choir, a gospel choir, and the Chapel of Hope choir made up of the best musicians. Used to take them to competitions around the state." He shakes his head. "They don't do that anymore."

"How did you feel about the death penalty?" I ask.

"That's one of those things you don't ever let on how you feel. If you tell a convict you're in favor of the death penalty, then you can't talk to him. And he sure won't talk to you. If you come out publicly against it when you're working for the prison system, then you lose your ministry. I won't call it a job. I think it's horrible, you know — I think it would be horrible, not just for me, but anybody else. I don't like the way people say, 'it's my job.'" He pauses to add with a qualifying shrug, "Of course, that's their business, but I don't think it's anybody's job to kill. You might do it for other reasons. But it's not a job."

8

Psychology

Let us call it by the name which, for lack of any other nobility,
will at least give the nobility of truth, and let us recognize it for
what it is essentially — a revenge.

ALBERT CAMUS

I ARRIVED AT Mary Alice Conroy's small and unassuming office in a building on the edge of campus, expecting a forensic psychologist to be a figure out of some Patricia Cornwell mystery, a professional delver into the darker recesses of the criminal mind. Someone who figures out what makes one person a serial killer and another a solid citizen. Someone who constructs, almost magically from the faintest of clues, a picture of a probable perpetrator. It didn't take Dr. Conroy long to set me straight about that.

"Oh, no," she said, shaking her head emphatically when I asked her about building a psychological profile of a killer. "Forensic psychologists don't do profiling. That's handled by the Behavioral Science Unit at the FBI. Profiling belongs to law enforcement. Forensics has to do with what takes place in the courtroom. Sometimes it's hard to get people to understand the difference."

"Okay. So what about jury selection?" I was thinking of John Grisham's novel *The Runaway Jury,* in which tobacco companies spend a fortune to assess potential jurors in a damage suit.

But Dr. Conroy merely lifted a dismissive eyebrow at the question. "*Some* forensic psychologists do that. *I* don't," she replied.

When I asked what had led her into this line of work, her response reinforced my impression of unassailable professional integrity.

"As a graduate student at the University of Houston in the 1970s — back when dinosaurs walked the earth," she said, "I knew I wanted to be a psychologist. The field of psychology is quite specialized — another thing most people don't realize — so I had to decide just what kind of psychologist. I didn't want to just make a living. I also wanted to make a social contribution. Since I had always been interested in criminal justice, I took some practicums in that area. I even came up to Huntsville several times. After I got my degree, I went to work for the Federal Bureau of Prisons."

And there she remained, working in the forensic division of the Federal Bureau of Prisons for twenty years, the last six as Director of Forensics.

"My students ask me, 'Do you *really* testify in court? Do you *really* talk to criminals? Have you *really* been on death row?' She pauses to laugh. "I tell them, 'Oh, yeah, I really have.'"

Though she went to graduate school at the University of Houston, Conroy is not a native Texan. Her speech is quick and clipped, with no identifiable regional accent. The directness of her demeanor verges on bluntness. Despite her small size, she is obviously a woman who expects to be reckoned with.

Conroy joined the faculty of Sam Houston State University five years ago. Its College of Criminal Justice appeared to offer a good fit for someone with her background. In addition to her academic work, Conroy runs an impressive number of seminars and workshops every year to which flock lawyers, judges, and criminologists from around the country.

She modifies her earlier disclaimer about jury selection now, as if intent on keeping the record scrupulously straight. "I do sometimes do assessments of juries that have already been chosen," she says, clasping her hands over one knee. "You see, jury selection consults are really quite rare. Only a very high profile, very expensive trial would get involved with that. After all, each side has just so many challenges. It's a great waste of time anyway. The ideal jury probably doesn't exist. The jury you get is the jury you get. The real work comes in assessing that jury after it's chosen. I help lawyers figure out what arguments will appeal to the people on the jury — what those twelve people will care about, what they'll need explained, and in what terms."

The phone rings and she turns back to her desk to answer it, dispatches the caller with a few words, then turns to resume our conversation with an example. "I was working on a death sentence case a couple of years ago. I talked to the attorney about how to present my credentials. He told me that on the jury were a prison warden and four TDCJ employees. That's five of the twelve. The lawyer wanted me to talk about my associate professor rank and the books I've written. I told him, 'You know that's not going to mean anything to these people. They're going to care about the fact that I worked for the Federal Bureau of Prisons for twenty years and that I spent ten of them in men's max where I daily decided who got placed in open population and who didn't. They couldn't care less if I ever wrote a book.'"

Consulting as an expert witness accounts for most of Conroy's forensic work. And she stresses that she works mainly on criminal cases.

"You mean civil cases use forensic psychologists, too?" I ask.

"Oh my yes," she says. "Malpractice, insurance claims, child custody, family law. If you want to get rich, that's where the money is, you know."

I can tell from her tone that Conroy has little patience with such misuse of talent. Indeed, she holds to the highest standards of professional ethics.

"A prosecutor called me from El Paso the other day. She wanted to hire me to testify that a certain defendant was a risk." Conroy all but sniffs before she continues, "I told her, 'You don't hire my opinion; you hire my time and expertise. My professional judgment is not for sale.'"

"But don't most prosecutors and defense attorneys want an expert witness who will benefit their side?" I ask. "How do those negotiations work?"

"Very badly in Texas," she says with no hesitation. "I've had attorneys call who want to know if I'm a defense expert witness or if I work for the prosecution. I refuse to categorize myself that way." She pauses, then adds, "Others, however, do."

Conroy's consultations in criminal cases most often deal with issues of sanity and competency. The court, not the prosecution or the defense attorneys, appoints a neutral forensic psychologist to do those evaluations. If either side in the case doesn't like the results — which, of course, they won't if her findings do not support their side — they are free to call their own expert witness. "Which is why we have such a hired-gun culture in Texas," she adds.

Conroy had been in Texas only a few months when she was asked to speak at a luncheon for lawyers. In her speech, she mentioned that what they could expect from her was an objective evaluation. She says an attorney in the audience raised his hand and asked, "Why on earth would I want that?"

Attorneys, Conroy feels, have an especially hard time dealing with professional ethics. "The defense attorney's job is to zealously defend the interest of his client. If he thinks his client's guilty, if he thinks the client's a dreadful person, it makes no difference. That's his ethical obligation. My ethical obligation as an expert witness, however, is not to get this guy off, but to give my expert opinion."

Before she explains her work as an expert witness in capital cases, Conroy makes sure I know the difference between certifying for competency and for sanity. Competency applies to the person at the time of arraignment. The question to be answered is whether the defendant is mentally capable of participating in his own defense. For competency hearings, the court appoints a neutral expert to evaluate the defendant. Conroy, for instance, was called to do a competency evaluation of Andrea Yates in Houston.

Sanity evaluations, on the other hand, apply to the defendant's mental state at the time the crime was committed. In Texas, such sanity evaluations are never done by a court-appointed specialist. Each side hires its own expert witness, on whose credibility the trial's outcome often hinges.

"Pre-trial, you may be called on to do a competency evaluation or an insanity evaluation. But once the guilt or innocence phase of the trial has finished and you're ready for the sentencing phase, a mental health professional will consider three issues," Conroy says, ticking them off on her fingers. "Mitigation, aggravation, and risk. Of course, you will have started your preparations for sentencing long before the trial reaches that stage, because there's usually not much time between the verdict and the sentence. The defense attorney in the Andrea Yates case has long ago started looking at the penalty phase."

During the sentencing phase, when a jury is considering the death penalty, the defense attorney is allowed to present extenuating circumstances from a broader field of inquiry than in other cases. "You can bring in anything that tends to humanize the defendant," Conroy says. "You can look at everything from birth defects to learning disabilities, social problems they may have had, cultural difficulties, anything that the jury might consider mitigating — even if you don't."

Of course, the prosecution also has the right to respond to that evidence with its own witnesses who can testify to the aggravated nature of the crime, which means anything that emphasizes the gravity of the crime. The aggravated category most often covers murders committed in conjunction with other crimes such as rape or robbery.

"Finally," Conroy continues, "you look at risk. A forensic psychologist can get involved in risk assessment two ways: first, and most obviously, by evaluating the individual and whether he poses a future danger to society."

In death penalty cases, the prosecutor has the burden of proving beyond a reasonable doubt — which Conroy sets at a 95 percent certainty — that the person is going to be a future risk. "That means, if he is not executed. It doesn't mean if he is released to the streets. In other words, is he going to be a future risk within the prison system? Because that's where he is going to be for the next forty years. It's not like he's going home. So the choice here is between forty years or death. They are not making a choice to put him back on the streets."

The second question a forensic psychologist may be called upon to answer has to do with the means of measuring a convicted criminal's future risk to society. Here the expert may cite current research, statistics, or probability theory.

"If you're doing a risk assessment of people on the streets, the biggest predictor you have, which is perfectly logical, is their past history of violence," Conroy explains. "If I have someone who's killed a number of people, and you ask me if he should go back on the streets, I'm going to say no. He's obviously a high risk. But that history doesn't necessarily predict how he's going to act in prison. If it did, death row, even during the years when it was largely run by inmates, should have been a slaughterhouse. But it wasn't. In fact, for over fifteen years, 70 percent of the inmates had no serious incident reports at all."

She crosses her arms now and leans back, emphasizing her point. "The murder rate at TDCJ is lower than the murder rate in Dallas. You're safer walking a cell block than you are walking in the parking lot of K-Mart after dark."

While working for the Federal Bureau of Prisons, Conroy did a study in two federal maximum-security facilities and found that, in an average year, only 5 percent of the inmates get a serious incident report.

"So if we really went by the standard of 95 percent certainty that this person is going to be a risk, we would never execute anybody. Because the numbers don't support that. The data say that people are not likely to be high risk in prison. Unless, of course, the offender actually committed the murder in prison."

"But that does happen sometimes," I say. I mention Jermar Arnold, who killed another inmate while on death row.

"Oh, yes," Conroy says. "He's always the poster child they bring up. They say, 'See, this is what can happen.' But statistically, that doesn't mean much. Unfortunately, juries like for witnesses to be 100 percent sure. Then they can say, okay, here's an expert who's telling me something for sure that I can count on. That seems to lift the burden of responsibility they feel. They don't like it when witnesses qualify their answers — if you say, well, under this circumstance or under that circumstance, maybe, or there's a 40 percent chance under these conditions and a 20 percent chance under different circumstances."

During her years with the Federal Bureau of Prisons, Conroy did over 1400 risk assessments for the federal courts. "And," she adds, "I've never been successfully sued."

"Sued?" I repeat, surprised. "You can be sued for your testimony? By whom?"

"Oh, it happens. If you're wrong, and the person ends up killing someone else, the victim's family can sue you." She shrugs. "Another professional hazard."

An expert witness may also be investigated by the criminal justice system. When the unexpected happens — that other 5 percent — the courts will want to know what went wrong. Thus, forensic psychologists reduce their own risk of a lawsuit or investigation if they give a negative evaluation of an offender's future threat to society.

I bring up the two differing opinions rendered by the expert witnesses in the Triple Creek Ranch murders. The defense psychologist said he would pose no future threat, while the prosecution's expert said he was bound to kill again. The prosecution's witness, as it turned out, had never given a positive risk assessment in his long career.

"Oh, yes," Conroy laughs, "I know. The fellow's famous. That's why he's known by people in the field as Dr. Death."

"What about you?" I ask. "Do your evaluations generally tend toward benefiting the defense or the prosecution?"

"An interesting question," she says, nodding and putting a finger to her chin. "As it happens, I've only recently gone back and checked my consultations. They turned out to be about even for both sides." She smiles, obviously pleased by her discovery.

"Ask any attorney in the area, and they'll tell you," Conroy continues. "Both sides play all sorts of little games. The defense attorney will ask Dr. So-and-So to evaluate a client. Of course, he knows that Dr. So-and-So is really a dedicated prosecution witness. After Dr. So-and-So evaluates his client, the defense attorney says he's decided not to use him after all. But, because Dr. So-and-So has already done one evaluation on this defendant, the prosecution can't use him either. They play all these little political games."

She sighs in resigned disapproval. "Another unfortunate aspect is that mental health professionals, especially those who are new in the field, often get co-opted by attorneys who tell them that, for the sake of this case, we need this or that testimony from you. And the novice thinks, okay, I guess that's what I'm supposed to do. After all, they're paying me."

"What is it like on the federal level?" I ask. "Is the system better? What about the prisons themselves?"

"Federal prisons generally are a cut above most state systems. For example, the majority of officers hired in the last ten years have at least a B.A. degree, if not a Master's. I'm talking about correctional officers. Of course, federal prisons pay very well. When I saw what corrections officers make at TDCJ, I thought, good heavens, how do they manage to hire anybody?"

In the federal system, a psychologist must sit in on every hiring interview. "Of course, I had no veto power, and no one can do an in-depth evaluation from a brief interview. But the panel benefited because psychologists are trained interviewers and could help other members ask their questions. At least we were able to eliminate the worst cases." She cites as an example a young man who claimed his parents were controlling his "smoking behavior" through the rays emitted from the microwave oven.

"What about Texas?" I ask.

"I don't know," she says. "But I do know of a Texas law which says that any peace officer must be certified by a psychiatrist or a psychologist as," she pauses to make quotation marks in the air, " 'sufficiently emotionally stable' to handle the job. That's really the job of an industrial psychologist, though. And, of course, the applicant can go from one psychologist or psychiatrist to another till they a find someone who will certify them."

"You've been living here for five years now. How would you characterize Huntsville as a prison town?" I ask.

"Huntsville's really interesting," she says, folding her arms again and turning her eyes to look out the window at the autumn trees as she ponders the question. "It's a two-industry town. There's the university and there's the prison. They're linked, but they're very different cultures. And the two cultures don't cross that much. I was astonished to learn that professors in the criminal justice department here, many of whom have been here for twenty or thirty years and done all kinds of research, have never set foot in a prison facility. I was having lunch with about six criminal justice faculty, several of whom have done studies involving the death penalty. We were talking about death row, and it became clear by the middle of the lunch that I was the only one who had ever set foot on death row. People just don't go out to the prisons that much."

Conroy, however, does. She teaches prisoners on the units and finds them focused and motivated. "Unlike my students on campus whose eternal question is, 'Is this going to be on the test?'"

Knowing that Dr. Conroy was on the panel to assess Andrea Yates's competency, I mention a poll in this morning's *Houston Chronicle* showing most people in that city want Andrea Yates to get a life sentence, not the death penalty.

"But the DA didn't ask for the death penalty because he expects to get it," she says, dismissing this with a shake of her head. "The prosecution asked for the death penalty so he can get a death-qualified jury, people who say they have no problem with the death penalty. That way, he's more likely to get a conviction. He did not tell me that, you understand, but I'm guessing that's his strategy."

"How do you think that trial will come out?" I ask her.

She only shakes her head again. "There's a gag order on that case, you know. The only thing I can say regarding the Yates trial is what came out in the courtroom, because that's public information."

She doesn't mind sharing her opinion about the death penalty, however.

"I'm 100 percent absolutely against it." She uncrosses her arms and cocks her head to one side, considering. "Having said that, do I do death sentence evaluations? Yes. Do I do competency-to-be-executed evaluations? Yes, I do. But," she goes on, "we have absolutely no evidence that the death penalty is a deterrent. So what the execution is then is retribution. When you ask people why we have to keep this sentencing option, they say it's for the victim's family. But let's just take a look at what actually happens to that family."

She leans forward now and once more ticks off her points on her fingers. "First of all, we're assuming that revenge is healing. And I don't think we have any evidence that it is. Am I going to feel any better about my dead loved one if I can see this other person die? We have no evidence that it works this way, but we tell people that it will. So the victim's family follows this case for years and years, until the offender is executed. Because they think they're supposed to do that. They can't just let it go and heal and go on with their lives. They've got to be constantly concerned and checking up on the appeals. And when it comes to the end, years later, they think that unless they come to Huntsville and stand in that little room to witness the execution, they'd somehow be letting their loved one down. So they've got that trauma to deal with as well. I think that's a terrible message to give people. I think that when you've had a loss, whether from natural causes or murder or whatever, you need to grieve and to heal and to get on with your life and not be worried about what someone else is doing.

"Also, there's another set of people in the death chamber: the family of the murderer. They've probably beggared themselves trying to get legal help for their relative. Just imagine if you had a child on death row and you knew that execution was five years away, a year away, five months away, five weeks away, five hours away. I think that's a punishment that they don't deserve.

"I did an evaluation for a fellow who's on death row now. His father's a retired mail carrier, his mother's a nurse, and he has six brothers, none of whom have ever been in trouble with the law. This was a single crime — the guy had no prior record. He gets the death sentence. Now maybe you think he deserves it, but I know exactly what that family is going to do. They're going to be following him for the next ten, twenty, who knows how many years, trying to get him help, trying to come visit him, and then, finally, they will be here to stand there and watch him die. What did they do to deserve that? I don't think that's justice to anybody.

"And then there's also the issue of, what if they didn't do it? That group of legal students in Chicago has already found evidence to show that seventy prisoners doing time didn't commit the crimes they were scheduled to die for. If there's that many who've already been found, how many more do we have out there?"

"I'm having a hard time myself," I confess, "figuring out what justice is. Retribution, compensation, punishment, an eye for an eye, evening the score, restoring balance and order to the community? Juries have a really tough job to do. In some cases, it's not a matter of trying to guess who's telling the truth or if the defendant is innocent or guilty. Sometimes there's no question. Maybe there's even a confession. I know you can't talk specifically about the Andrea Yates case," I say, "but in that situation there's little doubt that she drowned all five children. On the one hand we wonder how she could do it. This is heinous. But on the other hand, there's a strong current of support for waiving the death penalty in her case, finding her insane. That jury is going to have a tough time deciding what is just."

Conroy nods thoughtfully. Then she tells me about a federal case where a woman had killed two of her children, not at the same time, but over a space of several years, and tried to kill a third.

"Those are the hardest kind of cases to explain to juries," she says, "because juries don't want to believe that this is a person like them. This woman was very much like Andrea Yates in that she was a middle-class, educated person. But the jury wants you to tell them the defendant is absolutely and totally deranged by some terrible mental illness. Then they can say, 'Okay, that's got nothing to do with me, that's not like anything that I have any connection to.' People who commit very weird sex crimes are in the same category. Juries don't want you to tell them that kind of person is in any way like them.

"The primary psychopath, the real, antisocial serial killer is rare, extremely rare. Most of the inmates in prison are a lot more like us than not like us. But most people are uncomfortable with that notion. My students sometimes want to know, is it okay if I like one of these guys? I tell them, yeah, I like my students in the prison units. That doesn't mean I approve of what they did, but I don't think I approve of everything I've ever done, either. I think people are better than the worst thing they've ever done in their lives."

—⁓—

ANDREA YATES, as it turned out, pled not guilty by reason of insanity. Several psychiatrists for the defense described in detail her descent into madness. Psychiatrists for the prosecution, on the other hand, claimed that, mentally ill or not, she knew she was doing wrong when she killed her children. Under Texas law, that ability is all that matters in determining guilt or innocence. On March 12, 2002, the jury agreed with the prosecution and convicted Andrea Yates of capital murder.

A few days later, however, that same jury quickly decided that she posed no further threat to society, which made unnecessary any deliberation over the mitigating circumstances of her mental state. Yates was spared the death penalty but sentenced to life in prison, where she must stay for forty years before she is eligible for parole at the age of seventy-seven.

Yates is now at the Skyview unit near Rusk, Texas, after having been processed in record time through the regular women's unit in Gatesville where she was photographed, fingerprinted, and given her prison whites and an inmate number: 1087566. She will spend at least a month at Skyview undergoing medical exams — including, no doubt, psychiatric evaluations.

Once the Yates trial was over, the gag order that had been imposed on everyone connected with the case was lifted. By the weekend, four jury members had appeared on NBC's *Dateline*. They explained that they had believed the defense lawyers when they said that the gaunt woman with long, limp hair had indeed been trying to protect her five children from the fires of hell when she drowned them in the bathtub. They believed that she was in a terrible state of psychological and emotional distress. But they could not say, finally, that she therefore did not know the difference between right and wrong — the only issue that mattered, according to Texas's strict interpretation of the M'Naughton rule that governs insanity pleas. Only by deciding that Yates was incapable of discerning right from wrong at the time of the crime could they find her not guilty by reason of insanity.

Murder of any kind upsets our sense of stability. When we can't come up with any other motive that makes sense to us, we call it insanity. But according to Mary Alice Conroy, most of the inmates in prison are a lot more like us than not like us.

Our county's district attorney, David Weeks, on the other hand, says that serial killers in particular are "just a different breed." But can we afford to say this of any human being without doing serious damage to our theology? Are some of us made in the image of God and others not? The jury deliberated only three and a half hours before reaching a decision. A columnist for the *Houston Chronicle* noted that Chuck Rosenthal, the Harris County district attorney, wore a What Would Jesus Do bracelet to court that day.

When the verdict was read, Russell Yates, holding his head in his hands, began to sob. His mother put her arm around him. Sitting behind them, Andrea's mother wept silently. Now they were all victims twice over.

Two days after delivering the guilty verdict, the jury returned to hear testimony from the defense as to whether Andrea Yates posed a continuing threat to society and if there were mitigating circumstances that might have affected her actions. The prosecution offered no rebuttal to any portion of the defense position.

It was not until the following Monday that Judge Belinda Hill formally pronounced sentence. The only people in the courtroom besides the judge, the defendant, and the lawyers, were Andrea Yates's two psychiatrists, both women, who have been treating her in jail. Russell Yates was in New York at the time appearing on *Larry King Live* and NBC's *Today Show.*

Judge Hill closed the case by saying, "Good luck to you, Mrs. Yates." Then Andrea Yates was led away to join forty-one other mothers in Texas prisons who have killed their children.

9

The Parents

Parents are the bones on which children sharpen their teeth.

PETER USTINOV

THE ACADEMICS we interviewed did not prove entirely dispassionate. Nevertheless, their viewpoints and assessments were abstracted from objective information — data, statistics, case studies. On the other hand, although prison employees have acquired their attitudes based on their direct personal experience, they do not — nor would it be wise for them to — become personally involved in the lives of their prisoners. But even criminals have families. And those families' lives are changed forever when one of their members is locked up, whether for life or eventual execution.

Doug and Bonnie Wilson were doing exceptionally well in Houston, even during the economic downturn of the 1980s when the Texas oil patch suddenly dried up. Doug's job at an educational consulting agency for the state's public schools seemed secure. The Wilsons lived in one of Houston's nicer suburbs north of the city, drove new cars, and took family vacations.

The couple had two sons. Michael, the older boy, had been born September 29, 1977; his little brother Tim, three years later. After the boys started school, Bonnie went to work at one of the priciest department stores in the Galleria, Houston's upscale high-rise mall. But she didn't let her job interfere with her life as a soccer mom. She and Doug had built their lives around their boys. Most of her spare time was spent ferrying them to their soccer matches and staying to cheer them on. The Wilsons were a 1990s version of the Cleaver family. Except that neither Beaver nor Wally ever got into drugs.

When he was fifteen, Michael started smoking marijuana. He was soon getting into trouble at school as well. After a series of suspensions, the principal finally sent him to an "alternative campus," where teenage troublemakers routinely end up. But this antidote didn't change Michael's behavior, so the Wilsons chose to enroll their son in a private school for children "at risk." They were determined, Bonnie says, to do whatever it took to get their son straightened out.

And, when the next school year started in September, Michael appeared to be doing well in this new environment. With smaller classes and more individual attention, his grades improved. He soon acquired a girlfriend, one his family thought would reinforce his new direction. He was going to rehab. As far as Doug and Bonnie knew, their older son was cleaning up his act, straightening out his life. What they didn't know was that he had graduated from marijuana to cocaine.

The Christmas holidays went well that year, they recall. Michael provoked no confrontations, got into no serious trouble. He appeared eager to start back to the new school after the holidays. Then, on January 16, 1995, the Wilsons' world suddenly collapsed.

BUYING COCAINE takes a lot more money than scoring a few ounces of marijuana. Several of Michael's drug buddies, Eddie Capetillo, James Duke, and his brother Curtis, were hard up for cash. Michael's marijuana supplier, eighteen-year-old Matthew Vickers, had recently received an insurance settlement of a thousand dollars for an automobile accident. Getting their hands on some of Matt's windfall seemed their best hope for coming up with drug money. They first tried to sell Matt Vickers a handgun and a scale for weighing marijuana. He told them he wasn't interested.

After that, the boys discussed robbing someone, maybe at an ATM. Then Eddie Capetillo had another idea. He knew that Matt Vickers's father was out of town on business. If they couldn't get Matt's insurance money any other way, they would simply steal it. Michael was dispatched to the Vickerses' house to scope out the situation there. The other three boys would steal a car, pick up a fourth friend and two firearms, a .22 rifle and a .38 caliber pistol. Then they would drive to the Vickerses' house on Apple Valley Lane and force Matt to hand over his money. Once the others adopted his plan, Eddie Capetillo became the leader of the group.

Eighteen-year-old Matt Vickers lived with his father, his twin sister Allison, and Allison's best friend Kimberly Williamson in a large two-story house. When the boys arrived at the Vickerses' home that evening, Michael Wilson reported that a fourth person was with Matt in the backyard — fourteen-year-old Grant Barnett. Then Michael got behind the wheel of the stolen car while the four other boys entered the house with the guns.

Allison was upstairs, helping Kimberly pack for a trip to visit her father in Michigan. Matt Vickers was out in the backyard smoking with Grant. Thus the four intruders found the living room empty. In the middle of the floor stood a partially disassembled artificial tree, left over from Christmas.

Eddie sent two of his accomplices outside to look for Matt. Meanwhile, the two girls, hearing noises, came downstairs to see what was up. Spotting two armed figures, they screamed and ran.

At this point, the chain of events becomes somewhat confused. Allison Vickers ran out the front door, escaping further harm. Her friend Kimberly, however, ran screaming through several downstairs rooms before she was dragged into the kitchen with Matt and Grant. Eddie was demanding the insurance money, but the only money the two boys had on them was eighteen dollars in Grant's pocket.

All three, Matt Vickers, Grant Barnett, and Kimberly Williamson were shot three times. Then the four intruders ran out of the house, jumped in the car with Michael, and fled.

Grant Barnett was the only shooting victim to survive.

The murders took place on Monday night, January 16. The five boys involved were arrested piecemeal over the next few days. Michael was driving to school with a friend on Thursday morning when he was pulled over by the police.

Meanwhile the Wilsons, who made a point of checking in with Michael several times a day, tried to reach their son on his pager throughout the day. He never responded. That evening they were growing ever more anxious when at last the girl who had been in the car with Michael when he was arrested told her own parents what had happened. They, in turn, called the Wilsons with the first news they'd heard of their son's arrest.

Bonnie and Doug rushed to the homicide division of the Harris County sheriff's department. They were not allowed to talk to Michael and only caught a glimpse of him as he was being put into a police car for transfer to the county jail downtown. Detectives had already interviewed Michael, and, of the five boys arrested, he was the only one who immediately told the detectives what had happened and what his own part in the crime had been.

The Wilsons' worst nightmare had come true.

As we sit around the dining table at our house on a rainy November day, they tell David and me what it was like, waking up and finding the nightmare was real, a reality that would come to dominate their lives.

"Of course, we were just like, oh my gosh, what did we do wrong? Yes, we knew Michael had been involved in drugs as a teenager," Bonnie says, "but it wasn't like he'd been a troubled child all his life. He'd made some bad choices, but Doug and I both felt like he was going to outgrow it. We felt we were on top of it. He was going to rehab. And then he made the nightmare choice to go with the guys that night, when he could have made the choice to go out with his girlfriend."

"We were involved at every stage," Doug adds. "We look back now and ask, what did we miss? We definitely knew there were drugs. It's not like we were blind to the fact. But there's just no way Michael ever had any guns in the house. I know I would have noticed that."

"So this thing," Bonnie continues, "it was just bam!" We jump as she claps her hands together. "Just like that."

In a state of shock, the Wilsons tried to think of an attorney to contact. Even though it was almost midnight, Doug called the firm who handled his company's legal affairs and asked for names of lawyers who dealt with criminal cases. He called every law firm on the list until he finally found an attorney willing to take the case. The Wilsons wonder now if Michael might not have been better off with a public defender.

Since Michael had stayed outside in the car and had never entered the Vickerses' house that evening, the Wilsons expected their son would be charged with a lesser crime, perhaps aggravated robbery at worst. They were stunned when the Harris County grand jury charged Michael with two counts of capital murder, the same indictment brought against Eddie Capetillo and the Duke brothers, under the law that allows capital charges to be brought against anyone involved in a crime that leads to a death. The boy who had joined the group last on the night of January 16 plea-bargained his way out of an indictment by supplying the police with evidence they needed to convict the original four.

Doug and Bonnie soon learned as well that only two outcomes were possible if Michael were found guilty of capital murder — the death penalty or life in prison. Nor did their uncertainty about conviction or sentence end soon. During the days and months they waited for the case to come to trial, Doug established a routine of rushing to the county jail in downtown Houston every day after work to see his son. There was usually a throng of other families waiting to see relatives.

"I would get there early and hold a spot in line till Bonnie could get there," Doug says.

And getting there early was less of a problem after Doug lost his job.

"Nobody ever said anything directly about Michael's arrest," he remembers, "but one day my boss calls me in and says the company was doing some reorganizing and that my job would be eliminated."

"I'm sure it was because of Michael," Bonnie interjects. "The education department didn't want someone working for them who had something like this in their family, especially if it got into the papers."

Michael spent almost two full years in the county jail, waiting for a court date. The Wilsons wonder now if a deal had been in the making during that time.

"After a year and a half, Michael's attorney and the prosecutor got together and presented us with a plan," Doug says, carefully rearranging his fork and spoon on the tablecloth. "They said, why don't you forego a jury trial and just have a hearing with the judge? If you do that, there's a possibility we can bypass capital murder and have the charges reduced to aggravated robbery."

The Harris County DA's office is famous for tough sentences and puts more people on death row than any other county in the nation. One-third of all the prisoners on death row were convicted in a Harris County court. And the same assistant DA was prosecuting the four other cases involved in the crime. Eddie Capetillo had already been tried and had received a death sentence.

This was incentive enough to convince the Wilsons to take the hearing rather than a jury trial. An aggravated robbery charge was open to a sentence of anywhere from three to ninety-nine years, but at least Michael would not be in danger of a death sentence. So both Michael and his parents agreed to the plan.

The hearing in Judge Bill Harmon's court, 178th District, Harris County, proceeded just as a trial would have. Lawyers on both sides presented their arguments. Witnesses were called. Evidence was presented. The only element missing was the jury. The only other person present was a young man still in his teens sitting in the jury box, listening to the proceedings.

As the Wilsons soon learned, Judge Harmon had another trial going on simultaneously in another courtroom. At the moment, the jury was out, deliberating a sentence. The judge was trying to take advantage of that downtime by hearing Michael's case before reconvening the other court. He was also signing papers brought to him by various clerks, and the bailiff frequently interrupted the hearing with updates from the other case.

"It became pretty apparent as our attorney got into presenting our case that the judge really wasn't hearing much of what was going on," Doug says. We knew that we could be interrupted at any time if the jury reached a decision. And actually, that's what happened. We had to go home for a while and come back later after the judge had finished with the other trial."

"We had left the decision about what happened to Michael totally in that judge's hands," Bonnie adds. "Finally our attorney told us, 'You know, Bonnie and Doug, I don't think it makes any sense to go any further.' And we agreed with him. We had more witnesses that we'd planned to call, but what was the point? It wasn't going to make any difference anyway. The judge had obviously already made up his mind."

When the hearing got underway again, the two attorneys made their closing statements and turned the case over to the judge. "It probably took Harmon thirty seconds at the outside to make his decision," Doug says. "Harmon said, 'I find him guilty of aggravated robbery, and I sentence him to two life sentences that'll run concurrently.' And that was that."

"And there was another weird thing," Doug adds eagerly, "that young man sitting over in the jury box. We don't even know his name. But we've been told that apparently he had been brought in to watch what was about to happen. The judge had told him if he didn't straighten his life up, he would be heading down the same road."

"Of course, we didn't hear about all this until later," Bonnie adds. "Afterwards, we did some investigation, tried to find out who that kid was. It turned out that he had been charged with a very minor drug offense, and Bill Harmon was just using Michael as an example. Which makes us wonder if everybody — the prosecutor, the judge, even our lawyer — had an agreement at some point as to what was going to work out best for all of them? We don't know."

The older Duke brother got the same sentence as Michael Wilson. The younger brother, sixteen at the time of the crime, was nevertheless certified to stand trial as an adult and got twenty years for robbery. Nor was that the end of the Vickerses' tragedy. Matt Vickers's younger brother, Jack, committed suicide nine months after his brother's murder.

The Wilsons remember the day, a month after Michael's hearing, when they arrived at the Harris County jail as usual to see their son. "I remember because it was an election day," Doug says, "early November. They told us Michael had 'caught the chain' that morning" — prison talk for being transferred by TDCJ bus.

Seven years have gone by since that January night when the Wilsons' world collapsed. It will be another thirteen years before they can hope to see their son outside the prison visiting room.

Nevertheless, Bonnie and Doug Wilson now believe that January 16,

148

1995, marks not only the collapse of their old world but the beginning of their blessings.

"We had always been very involved in our boys' lives," Bonnie says, "but mostly it was centered on soccer. That's where we went on Sundays, to the soccer field. We were only Christmas-and-Easter churchgoers. But when this happened, for some reason, we reached out to God from the first. A lot of the members of our church then were having trouble with the pastor, but ironically he turned out to be just what we needed. He had a heart for us. I really believe that God sends everybody for a purpose. We had a lot of, maybe, well, legalists in our church. I don't know who they are exactly. I don't want to know. Doug and I are such new Christians that we don't always see those things.

"We had a lot of friends," she goes on, turning to look at her husband, "or at least we thought they were friends. They totally deserted us. These were people who had known Michael since he was a little kid." She sighs and looks out the window behind me. "But we came to see that as God's protecting us, removing them from our lives, because we needed to be around people who could strengthen us and get us through this. So other friends showed up, ones who could help us."

Doug is nodding. "Thank God, we went that way and not another way. We could have easily gone in another direction, wondering why this happened to us."

Not that their troubles ended with their son's incarceration. After being processed through the Diagnostic unit in Huntsville, Michael was sent to the Allred unit five hundred miles away in the Texas panhandle. That meant long trips to see him twice a month. Then the parents of one of the shooting victims learned that the Wilsons' homeowners insurance might cover damages and brought a civil suit against them. They had already mortgaged everything they owned to pay Michael's lawyer's fees. Doug did get another job, but they no longer lived the well-padded life of suburban affluence.

They also discovered a glitch in their choice of a hearing over a jury trial. While a jury verdict can be appealed, a judge's ruling cannot. They are looking into the possibility of a time-cut, a reduction in the amount of time required to be served, though they are still hazy about the requirements and procedures for requesting one. Like most middle-class people, they have never had occasion to deal with the criminal justice system, and they are groping their way through the thicket of law codes.

"We're not saying that Michael doesn't deserve to be punished," Bonnie says earnestly. "Obviously, he was involved in something where two young people were killed. But the severity of his sentence is our concern. And how we were dealt with in the court, it just seems like . . ." she breaks off and shakes her head.

"What makes time-cuts so difficult," Doug explains, "is the process you have to go through to get there. As we understand it, you have to get three people from the county where you were convicted to agree before it can even be considered." He ticks these off on his fingers. "The judge who handed down the sentence, the prosecuting DA, and the head sheriff. Then it goes to the parole board. We're not sure if they have to agree unanimously or not, but if it gets past them, then it goes to the governor, who makes his decision."

"But it's not like we've done any major research on it yet," Bonnie puts in. "We still have a lot to find out."

"Is Michael accumulating any credits?" David asks.

"Not really, because of his sentence," Doug says. "With a life sentence you can't accumulate any good-time."

"I meant just personally," David says. "Positive credits from this experience."

"While he was in jail, waiting for his trial, he read the whole Bible through," Bonnie begins, "but when he got the outcome he did, in his immature mind it meant God had deserted him. I'm not so surprised, I really am not," she pauses and searches for the words, "but he took on the attitude, why did God do this to me? Then he gets in the prison system where people abuse religion. Going to the church services and then using that as a tool to get to something else. He doesn't want to be labeled as one of them. He doesn't understand that God can love him where he's at, that he doesn't have to be perfect overnight." She smiles ruefully. "And he doesn't want to be perfect overnight. He says, 'What happens if I still want to cuss?'"

Suddenly Bonnie brightens and turns to her husband. "I forgot to tell you what Tim said, Doug." She turns back to me to explain that Michael's younger brother Tim, in college now, had recently visited him. "And what Michael told him — this is answered prayer, it's nothing more than answered prayer — Michael said he wanted to get the names of the families of the two kids who were killed that night. He wants to write them. He wants them to understand a little bit about himself and his background. So without him even realizing it, to me, he's taking steps in coming closer to God."

"Like Alcoholics Anonymous," David puts in, "where you have to go and make it right with the people you've harmed."

"Yes," Bonnie agrees. "I told Michael, even if the people have moved or something and I can't find them right away, go ahead and write that letter. The important thing for him is writing it. Anyway, that's a step."

Michael knows that his parents are now deeply involved in Kairos, a prison ministry that sponsors weekend spiritual retreats led by lay-people. The retreat team follows up with monthly visits to the prison. Participation on the part of prisoners is entirely voluntary, and the retreats are almost always over-subscribed. Partly this is due to the extreme boredom of prison and partly because the food, which is prepared and served by the team's kitchen crew, is a welcome change from prison chow.

"After Michael was moved to the Ferguson unit, I told him to sign up for the next Kairos retreat, even if just for the food," Bonnie says. "We know that's why some of them come, but that doesn't matter. They don't leave the same."

"What has prison life been like for him?" I ask.

Doug answers quickly. "I'd say it's been pretty good. Of course, he's a small kid. And he's white. The majority of the prison population is Hispanic and black, and there's still heavy discrimination in the men's prisons. When he first went in, he was fearful, I think. He was involved with, really, the white hate group, is the only way to put it. The Aryan group. It was pretty prevalent in the Allred unit. The last couple of times we've been to visit, he's mentioned that he doesn't want any part of the Aryan group anymore. He recognizes that he doesn't need them for protection."

The Wilsons say that at home Michael had no racial or ethnic prejudices, citing the fact that the leader of his partners in crime was Hispanic.

"But he's mentioned to us several times lately that prison is making him prejudiced," Doug says. "He's gotten some tattoos, part of the prison scene."

Michael has also taken training courses in small engine repair at Wynne, his current unit. He's taken some academic classes, too, and finished his GED.

"He had a super job in the boiler room at the Ferguson unit," Doug says, "a job with a lot of responsibility and limited contact with COs. Basically a job of trust."

But after the Texas Seven prison break during the Christmas holidays in 2000, the prison administration removed prisoners with life sentences from positions that afforded an opportunity for escape. So Michael lost his job at Ferguson and was transferred to Wynne, where he has been learning small engine repair. He's planning on signing up for college courses next semester.

"Overall," Doug says, "I'd say it's been a good experience for him. We've not seen that he's been involved in fights or been attacked or had any physical injuries."

"Or if he has," Bonnie puts in, "he hasn't spoken about it. And I really believe he avoids telling us stuff to protect me."

"He's done a lot of work with weights," Doug continues. "Physically, he's a lot stronger. I don't think he's been abused. I've visited him several times by myself, and I think if something like that had happened, he would share it with me. I think he would fight if he had to. But he's reached a point where he knows the system, and people leave him alone."

"Except that he has shared with us," Bonnie adds, "he's said, 'Mom, if a circumstance happens where it's the whites against the blacks, I'll have to go with my race.'" Her voice tightens a little. "I just pray that doesn't happen. That's my prayer for him daily." Clearly, the possibility of such a disturbance weighs on her.

Later, while we're drinking coffee in the living room, David asks the Wilsons if, from their perspective as the parents of the convicted criminal, they have particular concerns about the justice system or think certain aspects of the system need to be addressed.

"I think people just need to realize that we hurt too," Doug says immediately. "And it wasn't us who committed the crime. We didn't do what Michael did. But we are condemned as if we did. Like the other day, we were listening to a Christian radio station in Houston, and they were talking about the trial of a young man accused of shooting a police officer. They were asking for prayers for the police officer's family and the jury and judge and everyone involved in making a decision. And never once did they mention the shooter's family, much less the young man himself. That son, that brother, he did that, and he will have to suffer the consequences of what he did. But what about his family? They've been ostracized. They've been pushed aside. No one cares about them, but they, we, need something just like everyone else does. On January 16, 1995, our life changed forever. And it will never be the same."

"You asked us what the system could do," Bonnie says. "You know, we always go to visitation, and by and large the staff is good to us. We stand in line with a whole lot of people who come from all different walks of life. For some of them, it's not the first time they've had someone in prison, and they're very opinionated about how it should be run or what it's doing wrong. They're full of anger. And I can see why. You don't get treated very well. But I will not let myself get hardened like that. I will not. I always have the attitude, kill them with kindness. Doug — and Michael too — sometimes get their dander up. Michael says the only reason he disrespects someone is when they treat him with no respect. For some reason, I don't know why, some of the guards think they have to be gruff, hard-nosed, abusive to people. Maybe the church should do Kairos weekends for the guards. Because they would be changed."

The Wilsons explain that an inmate makes his own visitation list of up to ten names. The list can only be changed at specified periods. Only immediate family members are allowed contact visits. Families can visit either Saturday or Sunday, but not both. Because of some demerits Michael picked up, he's now allowed only two contact visits per month. At first the Wilsons also went to see their son on the other weekends, when they were permitted to talk by phone through the glass barrier that separates the inmates from the visitors. However, neither they nor Michael found that arrangement very satisfying, so he eventually asked that they come just for the contact visits.

Doug and Bonnie usually arrive early in the morning, so that Michael doesn't miss his time in the rec yard. He's on the soccer team at the Wynne unit. Also, if the Wilsons arrive early Saturday morning, they can get their two-hour visit in and Bonnie can still make it to work only a little late.

When the couple arrives at the unit, they must stand in line to check in and be searched. Being early helps shorten that wait, too. They are allowed to bring coins into the unit for the vending machines, but can bring no currency.

"Folding money's a precious commodity in prison," Doug says. "You can buy everything from sex to drugs with it. It's amazing what people will do to pass that money off. Sometimes a wife will come in and kiss — you're allowed that kind of contact once when you get there and once when you leave — and she'll pass her husband money via the kiss."

In fact, it was an incident involving money that led to Michael's demotion in security grade — called "catching a case" — and thus to the reduction in number of visits he's allowed. A fellow inmate had hidden some money down in the boiler room where Michael worked and had asked him to look out for it. Michael was caught with the money in his hands when an officer walked in.

After visitors get through the gate, they must check in again at the visitation room. Then they wait, usually for twenty or thirty minutes, till the inmate is brought in. An inmate can have only two adult visitors at a time, so, because Michael's younger brother is now over eighteen, they can never all four visit together at the same time.

"But you can bring any number of little kids in — if they're less than sixteen years old. I've seen up to eight," Doug says, folding his arms over his chest.

At the Ferguson unit, the visitation room had picnic tables, both inside and outside, where families could sit together, affording some degree of privacy. But the Wynne unit is so short of personnel that all the visiting families must meet in a large, echoing room, in two rows of chairs, one side for families, the other for inmates.

"I kind of get wrapped around the axle with the way we get treated when we go in sometimes," Doug says a little hotly. "Bonnie deals with it pretty good, and I don't. But here, maybe a month ago, we were up to visit, and one of the ladies that works the visitation area — we see her all the time, so that's probably her regular assignment — she had the responsibility that day of saying where everyone was going to sit. Usually they keep at least one chair between the different family groups so you can hear one another better and have a little privacy. But she put everyone right together — chair number seven, chair number eight, chair number nine, chair number ten. Right in a row, nothing between. And this was at eight o'clock in the morning. There was hardly anybody there at that point and plenty of room. There was no reason to do it that way, but it's a power thing. She's in control, she's going to put you where she wants you. You can't talk, you can't hear. And all she had to do was spread us out, leave an empty chair between the groups."

No other family members have ever expressed any interest in visiting Michael. Doug's parents are in their eighties. "They're never going to see him again outside of those walls, but they've never even asked about visiting their grandson. We've struggled with how do we even broach that topic with them," Doug says.

"Doug's mother writes to Michael on a very regular basis," Bonnie says, "but it's all on a very surface level. And when she asks us about Michael, we just say he's doing pretty good. That's all they really want to know. It's the same thing with my brother. He'll ask how Michael's doing, and I'll just say fine. Nobody's going to ask me more than that. You realize there's no interest there so you don't say much. We just tell them stuff they want to hear."

"We gave my folks a tape of one of the Kairos retreats," Doug adds, "hoping maybe they'd be interested. But they think it's just a passing fad, something we'll get over."

On her first weekend retreat with Kairos, not long after her son had been taken to the Allred unit in West Texas, Bonnie was assigned the job of delivering cookies to all the inmates in their cells, a regular feature of the retreats. "At first I told the team no, I just couldn't do that. I'd work in the kitchen or whatever, but I didn't think I could stand to see where they lived and picture Michael there. But when I got to the unit, I somehow was given unbelievable strength. I told the leader I'd changed my mind. I went in and I was fine. I really needed to do that.

It's like God wants us to be so strong. He wants to strengthen every inch of us. He wants us to see. He wants us to talk to people, so that we know what it's like. Not that we know everything, because we don't live there."

But the Wilsons know more than the rest of us. Maybe more than most of us want to know. I think how easily any seventeen-year-old boy, whether from a privileged, intact family like the Wilsons or growing up in the projects, can, in the twinkling of an eye, have their future destroyed. Napoleon Beazley, president of his high school class, was also only seventeen when he shot an elderly man for his fancy car. As was Raymond Cobb, who killed Margaret Owings and her little girl. My eldest grandson turns seventeen this year, Michael Wilson's age on that January night when his life — and those of a dozen other people, including his devoted parents — changed forever. What if my grandson goes out with the wrong friends one night?

And we need not think that stable homes, not even fervently religious ones, are immune. A young cousin of mine, home-schooled by his devout parents in order to guard him from the very influences that affected Michael Wilson, is currently on parole for drug-related crimes. The son of a pastor in a nearby small town is serving a life sentence for murder.

I know all these parents. I know the way my mind wants to scratch around in their habits, their childrearing, their family history, trying to find where they went wrong, just as the Wilsons searched for ways to blame themselves. No doubt they all "went wrong" at some point. And what parent doesn't? Some wrongs are more blatant and long-lived than others. But anyone who is a parent knows the inevitability of failure. And the unforeseen moments when one's failure coincides with a convenient aperture for evil. An angry parental outburst followed by the consolation of a cocky friend. The tired acquiescence that leads to tragedy.

Crime — evil, in fact — is a web that enmeshes many more people than simply the perpetrators. More, even, than the family. Co-workers, teachers, shopkeepers, church members. None of us is untouched by its causes or its effects. But those who suffer most are those who love most, whether Matt Vickers's father and sister, Kimberly Williamson's parents, or Bonnie and Doug Wilson. Here is yet another injustice.

AFTER THE Wilsons had left that November afternoon, I remembered the man who was sentenced to fifty years for stealing a microwave. Scott Watson, who runs the woodshop at the Ellis unit, told us about him. He mentioned the man again at the end of our visit when we asked him for his views on the death penalty. Watson said that the fellow had in fact been a habitual offender, almost a compulsive thief. That was why he'd gotten such a stiff sentence. Watson had overheard a conversation between the man and his exasperated father during one of their visits. The son was spelling out at some length and with a good deal of enthusiasm a new strategy for appealing his case.

The father, obviously frustrated, finally cut him short. "Damn it! If you wanted to be a lawyer, why didn't you be one instead of a thief?"

Watson added that, from his experience, the best reason, maybe the only good one, for the death penalty is to give the parents a break. "They carry around such a load of guilt. They mortgage their homes, work extra jobs, suffer humiliation, many times ruin their health. But to their kid there in prison, it's never enough."

10

The Death Chamber

*I do not know whether capital punishment should or should not
be abolished, for neither the natural light, nor Scripture, nor ec-
clesiastical authority seems to tell me.*

C. S. LEWIS

WHATEVER THE opinions or emotions of others, it is the warden on duty
at the Walls on execution day who must feel the weight of responsibility most deeply for putting a prisoner to death. Jim Willett never intended to become the man responsible for overseeing Texas executions.
When he first went to work for the prison system thirty years ago, the
death chamber had already been shut down. But during his three-year
tenure as warden at the Walls unit, he supervised the deaths of eighty-
nine prisoners, more than any of his predecessors.

As a kid from a small farm town in central Texas, Willett came to
Huntsville to work toward a business degree at Sam Houston State University. Like many students at the school, he supported himself by
working as a prison guard. By the time he graduated, he had risen to
the rank of sergeant, so he decided to stick with the job.

He continued to rise through the ranks, assigned to different units,
until in April of 1998 he was offered the job of warden at the Walls.
Willett had fond memories of his college years and was eager to return
to Huntsville. On the other hand, the state had begun executing prison-

ers again in 1982, and, since the mid-nineties, at a rapidly increasing rate. Despite his long career in corrections, Willett wasn't sure how he felt about the death penalty. So he turned the offer down. His refusal, however, was qualified. "I left the door open," he told *Houston Chronicle* reporter James Kimberly. "I told my boss, 'I don't want it, but if I'm the one y'all really want to put over here, I will come and do it and I will do the best I can.'"

That mixture of aversion and accommodation is peculiar to certain Texas men, easygoing types who are nevertheless determined to pull their share of the load. When the prison board could find no one else to take the job, they came back to Jim Willett. This time he acquiesced.

Willett dealt with his mixed feelings about capital punishment by telling himself that he was just doing his job. "I convinced myself," he wrote in the *Washington Post* shortly after his retirement date, "that my job was simply to see that the process was carried out smoothly and professionally and with as much dignity as possible."

He also made a point of never reviewing the prisoner's file before an execution: "I found it virtually impossible to keep my mind on the job at hand if I associated the person on the gurney with the brutal, atrocious crime for which he had been convicted." He adds, "I doubt that I could have supervised more than one or two executions if I had chosen to be unforgiving, vengeful, or zealous about watching someone die."

Despite all his precautions, however, those three years at the Walls took their toll. How did those eighty-nine executions make him feel? The word he uses is "weary." In April 2001, he decided to retire.

Willett still doesn't know what to think about the death penalty. "If I pick up the paper tomorrow morning and I see where somebody has abducted, molested, and murdered an eight-year-old girl," he told Kimberly on his last day at the Walls, "the first thing that pops in my mind is, that guy deserves to die for that." On the other hand, he calls executions an "unnatural" act. "There's a part of me that says, 'I don't know as a human being that this is right.'"

For one thing, some of the men he stands beside as the toxic chemicals begin to flow into their veins are not the same men who committed the crime. Death row has changed them. Willett admits it bothers him to waste those changed lives.

And then there are those who, quite literally, are not the men who committed the crime. Willett thinks that innocent people have been executed. Such errors are not necessarily malicious. But, since the judicial system is a human institution, he believes that it can never be free of error.

He describes the execution routine this way: On the day of an execution, he meets with the prisoner — with only a handful of exceptions, a man — shortly after the transport van delivers him to the Walls at one o'clock. The meeting takes place in a cell where the prisoner will wait until a few minutes before six. It is only a few steps to the death chamber. Willett answers any questions the prisoner has — when he can see family members, make telephone calls, consult with his lawyer and spiritual adviser.

But Willett also uses the time to assess the condemned's mood. A number of the men are surprisingly jovial, though once in a while someone will turn defiant. The last thing Willett wants is to be forced to order a cell extraction, prison code for the tie-down team, protected by face shields and armor, dragging the prisoner kicking and screaming from the cell. At times, tear gas must be used to subdue the condemned man.

Such a scene is seldom necessary, however. Most of the men are determined to face their fate with whatever dignity they can muster, though a few are so weak in the knees that they must be supported down the corridor to the waiting gurney.

As six o'clock nears, Willett returns. Even though the appointed hour has arrived, the procedure is held up at times while the team waits for a judge to rule on a last-minute appeal. Those are some of the worst moments, Willett says, for the man whose life hangs in the balance.

After the prisoner has been led into the death chamber and strapped down — each man on the tie-down team being responsible for securing a separate segment of his body — the IV needles are inserted. Then the witnesses are led into two rooms, each with a window facing into the death chamber. The victim's family members and those of the prisoner are, of course, in separate rooms. Also watching are prison officials and five media representatives, preference being given to the newspaper in the town where the crime was committed.

The Death Chamber

At this point, Willett asks the prisoner if he has any last words. Surprisingly, an analysis of these final statements shows that about a quarter of them have nothing left to say. They just want to get on with it. As for the others, most have simply thanked their friends and family for their support. A few even thank certain of the prison personnel, whom they may have known longer than their own family members.

A little over 10 percent of the condemned protest their innocence, though they may also offer words of condolence to the victim's family. Only slightly fewer express some religious sentiment along with the farewells to their families. Sometimes they also add a few words of apology to their victim's family while not explicitly admitting their guilt. An equal number express their general regret that the crime has occurred and their sorrow for the pain inflicted on the victim's family, but again without confessing their own responsibility, though some imply this when they include a request for forgiveness. A little under 10 percent frankly admit their guilt and ask to be forgiven. About the same number limit themselves to quoting Scripture, offering spiritual encouragement to the witnesses, praying, or singing religious songs. A handful have launched into lengthy speeches whose meanings and references are confusing and obscure. A couple have delivered diatribes against individuals. Two more have claimed to be the victims of racial prejudice.

Jim Willett always let the condemned have their say. When they finished, he would take off his glasses, the signal for the IV to start flowing.

First comes the sodium thiopental, a lethal sedative, then pancuronium bromide, which collapses the lungs and diaphragm. Last, potassium chloride stops the heart from beating. It usually doesn't take long, about twenty minutes.

Jim Willett's first execution didn't go so smoothly, however. The medical technician had to work hard to find a vein in the prisoner's arm. The prisoner made his last statement. As he finished, the needle fell out. Willett and the chaplain pulled the curtains across both windows, and the witnesses were led away. Another struggle to insert the needle ensued. Finally, the technician was able to find a decent vein, Willett took off his glasses, and the IV began to flow. After a few more minutes, the doctor pronounced the prisoner dead.

After that first difficult experience, Willett consoled himself with the thought that executions "would get easier with routine." It didn't take long before he saw that it would never get easy.

Another execution Willett found particularly painful was that of Robert Earl Carter, who had killed six people in one family in Somerville, Texas. Willett had known him when the man was on the other side of the law. In fact, Carter had worked for Willett as a correctional officer in a prison in another part of the state. Willett remembered him as a hard-working, reliable employee who took pride in doing his job. During the cell visit with Carter on the day of execution, Willett asked his former employee if he remembered him. Carter said he did. But "he wasn't very talkative," Willett recalls, "which made things easier. We didn't talk about old times."

Willett makes the argument that, whatever part he played in them, the responsibility for those eighty-nine executions is spread among a large number of people, diluting it the way a drop of ink is dispersed in a glass of water.

"Because I am the man who had to carry out the somber business of the state more often than anyone else alive," he says, "I get asked lots of questions. People wonder how I could do it. I remind them that mine was but the final contribution to a long and complex process. Each member of the jury had a part, along with the attorneys and witnesses and judges. I have never lost a loved one to a brutal murder. I have never spent months or years investigating a case. I've never sat on a jury and had to decide whether to put someone to death. I've never sat in judgment."

Nor, he might add, is he personally responsible for the Texas laws that prescribe the death penalty. Nevertheless, three years of carrying out the courts' execution orders hasn't resolved the issue in his mind. "Getting me closer to it, I guess as close as you can get, hasn't caused me to decide one way or the other," he says.

It's easy enough to see Jim Willett as just another example of a person who rationalizes some "unnatural" act by telling himself he's just doing his job. But the system is intentionally designed to so distribute the accountability for executions that no single individual need ever feel the full force of responsibility. Each person, from guards to wardens to chaplains to the medical personnel, participates in only a small part of the procedure. In fact, the medical technicians who insert the needle and set up the IVs are actually in an adjoining room when they start the flow of chemicals through the tubes. The American Medical Association forbids doctors to inject people with lethal drugs, though a rotation of MDs in the city are on call to pronounce the prisoners dead.

———

IT'S RAINING the day David and I take the interstate exit twelve miles south of Huntsville that leads to the Gulf Coast Trades Center, a residential facility for minors who have had a brush with the law and are headed for a collision with TDCJ unless someone intervenes to change their options. At the facility, youth officially designated as "troubled" study toward their GED and receive vocational training as well as medical care and counseling. They are also kept out of harm's way by their location; Gulf Coast Trades Center is not so much nestled as buried in the national forest that surrounds Huntsville. The grounds look like a well-maintained park, all the underbrush cleared from beneath the tall pines. The main administration building, at least, seems almost brand new, though it's nearly twenty years old. On the day we visit, the receptionist tells us that 151 students are currently in residence, a number lower than usual, she indicates, because of the number currently furloughed home.

We have come to interview Leigh Anne Gideon, who works in the school's communication division. Described by a mutual friend as "no bigger than a minute," she is younger than our daughters. Her long gingery hair spreads over the shoulders of her down vest, and she props one booted ankle on her knee as we talk. Gideon worked at the Huntsville newspaper as a student intern while she was majoring in journalism at Sam Houston State University. After graduation, she continued at the paper as their criminal justice reporter, and, during her two years there, witnessed fifty-two executions. Karla Faye Tucker's was her first.

"The editor did not feel I was ready to cover that execution on my own yet," she says after the three of us have settled in on one side of the long conference table in the facility's boardroom. "The reporter whose place I was taking was still there to cover the actual execution. I was there to observe and cover the press conference afterwards and the circus that was taking place outside. So the first time, I saw it all, but I didn't have to write about it."

The next execution was scheduled six days later, and this time Gideon was on her own. "At first, I was excited," she recalls. "This is one of the biggest stories you can cover, especially in Texas."

Determined to do a good job, she had researched the case closely. "I had thought about it a lot, you know, how I was going to feel. I'd read everything I could get my hands on. So, I just kept telling myself, 'Focus on what he was accused of doing and it'll be okay.' I was more scared of not being upset by the execution than anything else."

Executions weren't altogether unfamiliar to Gideon. Her father had worked for TDCJ for thirty years. She had grown up in prison employee housing on the Ellis unit, still home to death row then. Nevertheless, she was surprised when all she felt as she left the Walls that day was numb. "I was almost scared because I didn't feel anything."

Whatever she did or didn't feel at the time, however, it is evident from the tension in her voice now that the experience has stayed with her. "Later on I realized," she goes on, "that numb is a feeling."

For one thing, seasoned veterans like AP reporter Michael Graczyk, who had already covered well over one hundred executions, assured her that feeling numb was normal. On the other hand, Gideon says, the numb feeling never went away. Every execution left her with anesthetized emotions.

"I had gotten to know some of them through interviews or letters. Some of them, I knew their families. Sometimes I'd gotten to know the victim's family. But, as a reporter, I couldn't show any of that, not how I felt. So, I'd write my story for the paper, then I'd go home and write my own story."

Gideon says that covering executions wasn't the reason she left the paper; she simply got a better job working for a state representative in the Texas legislature. She also worked for a while as the civilian editor of the Echo, the inmate newspaper for TDCJ. The *Echo* was originally intended as a means of informing inmates about policy changes, procedures, health issues, and general inmate affairs. The publication had been shut down for a while because prison authorities decided it was doing more editorializing than informing.

Also, the TDCJ administrators had security concerns, Gideon tells us. The paper had been shut down immediately following the Thanksgiving escape of inmates from death row at Ellis. Gideon was hired "to help get it back on its feet again."

As editor, however, she was officially both a TDCJ and a Wyndham school system employee. As such, she had to follow state regulations for both entities. She soon found the stress of operating under multiple sets of rules too much.

"The inmate writers were wonderful, though," she says. "I never had any trouble with them."

"What about media coverage of executions?" David asks her. "Who gets to cover those?"

Gideon lists the five spots reserved for the press: one each for the AP and UPI representatives, one for the Huntsville paper, and two representatives — one print and one broadcast — from the town where the crime was committed. If the town has no newspaper or radio or TV station, they can give up their spot to someone else, usually the nearest town with a paper.

Gideon, along with Michael Graczyk and the UPI reporter, developed their own insider rituals for coping with the emotional demands of the job. "You have to do something to relieve the tension," she says, "and we sometimes made jokes, but never anything that showed disrespect for either the inmate or the victim. Just reporter-type stuff." European reporters covering the high-profile executions were shocked and offended by their dark humor, however. Gideon remembers being criticized in a European magazine for putting on "her bright red lipstick" before going into the execution chamber.

"For any of the fifty-two executions," David asks now, "was there ever so little interest that just you and maybe one or two other people were the only ones there?"

"I think at the one right after Karla Faye Tucker there was just us three. No other media." She clears her throat before she goes on. "There were so many executions that, unless I knew them or something out of the ordinary happened, they tend to just blur. It's terrible, I know, because they were all human beings. But I can't remember them all."

"Which ones stand out in your mind?" I ask her.

"Joseph Cannon. He's the one where his vein blew and the needle popped out and they had to start all over again."

The next one she mentions is Jonathan Nobles, with whom she had become good friends. "The media made a big deal out of Karla Faye turning her life around, but other inmates would tell you Jonathan was one of the most religious people they knew. He started Bible study groups and encouraged the others."

Next, she mentions Kenneth McDuff, whose crimes later motivated the Texas legislature to pass the serial-killer bill. "In all honesty," she says, "I have to say that was a good execution."

"I've heard that even death penalty opponents approved of that one," I say.

Gideon nods. "I had done as much research as possible on him before the execution," she says, "and I found out that he preyed on small women like myself. I did not realize until I walked into the chamber and saw him strapped to the gurney how big of a man he was. He was a very large man. And he was lying there trembling, visibly trembling. The first thought that came into my mind was, good — now you know how it feels to be scared, to be one of your victims. Of course, I couldn't write that in my story," she adds with a nervous laugh, "but that's what I thought."

Then there was James Beathard. "He was one of my last ones," she says. "He and I had become acquainted. He wrote me quite a lot. I probably knew more about his life than most people. He had just reunited with his daughter not long before his execution. That was a very difficult one. It was probably the only execution where we were all extremely quiet afterwards. We just sat there. Then Chaplain Brazzil came in. He told us, 'One of Beathard's last requests was to pray for y'all and to make sure that you're okay.'"

But there was another prisoner whose name Gideon cannot now recall, perhaps because she found herself hating the man, because he had asked his eighteen-year-old daughter to witness his execution. "What kind of father would do that?" she asks.

After the execution, as they were leaving the viewing room, the daughter collapsed. "You could tell she was trying to be strong and not cry. The correctional officers handled the situation very professionally. They made everyone move back and give her space. They didn't rush things. They very quietly got a wheelchair for her. She didn't use it though. She got up on her own and very proudly walked out of that prison."

When she got outside, a woman with the Salvation Army who often acts as spiritual adviser at executions caught the daughter by the arm and turned her around to face Gideon. "Here's someone who knew your father," the woman said.

"Really?" the daughter said, her eyes lighting up.

"You see," Gideon tells us now, "her father had been in prison so long she never really knew him. I was really on the spot. I didn't know what to say. So I just said, 'He talked about you a lot. He was very proud of you.' She seemed to be really pleased with that."

"Do you still think about it?" I ask.

"Yes. In the middle of the night, do I still have dreams? Yes, sometimes I do." Unexpected things, Gideon finds, can trigger a memory. "For instance, Jonathan Nobles sang 'Silent Night' as he was being executed. I hate to hear 'Silent Night' at Christmas now. I cannot stand it because it brings back that flood of memories. You try to put it out of your mind, but I can't. If I think about it much, I still get that feeling of numbness. It's become such a part of me."

Gideon once spent two or three hours interviewing Henry Lee Lucas, a serial killer who claimed to have murdered hundreds of people. "When I got back to the *Item*," she tells us, "everyone was like, 'How was it? What was he like?' I told them he's like that crazy old uncle in your family that everyone disowns. He was extremely cordial, a total gentleman to me. He gave me the information I wanted, you know, and that's all there was to it."

Gideon tells us that most of the female reporters at the newspaper didn't think they could handle the executions.

"What made you think that you could?" I ask.

"Because I'd grown up around it, knowing about it. That was one of my interview questions right off the bat. They asked if I could witness an execution. I told them I thought so. I didn't see any problem with it. I'm a very realistic person." She pauses, rubbing one finger along the sole of her boot propped on her knee. "Could I witness an electrocution or the gas chamber? I don't know. I have seen footage from electrocutions and the gas chamber, and I don't know if I could or not. On the other hand, in some ways it's really no different than going to a wreck scene where families have been killed or mutilated. Innocent people. You go and watch this other person at the prison peacefully die for something he has been convicted of by a jury."

"Did you ever have doubts about their guilt?"

"There were very few times that they came out and said, 'Yes, I did it,'" Gideon says. "Some did, but not all of them. So there was always that shadow of a doubt that they were actually guilty of what they were being punished for."

We ask Gideon about her own feelings about capital punishment.

"There's the two arguments. One argument says this is cruel and unusual punishment. But the act itself I do not believe is cruel or unusual — the execution process itself. We don't know what they actually feel, but it seems like they just go to sleep. The other argument is that they don't suffer enough. Family members will say, look what my father or my mother or my brother went through. But you have to remember, this condemned man knows exactly when he's going to die. So he has this Advent calendar where he knows in advance. What kind of mental torture is that?"

She stops and opens her mouth several times and shuts it again before she speaks, hesitating over words. "I haven't ever made up my mind, you know, which way's better. One side says this and the other side says that, and they will not even think about reasoning or seeing the other side. One group will quote the Old Testament — an eye for an eye — and the other group will quote the New Testament. It's kinda weird. You really see where people take it and make what they want of it."

David asks what the *Item*'s policy for covering executions was when she was employed there.

Gideon recalls that the first of every month she would get the execution schedule and set about trying to get interviews with the men. "Not too close to the actual date," she explains, "because they certainly don't want to be talking to a reporter right before they die. After the inmates on death row got to know me and realized they could trust me, I never had any trouble getting them to talk to me. If I got an interview, we ran with it, no matter what."

"Did the policy change after you left?" I ask.

She tilts her head to one side and purses her lips while she considers. "I noticed that there was less and less coverage. Maybe they just were not being granted interviews. The inmate gets to decide who he'll talk to. Or maybe they weren't asking for interviews. I don't know, but I noticed it. To me, it had been very important to get the condemned man's point of view. You get the attorney general's point of view and his summary of the crime. A reporter can try to get a hold of the inmate's attorney, but so many times it's pro bono and you simply can't find him. But I wanted that other side just to make things clear. I'd get the inmate's side and I'd get the state's side, and I'd let my readers draw their own conclusions."

"Are there some people," I say hesitantly, uncertain how to phrase my question, "because of the way their heads are wired or whatever, that are just beyond redemption?"

"I'd say yes," she replies quickly. "I'd definitely say yes." Then she continues more slowly. "I've talked to some inmates on death row when it really didn't seem to matter to them that they were there. Some of them had been institutionalized since they were youths. They didn't really know anything else. They'd been in facilities all their lives, in and out, in and out. Until they finally murdered. I've looked at some straight in the eyes and known they were lying to me about committing some of the most horrid murders. They could look me straight in the eye with a smile on their face and lie like a dog."

"To deny guilt or . . . ?" David leaves the question hanging.

"Yes, denying guilt. I'd seen the evidence. I knew that he was lying. I felt like yelling, stop it! That's been my whole fascination with serial killers — the why. Why, why, why?" She beats out the words on the side of her boot.

"And it's generally women that they kill," I say.

"And they are so good at what they do," David adds.

"Oh, you take some of them," Gideon rolls her eyes, "they could con the pants off Mother Teresa."

David asks whether she takes safety precautions, such as not telling people where she lives.

"I rarely tell anybody where I live. I live in an area that's not very well known, out in the middle of the woods, a farm and ranch community. My phone number is unlisted. But I look at it like this. If it's a criminal mind, and they want to find you, then they're going to find you. And . . ." She pauses a moment before going on. "I have always had a strong belief in God. That's what got me through a lot of those executions. Some of my colleagues would pick on me because I would go into a quiet spot in the office before an execution and I would pray — for everyone. The inmate, the inmate's family, the victim's family, the CO team, us. I did that every time. It made me feel better when I walked in there. And so," she shrugs, "I just trust in God to protect me. If it's my time to go, it's my time to go. Whether it's a former inmate distraught over something I wrote or it's a car wreck."

"How does your husband feel about it?" David asks.

"I decided, because my husband was very fearful when I took this assignment at the *Item,* just not to worry about it. I told him, 'Look, there's nothing you can do about it if one of them does show up. We can defend ourselves, but if it's meant to be, then it's meant to be. Don't worry about it.'"

She stops and smiles. "He's very supportive, though. After that first execution, when I got back to the office, there was a bouquet of flowers waiting for me. The note said, 'This is so you'll have something nice to look at.'"

That gesture started a tradition of post-execution gifts for Gideon, supplied each time either by her husband or her mother. "Something good to eat, maybe some candy, or a candleholder and candle."

Her usual debriefing routine went like this: she'd go back to the newspaper, call her mother if she was upset about how it had gone, then write her story. After that she'd call her husband. If it was a bad night, she'd say, "Have the tub ready when I get there."

The execution chamber, Gideon says, has a distinct smell. "I could always smell it on me afterwards." Sometimes she would thrust her clothes into her husband's face and say, "Can't you smell it?" No one else could, it seemed, but she knew it was there. As soon as she got home, she would get in the bathtub, trying to wash away the smell.

"It was like a cleansing ritual in some ways," she tells us. "My husband would sit there by the tub and talk to me. He patiently listened to me while I screamed or cried or did whatever I needed to do. I thank him a lot for that."

"Did you witness any executions where the condemned fought or resisted?" David asks.

"All of them, the ones I witnessed, went straight to the gurney. Of course, there were the ones who fought the execution itself, fought the drugs. They'd tense up and try to hold their breath. The others, they'd just try to relax and let it flow. That's what they're encouraged to do." She pauses and cocks her head to one side. "Those who fought it, they turned purple real quick. After so many, you look for those little details."

Gideon went to visit her mother, who lives near the Walls, the day that Gary Graham was executed. She had left the newspaper by then, but as she drove around the area, helicopters flying overhead, protesters outside, she felt a little left out, knowing she wasn't at the heart of the drama any longer. For a moment she says she missed the adrenalin rush she got from covering a big story.

Gideon had interviewed Graham, and though his case was hotly debated in the state, she didn't feel he was exactly the right person to display as an argument for abolishing the death penalty. Friends and colleagues called her afterward and asked if she missed covering the story. "I thought about it," she says, "and told them no. I really don't need that anymore."

David has another question for her. "With the execution of Karla Faye Tucker, people began to ask whether, if a person's life is turned around in prison, the state should proceed with the execution. After all, it seems counterproductive to execute a rehabilitated prisoner. What's your take on that?"

Gideon takes a deep breath and lets it out slowly. "I can't answer that in one sentence," she says. "Number one, our criminal justice system is supposed to be set up in order to rehabilitate. I think if there is a possibility of rehabilitation and proof of rehabilitation, then, yes, another chance should be given. But some of the inmates on death row have been there so long, years and years and years. That's where a lot of the problem comes from, is the wait. There are inmates on death row who have filed appeals, and the appeals have been lost in the system for fifteen years. On the other hand, I believe there's a need for the execution process and the death penalty. I believe we have to offer juries a full range of options, including the ultimate punishment. But I believe it needs to be handled in a swifter manner. That's torture, sitting there waiting to die for fifteen years."

As we're leaving, I tell her I have sent letters to twenty men on death row, asking if they would tell us their stories.

"If you hear from a guy named Jack Smith," she says, "tell him I'm still praying for him."

FRED ALLEN is a big, burly bear of a man. Born in Germany in 1959, Fred seldom saw his Army father, away in Vietnam, during his early childhood. Fred's German mother sent him and his brother to local schools, so that German was, for all intents and purposes, his first language. One would never guess that, however, to hear him speak today. He sounds and looks like a hard-working, forty-year-old East Texan with a physically demanding job.

I first heard Fred's voice on the NPR documentary, "Witness to an Execution," recorded in Huntsville a couple of years ago. Today I meet with Fred in the parlor at my church, recently and zealously decorated by the women's group. After a hard day on a construction site, he eases gingerly into a Queen Anne chair, saying he's already getting too old for this kind of work.

In 1977, when Fred Allen was a sophomore in high school, his family moved to Huntsville. His father, retired from the Army by then, went to work for TDCJ. After graduation, Allen followed in his father's footsteps and got a job with the prison system, working in the construction division. TDCJ was in the midst of its first big building boom, expanding rapidly to provide for the almost overwhelming influx of new prisoners. Allen was soon a labor foreman, operating heavy equipment and overseeing a crew of inmate laborers.

After a couple of years, though, Allen felt he was ready for something new. So he spent a couple of years at the Brown Oil Tool company, also in Huntsville, where he learned to weld, a skill that stood him in good stead when the oil bubble burst in the early eighties. He was able to get a job at another local company welding tanker trailers.

When he had been out of school for five years, however, Fred decided it was time to go to college. And, like Jim Willett before him, he went to work for TDCJ, this time as a correctional officer. After his stint at the training academy, Allen was assigned to the Walls unit in Huntsville, where he advanced steadily through the ranks to sergeant, then lieutenant, and finally captain.

But while he was still at the rank of Corrections Officer 3, he was assigned to security in the prison hospital, located then at the Walls. It was a cushy assignment, but for that very reason Fred felt the job lacked challenge. He wanted more responsibility, he tells me. And he got it. In fact, more than he bargained for.

Rev. Carroll Pickett, then chaplain at the Walls, asked Allen one day, "You want to help me out, Fred?"

Allen admired Rev. Pickett enormously. "I'd known Carroll since I was in high school," he explains now. "I used to go with a girl who was a member at First Presbyterian, and I got to know him pretty well. I'd give him the shirt off my back."

As the Walls chaplain, it was Pickett's duty to provide what spiritual and emotional comfort he could to the condemned awaiting execution. "I need somebody back there who I can depend on," Pickett told Allen. As I listen to him now, I quickly come to understand that "back there" is prison code for the death chamber.

"I told him, sure," Allen says. "So that's how I started sitting with the condemned." He rubs his big hands over the thighs of his jeans. "Back then, they would bring them in early in the morning, and I would relieve the first shift officer when I came in. Most of the men they used back there then were just COs; there wasn't much rank. My job was just to perform security back there and help Carroll. When the warden asked him who he wanted back there, he said he wanted me."

Two men were assigned to guarding the prisoner on execution day. "I wanted whoever was back there with me," he says, "I wanted us to make sure we were professional, that we got integrity and that everything's done sincerely. You know? Be sincere. We had some people back there — Carroll will tell you the same — they just, oh man, I couldn't wait for somebody to get them out of there."

This experience is hard for Fred Allen to talk about. He swallows and takes deep breaths, working hard to find words that make his point. "After all, you're dealing with a man who's got a limited amount of hours left."

"Did the prisoners feel desperate?" I ask uncertainly.

"There's been some back there," Allen takes another long breath, "who just didn't know how to talk."

He shakes his head. "You're trying to make him as comfortable as possible. But there's some of them back there, some kind of stereotyped individuals," (and now I understand he's talking about guards) "who're all gung ho. They say, 'Hey, I'd do it myself.' Everything that CO was saying was getting to that man sitting there. It was just getting him more and more agitated."

Allen shakes his head and rasps his hands together. "Back then, I would've told you right off the bat that what we were doing was just the law. We were just performing the last duty of the judgment. So, if anybody was going to do it, I was going to make sure it was done right."

This last comes out in a rush and more firmly, as if he were calling up a remembered pride in a difficult duty well done. But this wasn't Allen's only duty on those execution days. He was also a member of the tie-down team, one of the four correctional officers responsible for securing the prisoner onto the gurney. Along with the chaplain and a senior warden, they first escort the condemned man to the death chamber. Then they help him onto the waiting gurney. Two extensions for the prisoner's arms stick out on either side at shoulder height. Disconcertingly, the extensions turn the deathbed into a cross.

Each guard then secures different parts of the prisoner's body to the gurney with leather straps. Because of their practiced efficiency, the whole process takes little more than thirty seconds. After the prisoner is secured and the medical team is ready with the IV needles, the guards leave the death chamber. Then, the medical technicians insert the needle into the prisoner's arm, turn on the IV, and leave. Only the warden and the chaplain stay with the man till he is dead.

At about the same time that Rev. Pickett asked Allen to help him out, the number of executions began to grow at a rate commensurate with the increase in prison population. In the ten years that Allen spent on the tie-down team, he performed his assigned tasks at 130 executions. "It's not just that you put him up there on the gurney," he says, "but you got to take him out, too."

The last time Fred Allen escorted a condemned prisoner to the death chamber was on February 3, 1998. Except that it wasn't a man this time. Karla Faye Tucker was the first woman ever to be executed at the Walls, and for that and other reasons, the most famous in living memory.

Tucker had been convicted in June 1983 of hacking to death with a pickax twenty-seven-year-old Jerry Lynn Dean in Houston. Her accomplice and codefendant, Daniel Ryan Garrett, also received a death sentence but died on death row of liver disease ten years after his conviction.

Because of the publicity that Tucker's gender and Christian conversion had aroused, Allan B. Polunsky, chairman of the Texas Board of Criminal Justice at the time (and for whom the new death row prison has recently been renamed), took the unusual step of issuing a public statement immediately following her execution. "These issues here were not religious conversion or gender but rather culpability and accountability. Karla Faye Tucker brutally murdered two innocent people and was found guilty by the court and afforded all legal processes. Although I believe she finally found God, her religious awakening could in no way excuse or mitigate her actions in the world she just left, but hopefully will provide her redemption in the world she just entered."

Almost no one doubted Karla Faye Tucker's conversion. Least of all Fred Allen.

"The media were just bombarding us, you know, talking about her as a born-again Christian," Allen recalls. "But I sat back there with this young lady — I say 'young lady,' but she was about my age — I sat back there with this person, and all she had was a smile on her face. One time she looked at me and she said, 'We're going to all be forgiven.'"

"You had never met her before that day?" I ask.

"No. Never seen her before," he says shaking his head. "All this didn't sink in till two days later — because two days after the execution, the media was still bombarding us. Karla Faye this and Karla Faye that. So for some reason, something just snapped. It was six o'clock, the same time when we . . . you know. It seemed like the time and everything just fell into place. And all of a sudden I just . . . I lost it. Tears were running out of my eyes and I said, 'What is wrong with me?'"

"Were you at the Walls when this happened?"

"No, I was at home, two days afterwards. And I just said, 'I can't do this no more. That's it.'"

"What did you do?"

"Luckily enough, the first person I called was Carroll. He was already retired then, but he said, 'I'll be right there.'"

I let out my own breath of relief.

"We sat and talked and I was just trembling," Allen continues. "I couldn't even control my emotions."

He stops and coughs, reliving the sensation. "You know, I believe I'm a pretty decent size man, but this right here took me. I had no control. Nothing."

He pauses to clear his throat. "I'll never forget it. I'll take it to my last day."

Carroll Pickett knew just what to say to Allen. "You can only explain it one way," the pastor told him. "You take a vase and you put a drop in it. Let's consider the drop an execution. You put another drop in for another execution. Pretty soon that vase is going to fill up and, when you put that next drop in it, something's going to spill over. That's where you're at. You're full. You cannot do any more."

"No," I say.

"I went to the warden the next day," Allen goes on, his words coming faster now, "and sat down with him and I said, 'I can't do it no more.' Even when I was talking to him I was trembling. I said, 'I don't want to go back there. I don't even want to see it. I don't want to see it on television. I don't want to read about it. I want to get away from it.'"

He steadies himself with a slow breath now and proceeds at his former deliberate pace. "It was almost, I don't know, not haunting or anything, but I wanted it out of my mind. The sooner the better. I didn't want nobody talking about it. I didn't want to talk about it. I just wanted it out of my mind."

He clears his throat. "Not daily, but two or three times a week, I'd been taking tours back there. Taking people back there and explaining the process."

"Tours?" I blurt out. "You mean like a tour guide for the death house?"

"Oh, yeah. These people come from victims' families, Sam Houston students, you know."

"Classes?"

"Right. Criminal justice classes. And this one lady, I think she teaches in-service for the Houston Police Department and she'd always get a tour. We'd walk in the place and I'd say, 'This is what happens. This is what we do here, and this is what we do here.' Every minute, I could tell you exactly what happens. Clockwork. Precision. I knew that as a captain on the first shift I'd still be responsible for those tours. But I told Warden Jones, 'I can't go back there.'"

"What did he say?"

"He told me straight out, 'Don't set foot back there.' And he said, 'Now, I might forget sometime and tell you to take some people back there, but if I do, you remind me.'"

Allen relaxes a little more, but frowns now. "The bad part was that now the warden's got a captain that — well, he'd depended on me as the shift captain to take people back there, depending on my knowledge to make sure everything was right back there, but now he can't depend on me anymore. Almost to the point where he's thinking, 'Well, I really don't have no more use for Fred' — as a captain, you know."

He pauses now and shakes his head. "There was a slight. . . ." He can't find the word. "Sometimes I sensed that. It was never said, but — you know. Everybody was always, 'Don't worry about it.' But I wasn't really with the supervisors anymore, you know? It was to the point where, when an execution came around, I'd watch the van come in at noon, and I couldn't get out of there fast enough at the end of the shift. But everybody else was over to themselves talking about the execution this and the execution that, what they were going to do. But I wasn't a part of it no more. I definitely felt excluded within the supervisor ranks."

"Did anyone make any overt comments?" I ask.

"No," he answers instantly. "But I sensed it. Once I told the warden, 'You better talk to those others going back there, because there's going to be some individuals who — well, I don't want to see them go through what I went through.' Of course, you're always going to have individuals back there who say, 'This ain't nothing, this isn't going to bother me.' Almost computerized. But. . . ." He raises his hands from his knees as if to release his meaning. "That's not the kind Carroll wanted back there when he asked me to help him."

A hint of a smile appears for the first time on Allen's face. "My wife says the best thing that ever happened to me was when I quit going back there. You can ask her. I used to toss and turn. Talk in my sleep. And she says the second best thing is when I quit TDCJ altogether."

Allen left the prison system after two more years. He's never been sorry. But it took a long time before he could talk about the 130 executions he participated in.

A couple of years ago, Stacy Abramson and David Isay produced an audio feature, "Witness to an Execution," for National Public Radio. Fred Allen, his wife Sherry, and their daughters flew to New York for the production's premiere. The interview they did with Allen and the subsequent question-and-answer session following the premiere provided the breakthrough he needed to be able to talk about his experiences.

"At that premiere," he tells me now, "I was up there on stage with Carroll. 'What do I say?' I asked him. 'Just tell the truth,' he said. 'It's easier that way.'"

"You know," he says, "the funny thing is, I still can't talk about this with my parents. They just tell me, 'Well, it's the law. You were just following the law.' I don't argue with them. I just have to get up and leave. But I know that just because it's the law doesn't make it right." He lifts his chin and cocks his head at a determined angle. "I'll stand up and tell anyone any day that what we did back there, it's not right. It's just not right."

Allen has changed in other ways, too. "I was driving over to Riverside a little while ago and I saw this old guy walking beside the road. Before, I would have just buzzed right on by him, not even looked in the rearview mirror. But I pulled over and asked him where he was going. He said, 'Trinity.' I said, 'I'm only going as far as Riverside, but I'll take you that far.' He gets in, doesn't say much, but I notice all the time he's looking at my shoes. I had on a pair of tennis shoes I got at Wal-Mart, fairly new. I looked at his, and he was just walking out of them, they were coming apart so. Well, I always keep an extra old pair in the back of the truck when I'm working construction. So, when I stopped to let him out, I pulled off my tennis shoes and gave 'em to him. I figured he still might have to walk the rest of the way to Trinity, but at least he'd have a new pair of shoes to do it in."

"I hear you're going to New York for Christmas," I say.

His smile broadens now. "Leaving December 22," he says, "and coming back December 27. Sherry and I are taking the girls and staying with the fellow that produced the NPR documentary. We wanted to help out those people in New York after the terrorist attack there, so we're going to work in a soup kitchen there on Christmas Day. I want to get up at six o'clock Christmas morning and work, just work hard all day."

———

AT FIVE O'CLOCK almost every afternoon when an execution is scheduled, you can find Dennis Longmire standing beside the stop sign at the corner of Avenue I and Twelfth Street, across the street from the Walls unit. A strip of yellow crime scene tape, put up for the occasion, stretches across the street. Usually two or three media people are there also, more if the condemned or the crime has received a lot of attention in the news recently.

Several times a year, a band of protesters from an abolitionist organization in Houston comes, too. While Longmire holds a lighted candle, they hold bullhorns and stand directly in front of the yellow tape, shouting taunts and accusations at the security guards on the other side. Sometimes a handful of people stand in a knot on the other end of the corner from Longmire. These are usually family members, maybe brothers or sisters, who are waiting outside while their mother witnesses the execution of her child's killer. Longmire makes a point of approaching this group and introducing himself. He asks about their lost loved one and tells them that he's praying for the victim as well as the person dying across the street now. They are almost always in too much pain to give him much of a response.

At about five minutes to six, prison officials lead a contingent of witnesses from the administration building in front of the Walls, across the street, and through the front door of the red brick fortress. These are the victim's witnesses. Then come the five official media representatives, and finally the condemned man's witnesses. Longmire is still standing there, holding his candle, when they exit, again in separate groups, about thirty minutes later. Photographers from newspapers and TV stations, if their directors have found this particular execution newsworthy, snap pictures of the witnesses. Reporters take down the words of the victim's family. Then everybody goes home.

Dennis Longmire has been repeating this ritual ever since he came to Huntsville seventeen years ago as Assistant Dean of the School of Criminal Justice at Sam Houston State University. As we sit in his living room on a damp February afternoon, he says he's glad there's no execution today, since he wouldn't relish standing out in the cold rain. "But those in August, when it's over 100 degrees, those are hard on you, too," he grins as he hands David a cup of coffee.

Dennis Longmire is about our age, stocky, bespectacled, and gray-bearded. He looks the consummate academic, but one whose original ardor has not cooled over the past three decades. It's easy to imagine him on a 1960s picket line. Perhaps because he has spent a good many more hours in the classroom than Mary Alice Conroy, his answers to our questions tend to be copious rather than crisp.

He explains that he had trepidations about coming to Texas. The state had just reinstituted the death penalty, and he wasn't sure he wanted to live in a town where executions routinely took place.

"I gave myself a three to five year sentence," he says. "I felt I could stick it out for that long. But my three-to-five turned into life. And, actually, I don't find it a burden anymore. I really like Huntsville, the community."

"What particular grievances about the system lead you to oppose capital punishment?" David asks.

Longmire takes in a long breath and expels it slowly, then says, "The easiest position for me to take against the death penalty is the intellectual, academic, professional one. I'm a professor of criminal justice. I look at the system and ask how the death penalty is being administered and feel professionally obligated to challenge it — or any action taken by the system that is unjust. If you've taken even a casual look at the American system of justice, you know that it is not equally accessible to everyone. The higher you are in the economic order, the better the system works for you. The lower you are, the worse it works. The death penalty, the ultimate sanction, selects the poor people — who in our society are also minorities, young, and male. The system works pretty effectively on that group. But it isn't just and it isn't fair that it wouldn't affect you and me the same way. In fact, we're almost immune to it. Those folks higher up than us *are* immune to it. They literally can commit murder with impunity — and do. That alone, just the disparity in the application of the system, brings me to oppose it.

"All the research shows us that the death penalty is unfairly used against certain groups of people," he adds, "and is not any more effective than life imprisonment in terms of a reduction of homicides. We know that the sentence is subject to error. We know that innocent people have been sentenced to die and then released after long periods of time. Sometimes we only discover their innocence after they're executed. We know it's a system of man, and as such it's bound to fail at times."

"Don't we have appellate courts to catch errors in the lower courts?" I ask.

"Sure. But they cannot consider guilt or innocence, only the procedures during the trial. The United States Supreme Court itself looks to society to find the failure rate we're willing to accept. As long as the American people say they're satisfied with the status quo, the Court says the situation must be acceptable. But the death penalty is only one part of a larger problem. Until we make changes in the fundamental disparities in our social justice, we won't come close to fixing the problems in our criminal justice system."

"So," I say, feeling foolish for asking such a vague question, "What is justice and how do we get there?"

"A good question," he says. "I think when we talk about justice we have to recognize the retributive nature of that concept. Justice is about retribution; it's about giving people what they deserve. When we think about desert-based justice, we usually think about giving people pain. You do the crime, you do the time. And certainly that's a part of it. But we also promise that we will give people their just desert following certain rules and regulations ourselves.

"In a capital case, we can't give people their ultimate desert very swiftly. We have to pause at least long enough for the Court of Criminal Appeals to review the case. Which means at least three years' delay — if you're lucky. It's probably going to take closer to seven years. And that's when the system's working at top efficiency. In my view, that's just unconscionable.

"Also, we know there are going to be errors, and that those errors are irreversible with capital punishment. Justice, in this case, only arrives when we can tell people, if you commit the crime of murder, you're going to suffer this punishment, and everybody who commits that crime suffers the same punishment in a fairly swift, fairly humane way."

"Lethal injection," I say.

Longmire nods. "Because we also promise that, when we do put you down, we're not going to make you suffer." He crosses his arms across his chest. "Now a lot of people don't like that. Those aren't the retributive theorists — those are revenge theorists. Retributive theorists want to make sure we give you what we promised, no more, no less. Playing by the rules. That's justice, not revenge. The justice in the death penalty comes in its ability to be administered fairly, uniformly, swiftly, with a high level of certainty, and compassionately.

"However," and here his thick eyebrows rise to emphasize his point, "when you try to build a system that delivers all that, you realize it's just about impossible, given a society that doesn't have equality or compassion or a real sense of order."

"Supposing we did have this ideal society," I say. "What would you think about it then?"

"Then I move beyond answering the question of justice, because I don't think the response to crime should be driven by a sense of justice, but by a sense of compassion — in a spiritual context, by a sense of mercy. What man is called to is greater than justice. We're called to be caring and to try to create a system that models that hopeful, restorative relationship that we try to engender in one another.

"If I have the power and the authority to tell you that I can kill you with impunity," Longmire goes on, "that creates a chasm between you and me. Especially if I have the authority of the state behind me. Instead, I want to build a bridge across that chasm. I want to say, you've done something horrible to me, you've taken the life of my loved one, and I want an institutional support system in the state that will help me build a bridge to you, not deepen the chasm.

"But as soon as I can get you killed, you have to steel yourself against me. You have to say, I didn't do it or I wasn't really responsible for it or I was crazy or whatever. When what we ought to be doing is sitting across the table from one another, with help, trying to figure out how to restore the brokenness."

As an academic, Longmire cannot help supplying oral footnotes for his ideas. He mentions two books in particular as major influences on his thinking. One is *Pedagogy of the Oppressed* by the late Brazilian theorist Paulo Freire. David still has our 1970 graduate school paperback copy stuffed somewhere in his bookcase. The book has continued to sell so well that in 2000 the publisher brought out a thirtieth anniversary edition.

The other book that Longmire mentions, *Hopeful Imagination: Prophetic Voices in Exile,* is not quite so old — 1986 vintage. It is a study of Jeremiah, Isaiah, and Ezekiel, by Walter Brueggemann, a Lutheran professor of Old Testament studies.

Longmire, it is obvious, has taken a prophet's mantle upon himself. Like his Hebrew scripture counterparts, he works through words and symbolic acts. And only his hopeful imagination, I think, can account for those 240 vigils.

11

Another Way

"I can't understand you. Do you mean to say that you, and the Elves, have let him live on after all those horrible deeds? Now at any rate he is as bad as an Orc, and just an enemy. He deserves death."

"Deserves it! I daresay he does. Many that live deserve death. And some that die deserve life. Can you give it to them? Then do not be too eager to deal out death in judgment."

J. R. R. TOLKIEN,
The Fellowship of the Ring

WE MUST AT this point come back to the victims. Whatever the state of Texas does or does not do to convicted killers, those families whose lives have been ravaged by a loved one's violent death will go through long years of anguish. Despite all the optimistic talk of "getting on with life," they find their lives crippled and wounded by frustration, anger, and terrible memories that never fade.

David Doerfler believes there is another way, one that helps heal the wounds. It is not an easy way, though, and it requires extraordinary courage to undertake.

Doerfler, a Lutheran minister, was hired in the Victim Services Division of TDCJ in December 1993 based on his previous experience of working with victims of child abuse and sex offenders in group settings. His job at TDCJ, however, turned out to include both victims and offenders. He was charged with designing and operating a mediation program that would bring together seemingly irreconcilable people. With the Director of Victim Services for TDCJ, Raven Kazen, he searched for similar programs around the nation, only to discover he would pretty much have to invent the program himself.

The program is not highly publicized. Indeed, I only found out about the Victim-Offender Mediation program from a somewhat unlikely source — an assistant district attorney who praised the project. Yet it appears to be one of the most successful attempts to give the families of victims of violent crimes any surcease from their pain and loss. Not only that, but it also gives the murderer a chance to confront and acknowledge his own guilt and shame.

At first, as I thought about this latter part of Doerfler's work, the task seemed impossible to me. I could understand the victims wanting to confront their loved ones' killers, though mediation sounded like too mild a term for the way I envisioned such an encounter. I had already learned that some judges now allow Victim Impact Statements in their courtrooms. Most families, I figured, would find a certain satisfaction in unloading their grief and rage on the one who had taken away their daughters or sons or mothers or fathers. Certainly, that opportunity seemed more appealing than engaging in the kind of sustained, deliberate dialogue that mediation implied, though I could see that a few brave souls might want such a catharsis.

But the murderer — what possible incentive could he have for facing someone who undoubtedly hated him and wished he had never been born? My first question to David Doerfler, who now works as an independent trainer and consultant in developing this process, was just that: "I have a hard time understanding how you could ever get a murderer together with someone from the family of his victim. What does he get out of it? Why would he ever go through it?"

No doubt Doerfler has been asked this question many times, because his response came quickly. "For one thing, it doesn't happen overnight. In most cases, it takes twelve to fourteen months of careful preparation before I ever bring the two together. And sometimes that face-to-face meeting doesn't ever happen, but something else does. Letters and video statements, for example. Anything that can provide the victim with some opportunity to heal."

"But what's in it for the offender?" I repeat. "As I understand it, participating in the program isn't going to reduce his sentence or save him from the death chamber."

"That's true. Nevertheless, it's not as difficult as you might think," Doerfler says. "Most offenders really want to be accountable." In fact, Doerfler estimates that between 60 and 75 percent of offenders earnestly seek the opportunity to engage the process, and a good number of those eventually agree to the face-to-face meetings.

"Another 20 percent will say, 'Absolutely not,'" Doerfler says, "though deep down they really want to. And then there's a residual 5 percent who are so damaged that they cannot even begin to function on the rational or emotional level necessary for such a process."

Also, it is victims who must initiate the process, Doerfler tells me. But first they generally have to stumble across the program. They are not automatically informed that the opportunity is available to them. Doerfler finds that the obscurity of the program is its biggest weakness.

Considered something of a frill by the current TDCJ administration, mediation is not high on the system's list of priorities. Nevertheless, during his eight years of directing this program for Victim Services, Doerfler documented the requests of over six hundred victims of violent crimes to initiate this program, the majority of them homicide cases.

"And that's just the tip of the iceberg," he says. "The good part about the victims initiating contact is that then it's clear the motivation comes from them and that we aren't just fabricating some well-intentioned but worthless program. The victim is saying, 'I need to do this.'"

Only one mediator is assigned per case. And, during most of the years Doerfler was developing the program, he was the only professional available. At best, he was able to oversee only three or four full-fledged face-to-face mediations a year.

Mediation will fail or succeed, Doerfler maintains, on the strength of the confidence people can maintain as they work their way through the process. Both sides must discover come semblance of trust in the one person in the world whose good intentions they probably have the least reason to believe. In the beginning, neither side is willing to be in such a vulnerable position. So first they must learn to trust the mediator.

Doerfler explains that, during the first year, the victim and the offender never meet each other in person. The mediator, however, visits each of them alternately. At this point, the dialogue between the two begins, the mediator serving as the message-bearer.

And more than just talk is required. Both the offender and the victim do a good deal of writing. They keep journals in which they respond to probing questions. In each phase, Doerfler invites them to go deeper toward self-awareness and understanding their emotional needs.

"The first assignment is simply to tell about the crime, what happened, from their own perspective," Doerfler says. "Next, I ask them to write about their feelings. In the victim's case, they usually describe disbelief, numbness, rage, desire for revenge. Sometimes their bewilderment about why this happened to them."

Doerfler maintains that, when they read and reflect on what they've written, their awareness of just how this tragedy has affected them begins to grow. Often, they have never gotten clear in their own minds just what they have felt and experienced during this catastrophe. "So, whether or not the victim ultimately gets the response he or she wants from the offender," Doerfler says, "they still have gained in self-awareness. Just getting that far in the process is invaluable to them."

With each side's enhanced self-awareness, they can move on to asking another question: when the past cannot be changed, what do you do? The question struck me as one that could profitably be asked in any number of desperate situations. Both the victim and the offender have to deal with that conundrum. "What they usually come to see," Doerfler says, "is that you have to face life on life's terms."

Both parties are simultaneously undergoing the same basic experience, which Doerfler identifies as grief. The victim is mourning his lost loved one. The offender is mourning both the impact of his destructive behavior and the consequences of his own constricted future.

"Most people don't understand how much the victim of a crime is left out of the criminal justice system. Every homicide case is entered into court records as the state of Texas vs. the defendant. The state of Texas?" Doerfler exclaims. "No! It's me, an individual victim! I'm the one who is suffering and who feels the loss." He uses an illustration from the movie *Ocean's Eleven,* a scene in which an ex-con says defensively to his wife, "I've paid my debt to society." The wife replies, "That's funny. I haven't received my check yet."

Violation creates obligation, Doerfler maintains. "When we raise our hand against another human being, that changes the situation. It's not that I care less about the offender, but in order to get the offender's needs met, the victim's needs have to be met first. Everything else flows from that, including the community's needs. When the victim's needs are met, then everyone's needs are met."

What does the victim need? When Doerfler talks to victims, he finds that, underneath all the other feelings, what they need most is to have the greatest responsibility possible placed on the offender, whatever they imagine that to be. Only then can they say, I have now done everything I can possibly do. If that doesn't happen, they will feel they have somehow failed their loved ones.

"If they can grieve, they can heal," Doerfler says. "If not, the offense continues."

David Doerfler professes to be an abolitionist regarding the death penalty. "But I understand very fully the other side. In fact, most of the time people in the abolitionist movement are their own worst enemies. They start in the wrong place. They focus on the offender and not the victim."

This enterprise of mediating between, say, the mother of a murdered child and the child's murderer, strikes me as a Herculean task. So I ask Doerfler what he has found to be the biggest obstacle.

"First of all," he says, "you have to get past a lot of misconceptions and distrust. It's hard for either party to understand that you're not on the other one's side. They're both afraid of being manipulated. So first of all, they have to learn they can trust you as the mediator."

After that initial step, they have to face giving up their pain. In an article written for *The Crime Victims Report* periodical, Doerfler wrote, "For so many victims, all those hurtful feelings well up inside to shackle and paralyze. Abdicating responsibility to the judicial or correctional system by concentrating on the offenders' sentence and supervision usually provides some immediate relief. Eventually even those external preoccupations lose their benefit and the feelings first experienced at outcry resurface and most likely intensify."

"They live with the pain so long and so constantly," Doerfler tells me, "that it becomes familiar. They know what living with the pain is like, and they can no longer imagine their lives without it. Letting go of it becomes the unknown, and thus frightening. So it's hard to turn loose."

The third obstacle, especially for the victim, is the family. Other family members are not necessarily a part of the mediation process. They aren't going through the same experience, and it's hard for them to understand why anyone would. Often the victim gets little support from them. In fact, other family members may become quite hostile, believing that the one choosing mediation is betraying both the rest of the family and the dead loved one.

"During mediation, the victim begins to see the offender as human. But, when she expresses that to other members of the family, she may be met with disbelief and anger. So it becomes hard to maintain the integrity of the experience. She may begin to doubt it. Still, even with all these obstacles, I've seen forgiveness powerfully lived out in people's lives."

His article offers these principles for healing in the victim:

"Until you are honest with yourself and face the hurt and pain of your past, the past continues. Until you take responsibility for your own grieving and for your own reconstruction and recovery, the offense continues.

"Until you move beyond the past, beyond your story of victimization, to focus on yourself, your present relationships, and your future participation in the life of the community, your healing is incomplete."

"What about the offender?" I ask. "What are his obstacles?"

"Fear," Doerfler answers immediately. "The offender is scared of being torn up by the victim's rage. And the next biggest roadblock for the offender is shame. The last mediation I did at TDCJ, I was preparing the offender for his first meeting with his victim. He told me he was really nervous. I asked him, 'Why? Are you afraid she'll hurt you?' 'No, not really,' he said, and he started to tremble. 'I'm just so ashamed.'"

Doerfler tells of an offender at the Walls unit in Huntsville who at first agreed to meet with his victim, "but as we worked through more and more of the layers of his pain of shame and guilt, he became afraid and decided not to follow through with the dialogue preparation. He told me, 'What this process is asking me to do is too hard. I'm supposed to reach down deep inside and face all that I have done and all the pain I have caused. . . . And I just don't think my arms are long enough.'"

Doerfler agreed with him that facing such pain was probably the hardest choice anyone ever has to make. It is a tribute both to Doerfler's honesty and skill and to the inmate's courage that ultimately the man agreed to try.

"He decided to stay with the process, and is in fact facing the pain of his past and his present. As has been the case with other offenders who have committed themselves to facing all the pain they have caused, and all the shame and guilt that results, he has experienced and continues to face a deeper kind of accountability and thus a deeper sense of meaning, purpose, and healing."

Doerfler has devised a separate set of "Principles of Healing for Offenders":

"Until you are honest with yourself and face the pain and shame of your past, the past continues. Until you admit guilt and take responsibility for your offense, the offense continues. Until you become accountable beyond yourself to your victim and your community, there can be no healing."

David Doerfler has developed quite definite views on the criminal justice system as well. "I think we grab the whole business of justice by the wrong end of the stick," he says. "Currently we ask who did it and how we can punish them. But it makes more sense to ask who was hurt and how we can restore them. So far, when we've dealt with the question of restitution, we've only focused on money. But the victim's emotional needs, which are most important, have been totally ignored."

Restitution is particularly difficult in homicide cases. Unlike crimes such as robbery, the essential loss of a life cannot be restored.

"But what if we said to the offender," Doerfler suggests, "for the rest of your life you'll have to give back — not 'pay back' — in response to the irretrievable loss of a life? That would at least give the offender a sense of purpose. You know, the Quaker understanding of prison is that it should be a place to reflect on what you have done. I don't see that killing offenders accomplishes anything for either side."

"Both repentance and forgiveness are, for Christians, a requirement," I say. "The Lord's Prayer links our own forgiveness to our forgiveness of others. How do you deal with that during mediation?"

"I'm not sure that our English translations of the verse that says 'forgive us as we forgive those who trespass against us' capture the deeper meaning. I believe that 'as' should be translated 'so that.' Forgive us so that we may forgive. Because we have been forgiven, God's love so fills us and empowers us that it overflows into the forgiveness of others."

As illustration, Doerfler offers the story of the mother of a young woman who had been raped and murdered. The woman, a Christian, thought she had already forgiven the man who had savaged her daughter. And, on one level, Doerfler agrees that she had. But when she finally met the man five years after beginning mediation with Doerfler, she discovered she hadn't even come close to the deepest level.

Death ends the dialogue, Doerfler maintains, and, with it, a deeper experience of forgiveness. "When you think about it," he says, "for the thief on the cross it was short and sweet. He died shortly after being forgiven. But what about the adulteress they brought before Jesus? Or Zacchaeus? Or the mother of a victim whose murderer is one day released? They have to live out their forgiveness, maybe for many more years. Whether you're giving or receiving, living forgiveness has to be done moment by moment. But then nothing is ever lived, except moment by moment."

The man who had raped and murdered her daughter did indeed die in the death chamber. Asked for his last words, he recited the thirteenth chapter of 1 Corinthians. For his last meal he requested the sacrament.

—⸙—

JIM BRAZZIL has witnessed over 160 executions at the Walls. Not from either of the two viewing rooms from which the families of the victim and the inmate witness the execution, but from inside the death chamber. As a prison chaplain, he used to stand beside the gurney, his hand resting just below the knee of the condemned. His was the last human touch they ever felt in this world. But before that final moment he has stayed with inmates during the hard hours they waited in a cell just off the death chamber. Many of them he had known during the months and years leading up to their final day.

Recently reassigned to the Victim Services Division of TDCJ, Jim Brazzil still witnesses the executions — only now he spends those hours waiting with the victim's family.

"The first person I ever saw die was alongside the highway in Lampasas, Texas," he tells David and me as we drink coffee at the pancake house that has become the setting for many of our meetings with TDCJ personnel. "I was holding the woman's head up so she wouldn't choke on her own blood. She died in my arms. It was an awesome experience, in the true sense of that word. A religious experience." Brazzil hesitates, pressing his lips together before he continues. "And every death I have witnessed since then has affected me the same way as that first one."

Brazzil had already spent twenty-five years as pastor of several Southern Baptist churches across Texas when he signed up for a tour of Ukrainian prisons with other pastors in 1992. The experience convinced him that he was called to prison ministry. He resigned from his church and, taking a pay cut of 50 percent, joined the chaplaincy program at TDCJ.

Unlike Rev. Pickett, the "death chaplain," who never met the condemned man until the day of his execution, Brazzil was able to visit the person scheduled for death as soon as the judge set the execution date. Over the years, he got to know many of these inmates before they took that last ride to the Walls. Some were even in Bible studies he led.

Following the intense media attention Karla Faye Tucker's execution brought to Huntsville, Brazzil was featured in a number of articles critical of the death penalty and was interviewed for several radio and TV documentaries. Brazzil does not speculate about whether his high profile caused him to be reassigned late last year to the Victim Services Division. He is obviously pleased to be serving now as a victim-offender mediator.

In his new position, Brazzil travels all over the state to meet with victims' families, helping them work through the arduous and protracted process of absorbing and coping with the aftermath of murder. With one exception, a rape case, all the participants in the Victim-Offender Mediation program at TDCJ have had a loved one murdered. Because the process is labor- and time-intensive, and because so few trained mediators are available, a long list of both victims and offenders are waiting to get into the program.

Brazzil assures us that he does not feel his ministry has been diminished by his reassignment. "In fact," he says, his round face buckling into its characteristic smile, "I feel it has broadened considerably. I still have access to inmates, but I also get to work with the families."

Several months ago, Brazzil got a taste of what a crime victim experiences. He came home from a weekend of traveling to find that his own house had been burglarized. "The door was busted open, the windows broken out, glass everywhere," he tells us. "My TV, VCR, DVD — all the stuff that could be turned over quickly was gone." But the loss of those items was nothing beside the emotional toll the burglary took.

"I called the police," Brazzil said, "they came, looked around, and said, 'Yep, you've been robbed all right.'" That was the last he saw of them. About a week later he did get a call from the police department telling him that the thief had been caught, but that Brazzil's possessions had already been fenced. There was no chance of getting them back.

"I didn't mind that so much," he says. "Those things could be replaced. But the fact that someone had been in my house, someone I didn't know, continued to bother me. On top of that, I was never informed when the case went to trial, what the man was charged with, or what the outcome of the trial was. To this day, I don't know where he is. That experience gave me a deeper insight into just how much victims are left out of the criminal justice system. Because we focus almost exclusively on the criminal, our justice system is about retribution. People get all worked up about punishing the criminal, making sure we're tough on crime, but it offers practically nothing to the victim." The crime problem in this country, Brazzil believes, will not improve until that changes.

Victim Services at TDCJ has recently extended its mission by offering a program called Victim-Offender Encounter. Unlike the more intensive Victim-Offender Mediation program, which pairs a member of a murder victim's family with the victim's actual murderer, the Encounter program does not match victims with their specific offenders. This allows more people access to the process.

"What we do," Brazzil explains, "we take about twenty victims — bona fide, hard-core victims. Some of them have been raped, some of them have been shot or stabbed, some of them have lost loved ones. We also go in with about twenty inmates. These are all volunteer inmates. They know they're not going to get out any earlier because they're participating." After some initial training on both sides, the two groups are brought together. The victims form a Victim Impact Panel, and one by one they tell their stories.

Brazzil pauses and whistles. "I'm telling you, those stories are heartbreaking."

While the TDCJ administration states on its Web site that the purpose for the panels is "to assist victims with their recovery and healing process," the program also benefits the inmates. After the panel finishes speaking, all the participants break into small groups made up of two or three victims, an equal number of inmates, a facilitator, and a chaplain.

"We talk about anger, we talk about hatred, we talk about vengeance, we talk about mercy, we talk about forgiveness, we talk about healing," Brazzil enumerates. "And we go through ten weeks of this. It changes people."

To illustrate, he tells of a recent encounter in which an inmate, who had been incarcerated for eighteen years on drug charges, stood weeping while he told the group, "Ever since I've been in here, I've carried a chip on my shoulder. I've been angry at the state. But for the first time in my life, I've seen the face of my victim. For the first time, I'm sorry for what I did."

This failure of inmates to admit guilt and acknowledge the harm they have done, Brazzil believes, frustrates and angers their victims, standing in the way of their recovery from the crime's aftermath.

"Yet inmates often are resentful of the system for their treatment in prison," David says. "Do inmates generally carry a chip on their shoulders because they feel that they've been treated unjustly?"

Brazzil shakes his head, irony tempering his smile this time. "Inmates in prison don't focus on justice at all. They focus on punishment. Most inmates will tell you that they've been scammed, or that they're only doing what everybody else does."

Brazzil is familiar with David Doerfler's history with the Victim-Offender Mediation program at TDCJ. So I ask him if Doerfler's claim that most inmates actually want to be held accountable for their crimes rings true with his experience.

"Oh yes," Brazzil says. "We have a waiting list in our office of inmates wanting to meet with their victims. But the problem with the mediation process is that it's victim-driven. The victim must initiate contact with us. We can't go out and say to them, 'We have an inmate who wants to meet with you.' But on the other hand, most victims aren't even aware the program exists."

"So you've got victims wanting to participate and you've got inmates volunteering, but they don't necessarily match up."

"Correct," Brazzil nods emphatically. "And that's the reason that the Encounter program is working so well. It offers them at least a modified mediation."

"The inmate doesn't have to be the one who actually committed the crime?" David asks.

"In the Encounter program, they can't be."

"And you do find that the inmates in the program actually want to be held accountable?" I ask again.

Brazzil holds up one hand, palm out. "You can't, across the board, make any claims about inmates. Each one is individual. But I'd say that it's true for a large number of them. They want this opportunity."

"People in the free world will find that hard to believe," I say.

Brazzil sits back and smiles, all trace of irony gone now. "Let me tell you a story," he says. "I had one fellow on death row that I went to see. His eyes were dark, evil-looking, cold-blooded. I got to know him very well, working with him over a period of time. He had a really bad disciplinary record and had been moved around from prison to prison. I'd go over to see him when he was in [solitary confinement].

"At first he was unresponsive, but after a while he'd let me talk to him. I'd always take my Bible along, but I'd just lay it down beside me there while we were talking. I didn't open it or anything. I'd sit down on one side of the bars and he'd sit on the other side, and that's the way we would talk. I'll never forget, when it really got serious, he broke down and started crying. So I shared some scriptures with him, and he received Christ. He really got into it.

"The next week I went over to take some other books to him. As soon as he saw me, he said, 'I don't want to talk to you today.'

"I said, 'What's wrong?'

"He said, 'I'm just not sure you did me any good. I don't want to talk about it.'

"I said, 'Come on. We've got a problem here, we need to talk about it.'

"Well, to make a long story short," Brazzil continues, "he had been in another prison system in another state where there was a major riot. Over the course of his incarceration, he had killed seven people. He told me, 'When you walked in here to talk to me the other day, I could've killed you without blinking an eye and never even thought about it. Taking somebody's life meant nothing to me. But now that you've opened my heart to God, those faces of the people I killed keep coming back. And I can't take it.'

"So I said, 'We've just got a lot of work to do. You have to work through this process.'" Brazzil lowers his head over his coffee cup. "The guilt is heavy. I've found that so much on death row. They don't want the media involved in it. They don't want it in writing. They don't want the world to know about it. But they want to come clean."

"But does it take the death penalty to bring a person to that point?" I ask.

"I don't want to get into the pros and cons of the death penalty," Brazzil says. "But I can tell you this: Say you have a young man who's incarcerated for killing someone, and he gets a life sentence, which means he's going to have to do forty years. That's going to make him sixty-one before he's even eligible for parole. When you're twenty and looking forty years ahead, that's a lifetime. So these inmates are looking at their mortality, too, even without a death sentence. Of course, when they first enter prison, they have to prove themselves. They get belligerent, they get angry, they get cocky. But when they've been there

196

a few years, then the reality hits. This is going to be the rest of their lives.

"I have an eighteen-year-old boy who killed two people, and he got two life sentences, stacked. He's just a kid. At first he got into gangs, he got into fights, he got into the homosexual scene, just trying to prove himself, just trying to fit into the prison life. He got shipped from unit to unit. Just a horrible situation. Finally, a couple of months ago, reality caught up with him and it brought him to his spiritual depths."

We're all silent for a moment. I'm trying to imagine what it would be like to be confined to a six-by-nine space for the rest of my life. I think I can understand choosing death over that.

Finally, David says, "Yet even church members want to dismiss spiritual experience among people who've committed crimes like that. Some think it's just another one of their scams. What's your take on that?"

Brazzil nods his understanding of the problem. "I believe that our people — and I'm talking about churches now — want everything to be so clinical, so black and white. They want it to be on paper. They want to see the progress. But they don't want be involved. And I think that's where our churches are failing."

ON SEPTEMBER 15, 1999, forty-seven-year-old Larry Gene Ashbrook stormed into the Wedgwood Baptist Church in Fort Worth, Texas, with two pistols and a pipe bomb and began firing into the teenagers assembled for a youth rally. He killed seven people and injured seven more before turning his gun on himself. Jim Brazzil was part of the Critical Incident Response Team assembled to deal with the aftermath of the rampage.

"It was easy enough to minister to the young people and their families," he says. "Their need was so obvious, and you wanted to respond. But there were also the policemen who rushed to the scene. And there were the firemen, there were the medics. They've all been traumatized. You know, when you see kids killed, that's always hard on anybody. But the people who needed help worst were the ones who scrubbed up the carpets. They had to clean up the blood and guts. You can't depend on the state to help those folks. They're going to fall through the cracks. Killing affects a whole community.

"I believe that every church ought to have a criminal justice ministry team. I'm not just talking about the ones that go into the prisons. I believe there ought to be a team that goes to the crime scene or the fire. There needs to be a cleanup team. Someone for every aspect of a crisis."

"If a church were to do this," David asks, "how would it go about connecting to law enforcement agencies? You can't just show up."

Brazzil nods. "First off, you'll need some training, but that's easy enough. I can put you in touch with the people who do that kind of training — Critical Incident Stress Management. But you can get started right away with some fairly simple things. Some of them will take some legwork and a little bit of money, but not much. You start by having an appreciation dinner for policemen in your area. Or, even simpler, take a bunch of donuts down to the police or fire station on a routine basis. It's easy, but you'd be surprised at the impact that it makes. But you can't do it just once and expect a pat on the back. This is going to take a growing relationship. But once you establish that relationship, you tell them you have a team member who has a scanner. He listens to the scanner and finds out there's a major wreck out on the highway where somebody's killed. The police and firemen are going to have to go out there and pull the bodies out of the cars and wash all the blood off the highway. They're the ones that are dealing with it. After it's over, have a team that's ready to go down and serve them coffee and donuts, pat them on the back and say, 'Man, you must have had a tough day today. If there's anything you need, just let me know.' That's all you have to say. When they know that you're going to be there, when they know that you really care about them, then when there's a murder, you make it known to them and the EMS personnel, 'Hey, we want to help. Whatever needs doing, we're willing to do. If you need someone to take the family somewhere, if you need a cleanup team, you let us know.' Once you get in and develop the relationship, they'll know you're serious, that you do really care."

Brazzil tells about passing an accident scene a few weeks ago in which a pedestrian had been hit out on the highway. "It was a Sunday morning, and I got there right after it happened. They hadn't even covered the body yet. Already cars were slowing down to rubberneck, the wreck was so bad. They were flagging cars on by, so I couldn't stop. But when I came back six hours later, they were still washing the pavement down, and the family was standing huddled there beside the highway, traumatized."

As a TDCJ employee, Brazzil accepts the restrictions about publicly discussing his views on capital punishment. Doing so would probably lose him his ministry. Instead, he simply says that he is "not in the punishment business, but the redeeming business."

So I ask him if he believes there are some people who are beyond redemption.

"I believe that redemption comes from God," he says, "and there's nobody that God's ready to give up on until his last breath. From that perspective, I don't believe anybody is beyond redemption. But I do think that there are some people whose hearts are so darkened and so filled with hatred and bitterness that they can't see God's love."

I ask if he thinks, as some of my respondents have, that killers — at least particularly vicious ones — belong in a special category, that they are not like the rest of us.

Brazzil shakes his head. "I disagree with that. Of course, for some over there on death row, there were times in their lives when they were animals. I think of Karla Faye Tucker herself. You can't take away the hideous things these people have done. But when you put them in a cell by themselves and let them sit there for ten or fifteen years. . . ." His voice trails off.

Then, taking a quick breath, he says again, "Let me tell you another story. When I first came to TDCJ, I taught a class on death row, using the book *Experiencing God*. At that time, the death row inmates on the Ellis unit could congregate. So I was in this cell with just me and twenty death row inmates. I was a little apprehensive at first," he gives a low chuckle, "but I had the greatest time of my life with them. It taught me a lot."

The waitress appears to refill our cups. When she's gone, I ask, "Like what? What did it teach you?"

Brazzil cups both hands around the cup and stares into it a moment. Then he says, "You know, usually, when you teach a book about the spiritual life like that, you talk about how it's going to change the person's life in the future. You talk about when they go to college, when they get married, when they get a new job. But you don't do that on death row. They're not worried about what they're going to do after graduation, they're not worried about getting a job. They just worry about today and their relationship with God right now." He glances up, smiling again. "I wish we could all be like that."

12

Doing Justly

He hath showed thee, O man, what is good, and what doth the
LORD *require of thee, but to do justly, and to love mercy, and to*
walk humbly with thy God?

MICAH 6:8

TODAY, DECEMBER 12, 2001, we will have our last service at St. Stephen's
for an execution this year. Vincent Edward Cooks, a black man who
shot an off-duty police officer while robbing a Dallas supermarket, will
be arriving at the Walls unit in a couple of hours. A few minutes after
six o'clock this evening the fatal chemicals will begin streaming into his
veins, making his the 256th execution since Texas began executing
again in 1982, the seventeenth this year.

That's less than half the number we executed the previous year, the
Houston Chronicle pointed out this morning. In fact, for the first time in
twenty years, Texas does not lead the nation in executions. Oklahoma
took the lead away from Texas by one death.

However, as of today Texas still has 455 prisoners, including eight
women, on death row. Fifteen of those have been waiting to die for
over twenty years. It is estimated that Texas will keep its annual number of executions under twenty in the future, mainly because many
Texans, like citizens in other death-penalty states, are growing increasingly uneasy as new technology uncovers instances of false conviction.

Moreover, prosecutors are filing fewer capital charges, and juries are handing down fewer death sentences. Nevertheless, at the rate of twenty a year, it will take twenty-three years just to execute the people waiting on death row now, even if no new prisoners are sent there. For this reason, what we call "death by natural causes" will probably spare the state the trouble of executing several current residents of the Polunsky unit.

Law is our way of restoring balance in the social realm. The sculpture seen in many courtrooms of a woman, blindfolded and holding up a set of scales, represents our image of justice. We weigh the facts, calibrate the crime against the punishment, seeking to reestablish balance and fairness. So deep-seated is our need for order that we even struggle to make the chaotic conditions of war as orderly as possible. We have developed "rules of engagement," directives governing whom one may attack and under what circumstances one may kill an enemy.

Many of our legal metaphors point to our need to restore equilibrium to society after someone has acted in a way that throws it off-kilter. We try to "balance the books" when we make criminals "pay their debt" to society. We speak of "getting even." One of our oldest models for justice, the law codes of the Hebrew Bible, demand that symmetry be reestablished after wrongdoing has destabilized the community. Both Exodus and Leviticus spell out in surprising detail how the children of Israel were to set things right when violence tore the social fabric. They were to exact not only the often cited "eye for eye, tooth for tooth," but "hand for hand, foot for foot, wound for wound, burn for burn, stripe for stripe."

Interestingly, our modern legal system has chosen to impose only the first penalty in that list of retributions — "life for life." In this country, we don't cut off people's hands or feet anymore, or set them on fire, or flog them. Indeed, countries that still mutilate lawbreakers we consider barbaric, unenlightened. We like to think we have progressed beyond such rough justice. But in Texas, as well as in eleven other states, we still follow the injunction of the Hebrew Torah to exact a life for a life.

Some supporters of the death penalty rely on those verses in Exodus to confirm their position. But citing Scripture can be a risky business, yielding unlooked-for results. The same chapter containing the "life for life" clause also provides the guidelines for selling one's daughter into slavery and mandates death for the owner of an unruly ox if the animal fatally gores someone. Likewise, it decrees that a child who curses or strikes his mother or father shall be put to death. Are we willing to impose the death penalty for those actions too?

And for Christians, there's the additional problem of weighing those commands in the Hebrew scriptures against Jesus' teachings in the Gospels to love one's enemies and pray for those who "despitefully use you." To make matters even more complicated, Christians are enjoined to follow not only Jesus' teachings but also his example. Did he not forgive his own murderers from the cross? Of course in that scene, Jesus occupies neither the judge's bench nor the jury box, but the prisoner's place of punishment.

Nevertheless, a good bit of Christian theology rests on the notion of retribution — or to use the term more commonly applied in religious settings, atonement. Jesus died in our place for our sins, thus evening the score with God. If we say that retribution has no place in the struggle to achieve justice, not only does the basis for our entire system of jurisprudence crumble, it compromises a fundamental Christian understanding of salvation. Indeed, most of the world's major religions underscore the necessity for retribution, for reestablishing equilibrium in the moral universe.

Yet most civilizations, at least in the West, have gradually dropped many of the harsh punishments formerly imposed on malefactors. Slowly, we have inched toward what we consider a saner, better form of justice. In the sixteenth century, prisoners were executed by means of boiling, burning at the stake, hanging, beheading, and drawing and quartering. As late as the seventeenth century, the cloven heads of felons were still displayed on the palings of London's Tower Bridge until they rotted away. How many of us would like to live in a country that thrust such sights upon its citizens? We like to believe that we have moved beyond such excesses.

Indeed, those states that still retain the death penalty have worked hard to find more humane methods of performing the task. Texas confines itself to execution by lethal injection. States like Florida that still use electrocution and poison gas are currently rethinking those alternatives.

We have also, in the past fifty years, cut back on the kinds of crimes we deem worthy of execution. As recently as the twentieth century, we still hanged or electrocuted people for theft and rape. Then we limited the death penalty to murder. After that, we began to define more narrowly the kinds of murders deserving of the death penalty. Texas developed the charge of capital murder, whose requirements are even more exacting than those for first-degree murder. These step-by-step limits we have placed on the death penalty signal our general uneasiness about the issue.

Our disquiet has been further aggravated by the accumulating evidence that we have executed innocent or wrongfully convicted people in the past. The Innocence Project, a group of attorneys, clinicians, and law students at the Cardozo School of Law in New York, takes on cases in which DNA tests have not previously been done on physical evidence but could prove the convicted prisoner's innocence. The project has spread to other states. Because of this kind of legal and forensic work, a startling number of condemned prisoners have had convictions overturned.

Illinois, for example, has executed twelve men since the U.S. Supreme Court reinstated the death penalty in 1976. During the same period, thirteen men on Illinois's death row were exonerated. Deeply disturbed by those figures, Gov. George Ryan has declared a moratorium on executions in that state and is considering whether to commute the death sentences of all 163 people currently on Illinois's death row. As he recently told a symposium at the University of Oregon School of Law, "We freed thirteen innocent men who were nearly strapped to a gurney in the state's death chamber so that fatal doses of poison could be injected into their bloodstreams. That is the ultimate nightmare." Even a 99 percent accuracy rate isn't good enough, he says.

Some see the modulation of jurisprudence over the centuries as a positive movement in history away from barbarism and toward civilization. They believe this gradual but steady movement points the way to a higher conception of what it is to be human. Those who would abolish the death penalty are not only on the side of the angels but are also allies with history.

Supporters of the death penalty often say that their primary concern is the safety of all citizens. Society has a right — and its leaders, a responsibility — to insure safety for its citizens. They believe that catching the killer is only the first step. We must also forestall future acts of violence by making the cost for such acts so high that others will think twice before committing such a crime. In criminal justice lingo, this is called deterrence — a laudable utilitarian goal.

Abolitionists, on the other hand, claim that capital punishment does not deter murderers. And one can find statistics to support either argument. Obviously, putting killers to death reduces to zero the chance that they will kill again, but how many potential killers that punishment will dissuade from murder remains an unknown quantity. And, as with risk assessment in any field, a society has to decide what is an acceptable level of security and just how much it is willing to pay for it. Driving thirty miles an hour, for instance, would no doubt result in far fewer highway fatalities than we currently accept. But how many people are willing to drive at that reduced speed?

Basing our decision about capital punishment solely on deterrence means putting justice into the hands of social engineers, experts who supposedly can calibrate risk to outcome. I believe most people expect more from jurisprudence than mere social utility. We also want justice, a somewhat loftier concept. And maybe we want it even more than safety. As a society we remain vague about what precisely justice means, however, and even more uncertain about how to achieve it.

But again, is punishment a requirement for establishing justice? Must something — money or time or a body part or a life — be forfeited in order to achieve balance and order? Does justice demand retribution? And if so, is the point of retribution to punish criminals or to satisfy victims?

Many people believe that punishment, in and of itself, is an essential ingredient in doing justly. Interestingly, this argument is not utilitarian; it refers for its authority to a higher power. Justice as retribution appears to require a religious basis. God's covenant with Noah in the ninth chapter of Genesis, advocates of capital punishment point out, demands the death sentence. "Whoso sheddeth man's blood, by man shall his blood be shed: for in the image of God made he man." They also rely for guidance on scriptural law codes that expand the list of crimes for which death can be exacted. In Paul's letter to the Romans they find an affirmation that a ruler "beareth not the sword in vain; for he is a minister of God, a revenger to execute wrath upon him that doeth evil." In their eyes, this clearly refers to capital punishment.

Abolitionists counter those arguments by pointing out that God himself showed mercy to any number of biblical murderers, not least of them King David. Also, Jesus forgave the woman taken in adultery — a crime punishable by stoning under Mosaic law — as well as the thief on the cross beside him.

Of course, say the supporters. Jesus, owing to his divine nature, was free to pardon, as indeed was his Father, who can rescind punishment as he pleases. But that is a divine, not a human prerogative, they caution.

The value of the retribution argument lies paradoxically in the high value it puts on human life. Murder is not a crime that can be made up for. Not to punish the killer, or to mete out too mild a punishment, demeans and trivializes a life's incalculable worth. Justice is not simply a matter of effectively lowering the murder rate. A life, anyone's life, is so sacrosanct that it can only be properly esteemed by exacting the highest possible price for it. Anything less cheapens its unique value.

Then again, if every life is indeed sacrosanct, if every person carries something of the image of God within, then who are we to take even from the most reprehensible person what only God can give — life itself?

A more practical argument against limiting justice to retribution lies in its focus on the offender rather than the victim. Retribution operates by demanding that the criminal suffer some pain equal to what he has caused, or that he forfeit some or all of his life. Our current criminal justice system has developed a kind of rough calculus to determine how much of a life equals the crime. Assault and robbery may draw ten to twenty years, forgery generally less. But none of the prisoner's forfeited freedom is used to benefit the victim of the crime. Though the state may levy fines, if the offender has stolen property, he is rarely required to pay back its value to the victim. If he has vandalized a home, he is not required to clean it up and pay for the restoration. If he has assaulted someone, he is not charged with paying his victim's hospital bills or lost wages. Instead he goes to jail, where taxpayers provide him with guards and his upkeep.

His victims, on the other hand, get nothing at all, except the possible satisfaction of knowing the person who harmed them has given up a portion of his life to the state.

In crimes against property or criminal assault, restoration makes eminent sense. It restores social balance in a way that merely depriving criminals of their freedom cannot. And there is ample basis in the Hebrew scriptures for restorative justice. Exodus provides in some detail for repayment of damages.

But when the crime is murder, another problem arises. Even though Mosaic law requires a life for a life, how can that sum ever benefit the murder victim? The life of the murdered person can never be restored, at least in this world. Neither does exacting a life for a life take into account the collateral damage to people other than the victim. How do we calculate the loss to a family deprived of a father? Or a parent robbed of a child? A husband of a wife? And what if the murderer killed not one, but several people? He still can die only once.

I HAVE another suspicion about our motives for exterminating killers, one that has nothing to do with justice. I wonder if some other element, ill-defined and unarticulated, but stemming from the sheer randomness of most violent crimes, underlies the demand for the death penalty. We have little control over haphazard evil. Despite all our alarm systems, neighborhood watches, and self-defense classes, we know we are vulnerable to violence. Who among us does not harbor some deep-seated fear that we might one day be victims of violence ourselves? What if I had been working in that optical shop along the interstate from which Debra Ewing was abducted? What if I, instead of Mary Risinger, had decided to wash my car that Halloween night? Alongside the more logical reasons for the death penalty, are we perhaps also motivated by a superstitious impulse to placate whatever mysterious power of evil prowls the universe, one beyond our ability to comprehend or ward against? Instead of keeping murderers locked up the rest of their lives, do we kill them as a sacrifice to the god of Chance?

LAST YEAR at a symposium on the death penalty, I listened to Renny Cushing, a representative of Murder Victims' Families for Reconciliation, describe the call he got one afternoon from the emergency room of the hospital in his small New Hampshire town. His father, they told him, had been shot. He arrived to find his dead father lying on a gurney, his chest "blown to hamburger" by two blasts from a stranger's shotgun fired through his front screen door. Within minutes, the body was sent to the morgue. "It was no longer my father," Cushing said, "but just a piece of evidence."

He called his six siblings with the terrible news. Then, it fell to him to wash the blood off his mother's walls at home.

"I don't oppose the death penalty because I care about murderers," he said, "but because I care about their victims, including the families they leave behind." He agrees that a life for a life would be true justice, a trade he would gladly make if he only knew how. "If I could trade the life of my father for the life of the man who killed him, I'd do it in a minute. But I will never get my father back by killing his murderer."

"I don't need vengeance," he adds, "I need healing."

Not all victims' families feel like Renny Cushing, however. For several years now I have followed the local newspaper accounts of families' statements to the press immediately after their loved one's killer has been executed. Sometimes they say that they can finally get a good night's sleep. Or they say they feel like he didn't suffer enough. After all, their father or daughter or wife may have experienced a good deal more terror and violence than the condemned man did on the gurney. The calculus of restoration, the attempt to even the score, breaks down at that point.

When the past cannot be changed, what do you do? That is what David Doerfler asks people during mediation. Eventually, he says, you have to face life on life's terms. Some losses cannot be recompensed or restored. At best, the hole they leave may be healed.

IN 1986, Paula Kurland's daughter was raped and murdered. She spent the next twelve years trying, unsuccessfully, to get inside the prison to confront her daughter's killer, Jonathan Nobles. "Wardens didn't want me in there. Chaplains didn't want me in there. I kept telling them that all I wanted was to look this man in the face and have him see what he had done."

Then, in April of 1998, David Doerfler called and asked Paula Kurland to participate in his new mediation program.

"It was an answer to prayer," she says now. "My family thought I was crazy for saying yes. But I didn't do it for them. I did it for myself."

It would still be months, however, before Kurland and Nobles were ready for a face-to-face meeting. During that time, Doerfler worked with each of them separately, taking them by gradual stages to the place where they both felt ready to sit down in the same room with one another. When in September 1998 the meeting was finally scheduled, the CBS newsmagazine *48 Hours* decided to film it live.

The encounter between Kurland and Nobles was almost called off at the last minute. Only weeks before his scheduled execution, Nobles petitioned to be an organ donor. Since the chemicals injected to execute him would make his organs useless for transplants, Nobles would have to be hospitalized beforehand to have such organs removed first. This would, of course, delay his execution.

Paula Kurland was furious when she heard the news. She believed the petition to be nothing but a ploy by Nobles to avoid the death chamber a little longer. She considered opting out of mediation at that point, but after talking it over with David Doerfler, decided to go ahead with the meeting. She had too much invested in the process, had waited too long, to forego her opportunity now.

Kurland arrives at the Ellis unit on the appointed day, accompanied by several friends, including her daughter's one-time fiancé. None of her family wants any part of the meeting. An attractive fiftysomething woman with streaks of gray in her short hair, Kurland might be a businesswoman arriving at a Chamber of Commerce meeting, except that her anxious giddiness looks incongruously like bridal nerves. But the woman is also obviously resolute. Though her hands flutter to her hair and she speaks in small, rapid bursts, she is clearly determined to make the most of the coming hours.

Jonathan Nobles is dressed, as always, in prison whites. I have seen his prison mug shots, taken over ten years ago when he arrived on death row. He was in this mid-twenties then, and still had most of his hair. Now he is balding on top, and the smirk that hovered on his full lips twenty years ago has disappeared. He looks like he has added to the 202 pounds he carried into prison, and his skin, like that of all white people on death row, is truly white from lack of sunshine. He too shows signs of nervousness, clearing his throat and flexing his fingers.

Doerfler meets with both Paula and Jonathan separately first, once more talking them through the ordeal that lies ahead. Doerfler himself is a thin man in a polo shirt and spectacles. His voice is low, intentionally gentle and steady. But when Jonathan, in rehearsing the remarks he will make to Paula, uses the word "mistake," Doerfler immediately challenges him. He warns Jonathan that Paula will be understandably angered if he calls her daughter's rape and murder a mere mistake.

Doerfler also reviews with Paula what she wants from the encounter. She says she wants him to look her in the eye and see what he has done, how this loss has shattered her life. "I'm not going in there for him to say 'I'm sorry,'" she tells Doerfler, her anger rising again. "I mean, sorry won't cut it."

"You can't change the past," Doerfler reminds her. "You can only decide what you're going to do now."

Finally, the two — the murderer and the mother — are ready to come together, one on either side of a Plexiglas shield that separates them.

As Jonathan enters the interview room and sits down, he puffs out his cheeks to expel a long tense breath.

Paula says, "It's hard, isn't it?" Then she holds up a 3x5 photograph of her daughter, the young woman Jonathan killed twelve years ago. "This is Mitzi," she says and then breaks into tears. "She was a real person, Jonathan," she cries. "She was real, but she was nothing to you. She was my whole life. She was my baby. You can't imagine what you've done. You can't understand how much pain you've caused."

Jonathan responds shakily. "When you say I can't understand the grief and the pain, you're right. I can't. I wouldn't even suggest that I could."

"Well, thank you for that," Paula says, her voice dry and caustic now.

"But that's why I'm here," he says.

Paula's face hardens. "Do you know you stabbed my daughter twenty-eight times?"

"No, ma'am, I didn't remember the number."

"It was twenty-eight times. And you murdered me. My kids lost their mother. Can you give that back to me? Can you give that back to my kids?"

"No, ma'am," Jonathan whispers.

Paula breaks into tears again. "I don't know what to do with you, Jonathan," she cries, throwing open her hands to him. "I just don't know what to do with you." She takes a gasping breath, struggling to regain control. "It's been ripping me apart. It's just absolutely eating me alive. I just don't know what to do with you," she shrieks again.

At this point, Doerfler interrupts the meeting and takes Paula outside where the sun is just setting to give both her and Jonathan some breathing space.

When Paula reenters the visiting room, calmer now, Jonathan says in a low voice, "I'm a beast."

"I agree," Paula says evenly. "You've scared a lot of people, Jonathan."

After that, the tension eases a bit and the two are able to talk. The conversation extends for hours.

"I don't want you to die just to die," Paula says. "I don't want that for anyone. But it's not very satisfying, going to your daughter's grave and saying 'I love you, Mitzi,' to a piece of bronze."

At one point, Jonathan attempts to explain his desire to donate his organs for transplantation and asks Paula's permission to publicly state, if he's allowed to go through with his plan, that he's doing this in memory of his victims.

Paula hesitates and then says simply, "I'll have to think about that."

After five hours of intense conversation, the relationship between these two people begins to shift. "Are you OK?" Paula asks Jonathan at one point.

"No." He is barely able to get a single syllable out.

"I feel compassion for you, Jonathan," Paula says.

"I don't know that I deserve it."

"No, you don't. But you have it."

"Thank you."

"Do you have anything else that you'd like to say?" she asks.

"Not at this moment."

She gives a short laugh and says they're both more than a little tired.

After another short break, they come back together for one last time. David Doerfler suggests they use this session for their closing statements to one another.

"You first," Paula says quickly, gesturing toward Jonathan.

He takes a deep breath. "Sorry is not enough. I brutally murdered your daughter. I brutally murdered her friend."

"Mmhm," Paula murmurs in agreement.

"I brought absolute horror into your life," he continues. "I don't know what else to say other than I'm sorry, and sorry seems so . . . cheap. I have tried to change my way of thinking, my way of life, my way of living. And yet that's not enough either. Nothing will ever be enough. But I am sorry. I honestly am sorry." He hardly has enough breath to utter the last few words.

"I wish that I could say that it's okay," Paula says, almost gently now. "But it isn't okay. The best I can give you is my forgiveness. I can't ever forgive what you did, but the God that I believe in demands that I forgive you as a person."

"Thank you," he whispers.

"You're welcome," she says almost briskly. She hesitates a moment then adds gently, "Thank you."

After the meeting, Doerfler talks to Nobles alone. He asks him if he could sense the tension in Paula between hope and grief. Nobles replies that he can't even imagine how deep her pain goes. He hopes that one day she will indeed be healed. As for himself, he says, "If I live to be a thousand, I don't think I'll ever be healed of the actions that I perpetrated. I don't think that I could ever disassociate myself from what happened. Ever." He takes a trembling breath and names over the members of his victims' families. "I did this. And I can't undo it. But maybe, just maybe, I can help them by being here and by helping them unravel some of the knots I've placed in their lives."

Paula Kurland and Jonathan Nobles met for the first time on September 22, 1998. They saw one another only once more, two weeks later, when Paula Kurland came to Huntsville to witness Jonathan Nobles's execution.

"I had always said I wanted mine to be the last face he saw on this earth," she tells me the morning I call her. But after that meeting on death row, she meant it in more ways than one.

As Jonathan lay strapped to the gurney in the execution chamber, Paula stood at the witnesses' window listening as he thanked her for the blessing his last two weeks of life had been. He asked the chaplain to help him get through the scripture he had chosen for his last words.

"It wasn't closure," Paula says now. "That's not a word I use, because the loss never leaves you. You just end one chapter and begin another." Then she says again, "Mediation gave me my life back."

SPEAKING AT the symposium in Huntsville, Renny Cushing described the isolation imposed on victims' families, itself a hindrance to healing. "Neither side in the death penalty debate wants to talk to us. Supporters of the death penalty want to exploit our grief as an argument for execution." But Cushing questions the motives of death penalty advocates. Are they supporting capital punishment on behalf of victims or for themselves? Cushing fears that they want to be able to say to victims, There now, we've done all we can for you. We've given you justice, meted out the ultimate punishment. What more could you ask? Now please go away so we can forget about it.

"They don't understand that killing the murderer compounds the pain," Cushing says. "It only creates another grieving family."

On the other hand, death penalty abolitionists too often find murder victims' families an embarrassment to their cause. "It's as if there's only so much sympathy to go around. Any compassion spent on us means less for people on death row," says Cushing.

As for those victims' families who support execution, partisan opponents believe they are only out for revenge. "But in reality most of those families are motivated by deep moral convictions," Cushing says in their defense. "They are not hate-mongers, not for the most part. They just want to spare anyone else the pain they're living with, to make sure what happened to them doesn't happen to someone else."

Cushing says he doesn't know if he can ever forgive the man who murdered his father. "But I do know that if the state were to take his life," he adds, "my opportunity would be gone forever."

PAULA KURLAND does not fit easily into the usual categories of the death penalty debate. Going through the mediation program did not change her feelings about capital punishment. She makes clear her staunch support for the death penalty during our conversation. Nevertheless, her position differs in important ways from that of most death penalty supporters — and carries the weight of personal experience.

She had lost other family members to death, she says, some of them to violent death. But those experiences did not compare to losing a child. "It was a thousand times worse. You have to go through it to understand. That death had been consuming my life for years. I agreed to mediation because I wanted my life back."

Kurland is Catholic, but she says she found little support from her local parish.

"When a murder happens," she tells me, "no one asks how you feel, for fear you might tell them. They'll listen to the gory details of the murder, but what they don't want you to tell them is how you're feeling. They're afraid. Christians, unless they've had some training, want to tell you that your child is in a better place now, or that it was God's will, or that it's all part of his plan. You don't want to hear any of that. And what kind of God plans a rape and murder?"

"So where did you find spiritual support?" I ask.

Surprisingly enough, she says she found watching the Trinity Broadcast Network immensely comforting. "I kept it on twenty-four hours a day," she says. "If you overlook all the stage settings, if you can get past the big hair and overdone cosmetics, some of those people have wonderful stories to tell. I would even call their 800 number, just to talk to someone about my grief. No one at my church ever offered me that."

Not long after her meeting with her daughter's killer, she began to receive requests to speak about her experience. "I've talked about mediation to three different Dallas churches," she tells me. "Afterwards, people always came up to me and wanted to talk about their own victimization. No one else in their church had ever asked them about it, not even the pastor. These people were desperate to talk to someone. These were big churches, where the head pastor might not even know their names. When a church gets so big the pastor doesn't know what's happening with his parishioners, it's too big."

Paula now devotes a good portion of her time to working with Bridges to Life, the proxy mediation program that Chaplain Brazzil described to David and me. "We sit around a table in small groups, four or five offenders — they have to be within eighteen months of release — with two victims and a chaplain," Paula says. "The victims tell their stories. It's very simple, but it has an immediate impact. For the first time the offenders are able to put a human face to their victims."

As I had with David Doerfler and Chaplain Brazzil, I tell Paula I'm amazed that offenders are willing to take part in such a program.

"Oh, we have more volunteers from among the offenders than we can handle," Paula assures me. "It's the victims who are hard to recruit. A lot of people are afraid to go into a prison. I know I was at first. When you hear those gates clang shut, it has an effect on you. But when you actually go, you find out the offenders are more afraid of us than we are of them."

Paula testifies to the effectiveness of Bridges to Life. "There's nothing else like it," she says with conviction. "It's a life-changing experience for everyone involved. The numbers show it. Offenders who participate in Bridges to Life have only a 6 percent recidivism rate, while the rate for the general population is over 50 percent."

Paula Kurland finds especially unconscionable the glacial pace at which the wheels of justice move. "It should not take ten years to carry out the punishment of a convicted killer. That's ten more years of anguish for the victim's family," she points out. She also finds troubling the life sentence as it is currently administered in Texas. "They say a life sentence means at least forty years, but we don't need killers out on the street. Ever." Thus, she also supports the life-without-parole sentencing option, which the state's district attorneys corporately oppose. "Once we get that," she says, "we will have a true life sentence."

While Kurland supports the death penalty, she is equally concerned that it be administered fairly. Besides her dedication to the Bridges to Life mediation program, she is also a member of the board for the National Committee to Prevent Wrongful Executions, an initiative of The Constitution Project at Georgetown University. The committee includes, among many illustrious members of the legal profession, William S. Sessions, the former director of the FBI during the Reagan and first Bush administrations; a former president of the International Association of Chiefs of Police; a prosecutor in the Oklahoma City bombing case; a former Stated Clerk of the Presbyterian Church (U.S.A.); Rabbi Eric H. Yoffie, president of the Union of American Hebrew Congregations; a past president of the American Baptist Churches; and a former judge on the Texas Court of Criminal Appeals.

The committee's mission statement, found on its Web site, begins thus:

"We are supporters and opponents of the death penalty, Democrats and Republicans, conservatives and liberals. We are former judges, prosecutors, and other public officials, as well as journalists, scholars, and other concerned Americans. We may disagree on much. However, we are united in our profound concern that, in recent years, and around the country, procedural safeguards and other assurances of fundamental fairness in the administration of capital punishment have been significantly diminished.

"Because we believe that the risk of wrongful convictions and executions is too great, we have formed a bipartisan death penalty initiative. We are beginning the critically important task of examining our country's present course, and of recommending ways to ensure that fundamental fairness is guaranteed for all."

Paula Kurland is not overawed by the august company she finds herself among on the committee, and she retains her independence of thought. Recently, because of her affiliation with the committee, she was asked to endorse an HBO documentary about a condemned man whose lawyers claim he is mentally retarded. After reviewing the evidence, however, she finally decided it did not support those claims and withdrew her personal endorsement of the documentary.

On the other hand, Kurland has recently withdrawn from several victim's-rights organizations, such as Parents of Murdered Children. She finds them too full of anger. "They just keep one another's outrage stirred up all the time," she says. "I'm not saying you shouldn't be angry. Heaven knows I was for a long time. But you can't heal while you're angry, and I wanted desperately to heal, to be whole again."

WHEN JIM BRAZZIL told us about watching his first death, there beside the Lampasas road, he called it a religious experience. That feeling has never lessened, he says, despite all the many deaths he has witnessed since then and despite knowing that sometimes the person he was watching leave this world had committed irreparable crimes. Death, the doorway to what lies beyond this world, is still a mystery.

As SAMUEL JOHNSON is credited with saying, "When a man knows he is to be hanged . . . it concentrates his mind wonderfully." If David and I have found any value in the death penalty, it is in its ability to force offenders to confront their imminent mortality. When I first saw the movie *Dead Man Walking*, my sense of relief came when the killer was finally able to confront honestly what he had done — and feel remorse for it. He became, at last, a whole person. Or, to use another lexicon, he died in a state of grace.

Would he have been able to sustain that transformation? Who knows? In the end, the human heart and the working of grace is also a mystery we little understand, even when we witness it firsthand. Yet David Doerfler, Paula Kurland, and Jim Brazzil all testify to the fact that many offenders do deeply desire, just as Jonathan Nobles did, to "come clean." I find that the most astounding discovery David and I have made while working on this project.

I believe that both Jonathan Nobles and Karla Faye Tucker, despite their horrific deeds, became whole before they died. My question is, does it take facing the death penalty to bring about such a miraculous transformation? If it does, we're all in trouble.

ONE OF my aunts was reading the newspaper at my kitchen table one morning when she exclaimed over a story about a murderer with a particularly grisly record who had been executed after many delays. "Wonderful!" she cried. "He finally got what he deserved."

"Well," I said slowly, "so do we all."

She looked at me as if I'd lost my mind. My aunt was the widow of

LIVING NEXT DOOR TO THE DEATH HOUSE

a Baptist minister, so I quoted Scripture to her. "'All have sinned and come short of the glory of God.' According to the Bible, we all deserve death."

"But we're not all murderers. That's different."

"That's not what they taught us in Sunday School," I said.

She frowned and rattled the newspaper up in front of her face again.

ONE OF my principal reasons for not supporting the death penalty lies in the fact that I would not want to be responsible for pushing in the plunger that sent the lethal chemical flowing into another person's bloodstream. Or throwing the switch, or dropping the cyanide capsules, or pulling the trigger. Or any of the ways we seek to eradicate whatever of God's image is left in even the most wicked person. How can I then, in good conscience, ask someone else to perform that act in my place?

Another reason is that I do not want to live in a society so devoid of moral resources that it is forced to kill in order to counter the violence that afflicts it. That is a loss of freedom of the worst kind. The rest of Texas is only too eager to isolate the killings in my town. No one seeks to live next door to the death house. People react to executions like nuclear waste — not in my backyard. This attitude is in itself evidence that we are all in some way ashamed of this act. Certainly Huntsville does not advertise itself as the execution capital of the Western world.

As I write this, the U.S. military is holding over a thousand prisoners in a camp in, of all places, Cuba. I imagine that most Americans are greatly relieved that the prisoners are not being held near them or even anywhere inside our borders. Physical distance provides moral relief. Thus, Texas has Huntsville and the United States has Guantanamo Bay. But yesterday the U.S. attorney general announced he would seek the death penalty for Zacarias Moussaoui, accused of conspiring with the other nineteen terrorists who wrought such havoc on September 11, 2001. He is the only terrorist available for trial, the others having died in the planes they hijacked. Moussaoui was in federal custody on immigration charges at the time of the attack. He will be tried in Virginia in a judicial district known for its swift expediting of cases. France, Moussaoui's birthplace, has already announced it will not hand over any evidence to the U.S. courts because of the four capital charges. Once again, as with Timothy McVeigh, Huntsville will seem like everyone's hometown.

JUSTICE IS still an elusive goal for all of us, and we should not pretend that it is otherwise. I believe we need to pursue justice with greater modesty. Dennis Longmire says he searches for insight rather than answers. We think too much of choosing up sides on this matter, then hurling rhetorical grenades at one another, instead of taking the small steps that would bring us closer to each other in a no-man's land of common understanding.

We all believe we should make sure that we are not executing people innocent of the crime they are charged with. We all believe that defendants should receive adequate legal representation. And most people think we should examine not only racial bias in courtrooms but also why there are no rich people on death row. In other words, whether we believe in the death penalty or not, we all want fair trials for everyone.

Beyond that, I believe we need to refocus our attention on victims and their needs, both financial and emotional. A justice system that excludes victims, making them irrelevant to the entire process, can never come close to achieving justice.

Murder is an attack on an individual, but it also damages the community in ways most of us are unaware of. We need to be attentive to those secondary victims — the families, the neighbors, the emergency workers, and the police — who must deal with murder's aftermath.

There remains so much that could be accomplished by doing justly in that no-man's land that lies so desolate and neglected between the opposing sides of the capital punishment debate. There in the demilitarized zone, insights rather than answers are found. People who love justice should make it their new homeland.

The good Samaritan who found a man waylaid and beaten by thieves on the road to Jericho first treated the man's wounds himself and then arranged for his recovery. The Samaritan traveler did as the prophet Micah advised. Being a Samaritan, it took humility for him to come to the aid of a Jew who might very well have proved his enemy under other circumstances. We see from his actions that the Samaritan traveler loved mercy and did justly. Who knows whether he "believed in" capital punishment or its abolition?

Good Friday, 2002

A Liturgy on the Day of an Execution

LEADER: Almighty God, to you all hearts are open, all desires known, and from you no secrets are hid: Cleanse the thoughts of our hearts by the inspiration of your Holy Spirit, that we may perfectly love you, and worthily magnify your holy Name, through Christ our Lord. *Amen.*

O God, you have bound us together in a common life. Help us, in the midst of our struggles for justice and truth, to confront one another without hatred or bitterness, and to work together with mutual forbearance and respect; through Jesus Christ our Lord. *Amen.*

First Lesson

Psalm

Second Lesson

The Sermon (optional)

Confession of Sin

LEADER: Dearly beloved, we have come together in the presence of Almighty God our heavenly Father, to set forth his praise, to hear his holy Word, and to ask, for ourselves and on behalf of others, those things that are necessary for our life and our salvation. And so that we may prepare ourselves in heart and mind to worship him, let us kneel in silence, and with penitent and obedient hearts confess our sins, that we may obtain forgiveness by his infinite goodness and mercy.

ALL: Most merciful God,
we confess that we have sinned against you
in thought, word, and deed,
by what we have done,
and by what we have left undone.
We have not loved you with our whole heart;
we have not loved our neighbors as ourselves.
We are truly sorry and we humbly repent.
For the sake of your son, Jesus Christ,
have mercy on us and forgive us;
that we may delight in your will,
and walk in your ways,
to the glory of your Name. *Amen.*

LEADER: Almighty God, have mercy on us, forgive us all our sins through our Lord Jesus Christ, strengthen us in all goodness, and by the power of the Holy Spirit keep us in eternal life. *Amen.*

Litany for an Execution

LEADER: We pray for God's justice, mercy, and grace.

RESPONSE: Lord, hear our prayer.

L: For our brother/sister _____ for his/her sincere contrition and his/her confidence in Jesus Christ.

R: Lord, have mercy.

L: For his/her family, in their sorrow.

R: Lord, have mercy.

L: For his/her victims, _____, that they have eternal peace.

R: Lord, have mercy.

L: For their families, that they experience healing and find forgiving hearts.

R: Lord, hear our prayer.

L: For the Correctional Officers who guard and prepare him/her, that they be led to perform their duties with compassion.

R: Lord, hear our prayer.

L: For the chaplains who guide and comfort him/her, that you comfort them.

R: Lord, hear our prayer.

L: For the wardens and officials who oversee his/her punishment.

R: Lord, hear our prayer.

L: For judges, juries, and attorneys who argued, heard and decided his/her case.

R: Give them peace.

L: For the Board of Pardons and Paroles, and for the Governor, in all their deliberations.

R: Let loving justice be in their hearts.

L: For the executioners who represent us.

R: Give them peace.

L: For the people of the State of Texas, who carry out this sentence.

R: Show us the way to justice and mercy.

L: For the people of Huntsville, that we may remain distressed and avoid complacency.

R: Lord, hear our prayer.

L: For those awaiting execution, that they may find forgiveness for their sins and true faith in your compassion.

R: Lord, hear our prayer.

L: For those who have been executed. May their souls rest in peace.

R: Lord, hear our prayer.

LEADER: Lord Jesus Christ, in this dark night, we know that you are with us in our distress. Help us to see all the wrongs we do, to repent of them sincerely and honestly, and to build your kingdom here in our lifetime. Guide us to true justice, help us to move away from anger and retribution, and remind us that whatsoever we do to the least of these our brothers and sisters, we do to you — our brother who endured the last necessary execution. We pray in your name because you told us to. *Amen.*

LEADER: O Lord our God, accept the fervent prayers of your people; in the multitude of your mercies, look with compassion upon us and all who turn to you for help; for you are gracious, O lover of souls, and to you we give glory, Father, Son, and Holy Spirit, now and forever. *Amen.*

St. Stephen's Episcopal Church
Huntsville, Texas